COMHAIRLE C̶H̶ ̶.̶.̶.̶.̶ ̶.̶.̶.̶ ̶ṘO̶S̶C̶O̶M̶A̶I̶N̶
LEABHARLANNA CHONTAE ROSCOMÁIN

1. This book may be retained for three weeks.
2. This book may be renewed if not requested
   by another borrower.
3. Fines on overdue books will be charged by
   overdue notices.

09. JUN 17		IR
16 NOV 2018		

MISSING BUT NOT FORGOTTEN

THIS BOOK IS NOT A MILITARY HISTORY
OF THE BATTLE OF THE SOMME.
INSTEAD IT IS A SELECTION OF
SHORT BIOGRAPHIES OF SOME OF
THE MEN COMMEMORATED ON
THE THIEPVAL MEMORIAL TO THE
MISSING OF THE SOMME.

MISSING
BUT NOT
FORGOTTEN

MEN *of the* THIEPVAL MEMORIAL
SOMME

PAM *&* KEN LINGE

Pen & Sword
MILITARY

First published in Great Britain in 2015 by
Pen & Sword Military
An imprint of
Pen & Sword Books Ltd
47 Church Street, Barnsley
South Yorkshire
S70 2AS

ISBN 978 1 47382 358 7

The right of Pam & Ken Linge to be identified as
authors of this work has been asserted by them in accordance
with the Copyright, Designs and Patents Act 1988.

A CIP catalogue record for this book is
available from the British Library.

Printed and bound in England
By CPI Group (UK) Ltd, Croydon, CR0 4YY

Pen & Sword Books Ltd incorporates the Imprints of Pen & Sword Aviation,
Pen & Sword Family History, Pen & Sword Maritime, Pen & Sword Military,
Pen & Sword Discovery, Pen & Sword Politics, Pen & Sword Atlas,
Pen & Sword Archaeology, Wharncliffe Local History, Leo Cooper,
Wharncliffe True Crime, Wharncliffe Transport, Pen & Sword Select,
Pen & Sword Military Classics, The Praetorian Press, Claymore Press,
Remember When, Seaforth Publishing and Frontline Publishing.

For a complete list of Pen & Sword titles please contact
PEN & SWORD BOOKS LIMITED
47 Church Street, Barnsley, South Yorkshire, S70 2AS, England
E-mail: enquiries@pen-and-sword.co.uk
Website: www.pen-and-sword.co.uk

THIS BOOK IS DEDICATED TO THE
MISSING OF ALL NATIONALITIES
FROM ALL CONFLICTS AND TO THOSE
WHO CONTINUE TO REMEMBER THEM.

DONATION OF ROYALTIES TO THE ROYAL BRITISH LEGION AND ABF THE SOLDIERS' CHARITY

The authors' royalties from the sale of this book have been donated to The Royal British Legion and ABF The Soldiers' Charity. Founded in 1921 and 1944 respectively, they continue to provide support to service personnel and their families. Both organisations are to be commended for the work they have done over the years and supported for the work needed in the future.

The Royal British Legion, Haig House, 199 Borough High Street, London, SE1 1AA, registered charity no. 219279.

ABF The Soldiers' Charity, Mountbarrow House, 6-20 Elizabeth Street, London, SW1W 9RB, registered charity no. 1146420.

CONTENTS

FOREWORD

(BY SIR FRANK SANDERSON BT. OBE)

It was over ten years ago that Pam and Ken first approached me and said they would like to contribute to the Thiepval Project by producing a short biography of each of the Thiepval missing. This seemed such an ambitious task that I remember thinking of the old nightmare of being told to count all the pebbles on a beach. At the time of the opening of the Visitor Centre in 2004 Pam and Ken easily had the biographies and photographs necessary for that iconic panel of the 600 Missing that takes pride of place in the exhibition hall.

Since that time they have devoted much of their lives to assembling a personal record of thousands of those men who disappeared into the Somme battlefield. In retrospect this is the very least that should be done for each one of the 72,200 Missing. It has taken one hundred years and the dedication of an exceptional couple from the hills of Northumberland to begin this most important task. We will remember them is a form of words that we have all used many times; Pam and Ken are still working assiduously to enable us all to comply with that promise.

The Visitor Centre is designed to enable those who are interested to learn of the Battles of the Somme and of the men who fought there. The BEF's Somme losses were horrific - especially on the first day; whilst a German official history called the Somme the muddy graveyard of the German Field Army. In the late twenties histories began to be written claiming that the BEF's deaths had been a waste. That is not how they were seen at the time nor at the time of Douglas Haig's funeral in 1928. It must be remembered that the massive German withdrawal to the Hindenburg Lines in the spring of 1917 was a direct result of those costly Somme battles, which also commenced the transformation of Britain's untrained mass civilian army into the efficient fighting force that defeated the German Army in the autumn of 1918. They did not die in vain.

This book tells the story of some of the Missing of the Somme. We should honour them and, by extension, all of their comrades in arms. Thanks to the work of Pam and Ken this book will help us to do so.

It was through the vision and persistence of Sir Frank and others that the Thiepval Visitor Centre came into being in 2004. The creation of the Centre provided the authors with an opportunity to collect, and the setting to display, information relating to the men commemorated on the Memorial. Since 2006 the Centre has been managed by the Historial de la Grande Guerre in Péronne on behalf of the Conseil Général de la Somme. British interest and influence is now carried on by a Franco-British advisory committee that Sir Frank helped to set up in 2006. He retired from the committee in September 2014.

CHAPTER ONE

'MISSING'

One hundred years after the start of the Great War the Commonwealth War Graves Commission currently records 1.1 million British and Commonwealth servicemen and servicewomen who died during the conflict. People may be surprised to know that only 56 per cent of those have a marked grave. The remainder, some 470,000, have no known grave and their names are inscribed on over 100 different memorials across the globe. Collectively they are the **Missing**.

During the war, many others would also have been officially classified as missing at some time. Subsequent investigations would have revealed that some had survived and were being treated in one of the military hospitals or had been captured by the enemy and were prisoners of war. For others their death would have been confirmed and with that the knowledge that they had the dignity of marked graves.

For some of the missing it is true that no trace of their body has ever been found. This is particularly so for sailors who were lost at sea when their vessel was attacked or sunk. In land based forces the effects of shelling in some cases vaporised bodies or buried men sheltering in dugouts in such a way that their bodies could never be retrieved. In a letter to the father of **Robert Dillon**, of the Lancashire Fusiliers, **Captain James McAllister** initially wrote *I understand he was coming along the trench with some other servants when a shell came and burst right in the trench. He and another man were the unfortunate ones.* In a subsequent letter in answer to a request for more information he gave an unusually frank response, *I am sorry to say I have no further information regarding the death of your son. Of course the official minds at the War Office would record him as missing – that is all they know of the case. They have had no notice of his burial because (it seems brutal to speak to you like this) none was necessary. There is one consolation about this however, for you cannot possibly picture him as lying out suffering. The only way you can remember or picture him is as you saw him last.*

Where bodies were found their comrades were keen to ensure that they were given the dignity of a decent burial. There are many examples of letters to next of kin reporting that this had taken place. Of course, the practicalities of the day to day fighting influenced whether this was in one of the organised cemeteries behind the lines or in a more rudimentary location such as a shell hole or abandoned trench.

Many of the isolated locations were subjected to later bombardment as the fighting ebbed and flowed across the same ground. Even some of the organised cemeteries suffered the same fate during subsequent German advances and retreats.

Another consequence of the changing battlefront was that ground gained by the Allies revealed bodies of men killed in previous attacks who had remained in what had been No Man's Land. Such an example was highlighted in the *Salford Reporter* in November 1916, following the discovery of bodies of Lancashire Fusiliers killed in Thiepval Wood on 1st July 1916. Thirty two of the bodies were identifiable and were accordingly buried in marked graves. Even this resting place was not secure as by the end of the war only eight of the graves could be found.

Often bodies were found but without any means of identification. In these circumstances the grave marker would state that he was 'unknown'. The problem of proof of identity was also a factor in the post war battlefield clearances. Dedicated recovery teams scoured the area a number of times and thousands of bodies were recovered and reinterred.

At the same time there was a programme of cemetery concentration, which meant that bodies were exhumed from some of the smaller scale cemeteries and reinterred in large cemeteries in the area. Where nothing was found that could provide a definitive identification, then the body now lies in a grave with a headstone marked 'A Soldier of the Great War' and 'Known unto God'. Where other information, such as date of death, rank or regiment, could be determined then these might also appear on the headstone.

In the Somme area there are some 50,000 such graves which represent around 50 per cent of those who are missing.

Despite such numbers, it is a tribute to the work undertaken by the recovery teams that a number of hitherto unidentified bodies were positively identified.

As far as the families of casualties were concerned, they were told by the War Office that the individual had been 'killed in action' or 'died of wounds' or was 'missing' (perhaps adding 'believed wounded' or 'believed killed'.)

In the first two cases it was unlikely that there would be any further official clarification unless a mistake had been made and news of the death was premature! Such mistakes did happen in the so called fog of war. **Private Ernest Tuttle** of the Sherwood Foresters was reported killed in action on 3rd July 1916. After receiving the letter from the War Office, followed by others from his captain and at least one comrade, an article was published in the *Worksop Guardian* on 14th July 1916, together with an appropriate *In Memoriam* notice from the family. A month later his mother, to her obvious delight, received a letter from Ernest, who was by that time in a prisoner of war camp, stating that he was *quite well*. The *Worksop Guardian* carried the news under the headline, *HE WAS LOST AND IS FOUND.*

In the case of the missing, the War Office was at pains to explain that the term did *not necessarily mean that the soldier is killed or wounded. He may be an unwounded prisoner or temporarily separated from his regiment. Any further information received will be at once sent on to you.* It therefore needed some further positive information in order to provide clarity as to the individual's fate. It required them somehow to return to their unit, to turn up in hospital, to be included in the prisoner lists, or for a body to be found and identified. Without any of these then the status stayed as missing. The War Office did investigate each case as far as they could but, as time passed and no new information came to light, eventually they had to reach the conclusion that the man had died on or around the time that he was first reported missing. It was not uncommon for this official process to take a year.

Some idea of the anxiety being felt can be drawn from the letters in local and national newspapers as the Battle of the Somme progressed. Families expressed their understandable frustration at not knowing what had happened to their loved ones. The sense of frustration was increased by the feeling that the authorities were hiding the truth for some unknown reason. Surely the War Office must know what had happened to their soldiers, so why did they not pass on that information? Whatever it was it could not be any worse than being told the person was dead!

A letter written by the father of **Rifleman James Victor Scott**, to the *Territorial Service Gazette* in June 1917, gives an insight into the feelings of the families of the missing. He noted that, *The anguish of waiting day after day for months for some news is heartrending. Even the "killed in action" report cannot always be accepted as authentic… Unfortunately, many cases, where "Killed in Action" has been received, can only have one meaning, owing to established proof of the fact, or the receipt of the hero's belongings. But, when nothing but oblivion confronts one, there seems little reason to hope; or at any rate, to keep on trying to find out what happened. Take the case of my son… In his last letter to me he said he was "fit and well". Those words have burnt themselves into my mind. Since then all is blank. First I received a report that he was "missing" after an engagement in France on Nov. 13, 1916. A while afterwards two letters which I wrote to him were returned to me with the word "wounded" pencilled on the envelope Some months later I received a report that he was "killed in action" on Nov. 13, 1916.*

Now, if he had been "blown to pieces" – I have a harrowing struggle to write the words – surely no one would have written those notes "wounded". If, on the other hand, he was seen wounded, and could not be picked up by our men, he must either have been captured by the enemy, or else his poor body must have been found later, to justify the report "killed in action", following that of "missing". Comrades must have seen him; yet not a single detail can I get; nor has even a particle of his property been returned to me.

My case, with variations, is like that of thousands more. Where are our loved ones – or where are their bodies? Surely they are worth more consideration than is afforded by a mere printed form? The authorities ought to be able to tell us more. We can face the worst news, provided it settles the matter finally.

James's body was never found; he remains missing.

The true emotional impact of the uncertainty can, thankfully, only be imagined. It is understandable that some next of kin, particularly mothers and wives, never accepted that their son or husband was dead and, until their dying day, believed that they had lost their memory and would eventually return home once they had recovered from their trauma induced amnesia.

In a small number of cases this did happen. **Private Wilfred Churchill** of the King's Own Scottish Borderers was reported missing in action on 15th July 1916. His parents' anxiety was heightened when a soldier wrote to say that he had seen Wilfred fall. Despite inquiries at the War Office, nothing else was heard until Wilfred wrote from a hospital in France in late November 1916, apologising that he had not written sooner as he had been suffering from shell shock. This had resulted in a complete loss of memory after he was one of a group of men who were buried by a shell explosion. Other mothers and wives would have taken heart when they read about Wilfred in the newspaper.

Whether an individual is in a marked grave or still missing can be the result of a minute difference in circumstances. **Fred Roker**, a private in the Lancashire Fusiliers, was killed by a sniper on 12th October 1916. At the time he was acting as orderly to **Lieutenant William Aubrey Fortescue**, who was also killed at around the same time. Both men were reported to have been buried later that same evening. In the spring of 1934 five bodies were exhumed from a small area to the north of Lesboeufs. Three of the bodies were found to be from the Lancashire Fusiliers but the regiments of the other two could not be determined. The names of two of the Fusilier bodies were confirmed from the identity discs that they had been wearing; one was William and the second was **John Noon**. The third Fusilier did have some effects on his body but these were not specific enough to establish an identity. This body, or either of the other two, could have been Fred's but we will never know. If he was one of these three unknowns it is fitting that he now lies buried close to his officer's grave, which is in Plot I, Row 8 in London Cemetery, next to High Wood.

In the absence of that identification Fred is still classified as missing.

In their post war work the (then) Imperial War Graves Commission recognised that the deaths of all service personnel, whether or not marked by a named gravestone, had to be commemorated. In a letter to the father of **Percy Birch**, confirming that his grave had not been found, the Commission staff wrote: … *you can be assured that his name will receive permanent commemoration, as it is the intention of the Commission to erect memorials to those officers and men whose graves cannot be found. The dead who have no known resting place will be honoured equally with the others.* Percy's story appears later.

Although there are over 100,000 missing from the fighting in Belgium it is not surprising that the largest concentration of the missing is in France, where around 212,000 names are inscribed on twenty memorials. A third of those names are on the Thiepval Memorial.

CHAPTER TWO

THE THIEPVAL MEMORIAL

Of the British Memorials to the missing Thiepval is the largest, with the greatest number of names, and was the last to be completed. It is both a Battle Memorial and a Memorial to the Missing. As the former, it bears witness to the Anglo-French offensive on the Somme in 1916. As the latter, it now commemorates over 72,000 men from British and South African regiments and corps who have no known grave, and who fell on the Somme Front from July 1915, when the British Third Army was formed to take over the Front from the French, to 20th March 1918, the eve of the German offensive.

The choice of Thiepval as a location was dictated partly by the nature of the site and partly by historical associations. Standing forty five metres high on an open ridge just south of Thiepval village, the Memorial can be seen on the skyline from many parts of the battlefield. Other places had been suggested, including straddling the Albert to Bapaume road at Pozières; but these were rejected.

Sir Edwin Lutyens's design is a massive stepped arrangement of intersecting arches that culminate in a towering central arch twenty four metres high. Construction work began in 1929 and the Memorial was completed in early 1932.

Clad in brick, the Memorial's sixteen piers are faced with white Portland stone on which the names of the dead are engraved; other dressings are of Massangis limestone. The original facing bricks came from the Pérenchies Tile works near Lille. Over 10 million bricks and 100,000 cubic feet of stone were used in the construction, at an estimated cost of £117,000 (around £6 million in today's money).

When the work was nearing completion, it was decided that an Anglo-French Cemetery should be made in front of the Memorial to symbolise the joint efforts of the two armies during the war. On the base of the Cross of Sacrifice in the cemetery is the inscription:

> *That the world may remember the common sacrifice of two and a half million dead there have been laid side by side soldiers of France and of the British Empire in eternal comradeship.*

Each country provided the remains of 300 of its soldiers. Of the 300 Commonwealth burials in the cemetery, 239 are unidentified. The bodies were found between December 1931 and March 1932, from as far north as Loos and as far south as Le Quesnel; but the majority came from the Somme battlefield of July to November 1916.

A number of the identified burials are of men who were originally commemorated on the Memorial, such as:

Captain Alfred Henry Wellesley Burton, 7th Battalion, Lincolnshire Regiment, who was killed on 23rd October 1916. His body was initially buried north of Lesboeufs and was exhumed on 4th January 1932 and reinterred in grave I.F.7.

Second Lieutenant John Littlejohn, 2nd Battalion, West Yorkshire Regiment (Prince of Wales's Own), who was killed on 26th October 1916. His body, initially buried north of Lesboeufs not too far from Alfred Burton, was exhumed on 22nd December 1931 and reinterred in grave I.C.10.

Both men's names are still visible on the Memorial, Alfred on Pier and Face 1C and John on 2A.

It was originally planned to have the official unveiling ceremony on 16th May 1932. This had to be postponed following the assassination of the President of the French Republic, Paul Doumer.

The inauguration finally took place on the afternoon of 1st August 1932 in the presence of the Prince of Wales (the future King Edward VIII) and the new French President, Albert Lebrun.

The ceremony was widely covered in the national newspapers of the day. It was also broadcast by the BBC to listeners in Britain and across the Empire. In Australia, for example, it was the first major overseas event to be rebroadcast from a shortwave transmission.

By 1932, the post war optimism for the future had dissipated and it was only six months later that Adolf Hitler became Chancellor of Germany.

Seven years later the Second World War began and by 1940 Thiepval was again under German occupation. During this time the Germans respected the Memorial and the structure remained sound. The village was liberated by British forces on 3rd September 1944.

Post war inspections revealed problems with the brickwork. The original bricks were not engineering bricks and their inferior quality meant they had begun to flake. The disposal of rainwater from the numerous flat roofs was also causing problems. It was therefore recommended that the Memorial be completely refaced and this work was carried out between 1952 and 1955, during which time the drainage system was also improved.

More work was carried out in the 1960s; the low forecourt walls were rebuilt and reduced in height to a continuous low horizontal instead of gentle steps down from the basement level of the Memorial. The circular wall around the rond point was replaced partly by hedge and partly by a new curved seat. At the same time a monumental staircase was built from the eastern terrace down to the Anglo-French Cemetery below to replace the previous temporary wooden structure.

The brickwork continued to be a problem and in 1970 it was decided to reface the Memorial for a second time. An English Accrington 'Nori' sand-faced engineering brick was

chosen. Work on the refacing started in 1973 and was completed by 1975. Maintenance work continues and the Faces are cleaned at regular intervals.

THE LAYOUT OF THE MEMORIAL

Face B on Piers 1 to 4 and Face D on Piers 13 to 16 are smooth, recognising that names carved there would be extremely difficult to read.

Similarly, the increased size of the lettering used on Face A on Piers 1, 8, 9 and 16 and Face C on Piers 4, 5, 12 and 13 reflects the distance from which they have to be viewed.

The names on the Faces are grouped by regiment or corps (there are 137 different regiments and corps listed), by rank and then alphabetically within each rank.

The battalions of the London Regiment (with 4,303 names) and the South African Infantry are divided; but all other regiments are shown without sub-division.

The other regiments with over 1,500 recorded names are: Northumberland Fusiliers (2,917); Royal Fusiliers (2,484); The King's (Liverpool Regiment) (2,135); Middlesex Regiment (1,920); Manchester Regiment (1,863): Royal Warwickshire Regiment (1,768); West Yorkshire Regiment (Prince of Wales's Own) (1,747); Lancashire Fusiliers (1,685); King's Royal Rifle Corps (1,640); and Durham Light Infantry (1,582). Thus, approximately one third of all those

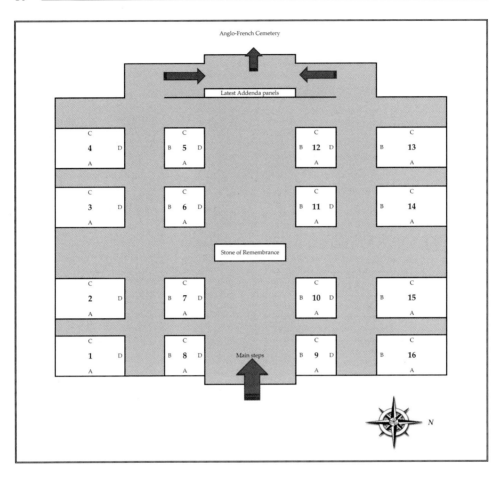

commemorated are from these eleven regiments.

Pier and Face 1A is interesting as it commemorates men from the Royal Navy, Royal Marines and Royal Naval Volunteer Reserve, these three totalling 791 men. It also features the Cavalry and Yeomanry Regiments (Household Cavalry, Cavalry of the Line, Reserve Cavalry and Yeomanry). In total, 105 men are commemorated from thirty four individual regiments.

Other regiments and corps also feature a small number of men. The Labour Corps (one) is on Pier and Face 5C, while 4C features a number of support arms: Army Chaplains' Department (two); Army Service Corps (four, there are a further six on 5C), Army Veterinary Corps (one), Army Ordnance Corps (one); General List (nine); as well as the West India Regiment (one). In addition, 4C also includes sections relating to the Royal Army Medical Corps (132) and the South African Infantry (830).

It is hardly surprising, given the need to compare the details of all the casualties with the known burials, that a small number of omissions occurred. Where it was discovered that men should have been commemorated on the Memorial, the details were verified and their names were added to the Addenda Panels. Initially these were on one column of Pier and Face 4C, with a few names added elsewhere; more recently the names were included on eight panels set into the walls of the western terrace.

THE MEN

Initially the sixteen piers were inscribed with 73,357 names. At the time of the inauguration the registers recorded the particulars of 73,077, the graves of some having been identified in the interval between the carving of the Faces and the printing of the first registers. In the following years other bodies were discovered and identified (including Burton and Littlejohn mentioned earlier) as the woods were cleared and farmers returned to the land.

A century after the start of the war the Memorial commemorated 72,195 men.

NUMBER OF NAMES COMMEMORATED

Pier	Face				
	A	B	C	D	
1	1,055		1,786	1,172	4,013
2	1,813		1,957	1,223	4,993
3	1,967		1,780	1,185	4,932
4	1,688		980	1,159	3,827
5	1,198	1,191	861	827	4,077
6	1,316	1,192	1,173	1,281	4,962
7	1,178	1,190	1,291	1,232	4,891
8	827	1,205	1,217	814	4,063
9	841	880	1,118	1,127	3,966
10	1,157	1,301	1,338	1,218	5,014
11	1,297	1,352	1,215	1,228	5,092
12	1,196	851	756	1,195	3,998
13	1,784	1,219	1,172		4,175
14	1,966	1,166	1,799		4,931
15	1,728	1,137	1,901		4,766
16	1,323	1,165	1,710		4,198
Addenda panels					297
					72,195

There can still be occasions when a name should receive commemoration elsewhere. The most recent example is **David Harkness Blakey MM**, a sergeant in the Royal Inniskilling Fusiliers, who went missing on 1st July 1916 during the fighting near Thiepval. For over ninety seven years David's body lay undisturbed until it was discovered (not far from the Ulster Tower) during road widening work in late 2013. In October 2015 David was given a full military burial in the presence of members of his family.

Within the registers new names have been added and other names, such as David's, deleted. Names are only physically removed from the Memorial itself when remedial work is required on a particular Face. The most recent work was undertaken early in 2014, when twenty four stone panels were replaced.

Although the Memorial covers the period from July 1915 until 20th March 1918, approximately 90 per cent of those commemorated died during the Battle of the Somme (July to November 1916). This includes some 12,400, or almost two thirds, of those killed on 1st July 1916. Amongst the men commemorated there are over 2,800 officers, the highest ranking amongst these being twelve lieutenant colonels.

As well as representing the various military ranks, the men are drawn from all sectors of society: the gentry to the worker (most types of employment are represented), sportsmen, musicians, artists, politicians, writers - all are here. Many individuals were connected through schools, universities, or employment as well as geographically, given the number of Pals battalions involved in the early battles.

The recorded age range is from 15 to 53, with an average of 25 years. Whilst many of the men were new to the Armed Forces, for others the war followed a period in the Territorials or the pre war Regular Army. A number had served in the Boer War or on service around the Empire. Many individuals of British birth were employed in the far flung regions of the Empire but returned to answer their Country's call.

Although the Memorial only commemorates men who served in the British and South African forces, amongst them are native born Canadians, Australians and Americans who enlisted in these forces.

Whilst each individual represents a separate loss to family and friends, there are many examples of multiple loss. Several sets of brothers are commemorated, some of whom were killed on the same day and with the same regiment; whilst others had differing dates of death and service.

GALLANTRY AWARDS

Over 1,100 of the men were recipients of gallantry awards.

This includes seven holders of the Victoria Cross and their individual stories feature later under the appropriate Pier and Face.

[3A] **William Buckingham**
Private, 1st Battalion,
Leicestershire Regiment.

[4C] **Alexander Young**
Lieutenant, 4th Regiment,
South African Infantry.

[4D] **Eric Norman Frankland Bell**
Captain, 9th Battalion,
Royal Inniskilling Fusiliers.

[11A] **Thomas Orde Lawder Wilkinson**
Lieutenant, 7th Battalion, The
Loyal North Lancashire Regiment.

[13A] **John William Mariner**
Rifleman, 2nd Battalion,
King's Royal Rifle Corps.
(Also known as **William Wignall**.)

[15A] **William Frederick McFadzean**
Rifleman, 14th Battalion,
Royal Irish Rifles.

[15A] **Geoffrey St George
Shillington Cather**
Lieutenant, 9th Battalion,
Royal Irish Fusiliers.

CHAPTER THREE

BIOGRAPHIES

As mentioned at the start of this book, it is not written as a military history but as a remembrance of these men as individuals. Although from many different backgrounds, they came together as part of the Armed Forces and have stayed together in their commemoration as the 'Missing of the Somme'.

We have selected the biographies in this chapter to illustrate their diversity. We can only provide a small number and space means that they have had to be summarised to a greater or lesser extent. A full version of each biography can be viewed at the Thiepval Visitor Centre.

Throughout we have used contemporary information, such as newspapers, so that the information is not affected by modern interpretation or hindsight. Similarly, all quotations have been included with the original spellings and punctuation.

For ease of use the individual biographies have been ordered by Pier, with at least four from each inscribed Face.

Where possible we have highlighted the number of siblings and children as an indication of the wider impact each man's death would have had on his immediate family. We have also included references where we know that close relatives died on military service.

Each individual biography is as important as the others and, as a collection, they stand as a remembrance of all of those commemorated on the Memorial.

The unwritten question at the end of each biography is:

What might have been had they lived?

PIER 1

A

- Royal Navy
- Royal Marines
- Royal Naval Volunteer Reserve
- 1st Life Guards
- 2nd Life Guards
- Household Battalion
- 2nd Dragoon Guards (Queen's Bays)
- 3rd Dragoon Guards (Prince of Wales's Own)
- 5th Dragoon Guards (Princess Charlotte of Wales's)
- 6th Dragoon Guards (Carabiniers)
- 7th Dragoon Guards (Princess Royal's)
- 1st (Royal) Dragoons
- 2nd Dragoons (Royal Scots Greys)
- 4th (Queen's Own) Hussars
- 5th (Royal Irish) Lancers
- 6th Dragoons (Inniskilling)
- 8th (King's Royal Irish) Hussars
- 9th (Queen's Royal) Lancers
- 17th Lancers (Duke of Cambridge's Own)
- 10th (Prince of Wales's Own Royal) Hussars
- 20th Hussars
- 21st (Empress of India's) Lancers
- South Irish Horse
- 1st King Edward's Horse
- 2nd King Edward's Horse
- Royal Wiltshire Yeomanry
- Shropshire Yeomanry
- Leicestershire Yeomanry
- Hampshire Yeomanry (Carabiniers)
- Duke of Lancaster's Own Yeomanry
- Northumberland Hussars
- Royal North Devon Hussars
- Queen's Own Oxfordshire Hussars
- West Kent Yeomanry (Queen's Own)
- Norfolk Yeomanry
- Sussex Yeomanry
- Essex Yeomanry

- Royal Horse and Royal Field Artillery - **Major A. I. Drysdale to Gunner J. R. Belshaw** *(continued on Pier and Face 8A)*

B

(Blank)

C

- Norfolk Regiment - **Private H. Green to Private M. G. Youngs** *(completed from Pier and Face 1D)*
- Lincolnshire Regiment
- Devonshire Regiment
- Suffolk Regiment - **Captain C. B. Bevan to Lance Corporal A. H. Benns** *(continued on Pier and Face 2A)*

D

- The King's (Liverpool Regiment) - **Private W. Livesey to Private W. Young** *(completed from Pier and Face 8B)*
- Norfolk Regiment - **Captain W. J. H. Brown to Private F. Green** *(continued on Pier and Face 1C)*

ALFRED FREDERICK MAYNARD

Lieutenant, Howe Battalion, Royal Naval Division,
Royal Naval Volunteer Reserve.

Died on 13th November 1916, aged 22, during an attack
on Beaumont Hamel.

Alfred was one of six children of William John (Durham
Probate Registrar) and Annie Maynard (née Smith) of North
Bailey, Durham. The family later lived in Dorset.

Educated at Seaford and Durham School, he then went
to Emmanuel College, Cambridge. Throughout all of this
time he was a keen sportsman and a member of the school and college cricket, hockey and
rugby teams. He also played cricket for Durham County. In one particular match he scored
eighty nine in what was described as *a beautifully free fashion* and then took a one-handed
catch on the boundary, for which even the dismissed batsman showed his appreciation. On the
rugby field he played occasionally for the Harlequins and in the 1913/14 season he was one of
the forwards in the England team that played against each of the home nations, although he
was not selected to play against France.

He graduated in 1914 but was absent on active service so could not attend to receive his
BA. He was commissioned in the RNVR in October and took part in the evacuation of Antwerp
and the raid on the Suez Canal. In 1915 he served on Gallipoli and was wounded in the leg.
He later served in two positions on the staff in Egypt and had temporary command of his
battalion at Mudros. He then took command of A Company of Howe Battalion in France in
April 1916.

He was killed between the second and third German lines.

In sympathising with Mr and Mrs Maynard, the battalion commander wrote: *I knew him to
be not only a zealous officer, but one in whom the greatest confidence might well be placed.*

A plaque at Twickenham Stadium commemorates the twenty seven **Rugby Internationals**
who lost their lives during the war. Alfred and six others are commemorated on the Memorial.
The stories of two of those, **Richard Thomas** [7A] and **Horace Wyndham Thomas** [16C],
appear later.

PETER JOHNSTONE SIM

ABLE SEAMAN, CLYDE Z/2277, DRAKE BATTALION, ROYAL
NAVAL DIVISION, ROYAL NAVAL VOLUNTEER RESERVE.

Died on 13th November 1916, aged 22, during an attack
on Beaumont Hamel.

Peter was one of seven children of James and Ann Noble Sim
(née Taylor), of Fraserburgh, Aberdeenshire, where his father
was a harbour master.

After an education at Broadsea Public School he joined a
firm of local joiners. He enlisted on 9th November 1914 and
was posted to the Benbow Battalion on 22nd February 1915.

He served on Gallipoli from 28th May before transferring to the Drake Battalion on 12th
June.

He went with his battalion to France on 31st May 1916.

Two older brothers died in 1915.

John Dingwall Sim, Able Seaman Clyde Z/610, Drake Battalion,
Royal Naval Division, Royal Naval Volunteer Reserve, died on 8th
May 1915, aged 27. He is commemorated on the Helles Memorial.

James Sim, Private 1930, 1st/5th Battalion, Gordon Highlanders,
died on 15th July 1915, aged 25. He died in hospital from wounds
received on 4th June 1915 and is buried in grave II.A.7 in
Longuenesse (St Omer) Souvenir Cemetery.

WILLIAM RICHARD THEW

SERGEANT, 665, NORTHUMBERLAND HUSSARS, ATTACHED TO
2ND BATTALION, ROYAL BERKSHIRE REGIMENT.

Died on 25th October 1916, aged 20, during an attack on
Zenith Trench, near Lesboeufs.

William was the only child of Philip and Dorothy Thew (née
Short), of Hexham, Northumberland.

Educated at the Queen Elizabeth Grammar School,
Hexham, he was assistant scoutmaster of the Hexham Troop
of Boy Scouts. He joined Lloyds Bank on 21st April 1913 and
worked in the branch at Collingwood Street, Newcastle-upon-Tyne.

He enlisted in the Hussars at Hexham in 1913; they were the first Territorial unit to go to
Belgium in October 1914 and the first to go into action. He fought at the First Battle of Ypres,
the battles of Loos and Neuve Chapelle, and was fortunate in never being wounded or having
any time in hospital. His only mishap was after Loos, when his horse fell and dragged him for
a distance, thankfully without injury. During his time at the Front he had twice refused the
offer of a commission.

For eighteen months he had been attached to the Berkshires and acted as confidential clerk
to the commanding officer, **Lieutenant Colonel Roland Haig DSO**. In writing to William's
parents, the latter said: *I am most terribly sorry as in him I lose a personal friend, and I can
thoroughly sympathise with you in your great loss. I have known him now for eighteen months, and
a more charming disposition I have seldom met. He and I were both coming on for a few hours rest
from the battle, and he was hit with a shell and killed.*

In 1919 his parents presented a portable Holy Communion set dedicated in his memory to
Hexham Abbey.

The **Tynedale Rugby Football Club's Roll of Honour** commemorates forty nine members
who fell during the war. William and three others are commemorated on the Memorial. The
stories of two of those, **John Wilfred Robinson** [12B] and **William Braidford** [14A], appear
later.

HENRY JOSEPH DOBNEY

BATTERY SERGEANT MAJOR, 33623, 105TH BATTERY, 22ND BRIGADE, ROYAL FIELD ARTILLERY.

Died on 25th September 1916, aged 32.

Henry was one of four children of Joseph (a gardener) and Mary Caroline Dobney (née Johns), of Tottenham, London.

After his education at West Green Board School he worked as a joiner.

He enlisted on 12th February 1904 and served in South Africa from September 1912 to September 1914. In 1913 his captain recorded that he was: *Trustworthy. Good with horses and a good rider. Hardworking. A very satisfactory man.*

He went to France on 4th October 1914 and was mentioned in despatches on three separate occasions for gallant and distinguished service in the field. He was promoted to battery sergeant major in June 1915 and was slightly wounded on 16th November.

He was killed during the fighting at Ginchy; his original burial place was recorded at the time but the grave was lost as a result of subsequent fighting.

Lieutenant Thomas Baxter wrote: *To say Battery Sergt.-Major Dobney was appreciated by us is too little. His qualities as a soldier of the brightest calibre were continually in evidence during those operations on the Somme from 1 July onwards. He was highly respected by his men; he was greatly appreciated by his officers. His loss to us is infinite.*

His youngest brother, **Ernest Victor Dobney**, Private 49624, 32nd Battalion, Royal Fusiliers, attached to the Machine Gun Corps, died on 7th June 1917, aged 30.

He is commemorated on the Menin Gate Memorial.

FREDERICK WILLIAM BENNETT

and his pal,

WILLIAM BENTLEY

PRIVATE, 18022, 6TH BATTALION, LINCOLNSHIRE REGIMENT, AGED 19.

PRIVATE, 18023, 6TH BATTALION, LINCOLNSHIRE REGIMENT, AGED 20.

Both died on 30th September 1916, in fighting near Thiepval.
They were killed by the same shell.

Frederick was the son of Mary Lavinia Bennett.

William was one of seven children of George William (a labourer) and Harriett Bentley.

Both men lived in Burton Street in Tutbury, near Burton-on-Trent. They worked together in Nestlé's Condensery in the town, they enlisted together and both went to Gallipoli on 21st November 1915. Later the battalion served in Egypt and went to France in early July 1916.

NESTLÉ & ANGLO-SWISS CONDENSED MILK COMPANY ROLL OF HONOUR

The Company's book, *Lest we Forget* lists 1,213 members of staff who served in the forces of Great Britain, Australia, New Zealand, France, Belgium, Italy, Serbia, Greece and Romania. A total of 104 died and are commemorated on the company's war memorial.

At least sixteen members of the Tutbury Condensery were killed, including William's brother, **George Edwin Bentley**, Private 11004, 7th Battalion, Lincolnshire Regiment, who died on 2nd March 1916, aged 27. He is buried in grave VIII.AA.34 in Enclosure No. 4, Bedford House Cemetery.

FRANCIS BAKER COLDWELLS

SECOND LIEUTENANT, 3RD BATTALION ATTACHED TO 2ND BATTALION, DEVONSHIRE REGIMENT.

Died on 1st July 1916, aged 24, during the attack on Ovillers.

Francis was the eldest of four children, all sons, of Joseph George (an accountant) and his first wife, Elizabeth Coldwells (née Baker), of Sutton, Surrey.

Educated at Whitgift Grammar School, Croydon, he was Captain of School in 1910, captain of the 3rd XV and editor of the school magazine. He gained a scholarship to Wadham College, Oxford, where he graduated with First Class honours in Classics. While at Oxford he served for four years in the OTC and was in the Wadham Hockey XI, as well as being a member of the Literary and Debating Societies. A contemporary described him as, *A fine scholar and modest man.*

Having enlisted in the Royal Fusiliers in September 1914 he rose to the rank of sergeant before receiving a commission in July 1915. Initially he was on the staff of the Officers' Training School in Oxford but was keen for action and in May 1916 he was posted to the Devons' 3rd Battalion.

All his brothers served and Francis was the third to die in action.

Leonard George Coldwells, Private 1745, 14th Battalion, London Regiment (London Scottish), died on 31st October 1914, aged 20. He is commemorated on the Menin Gate Memorial.

Charles Albert Coldwells, Second Lieutenant, 108th Brigade, Royal Field Artillery, died on 28th September 1915, aged 20. He is buried in grave VII.F.16 in Dud Corner Cemetery.

The youngest brother, **Edward Greenwood Coldwells**, served as a second lieutenant in the Leinster Regiment and was wounded.

ARTHUR LESLIE PLATTS

CAPTAIN, 2ND BATTALION, SUFFOLK REGIMENT.

Died on 20th July 1916, aged 25, while going to the assistance of a wounded man during the fighting at Longueval.

Arthur was one of at least eight children of Arthur (a warehouseman) and Julia Mary Platts (née Hardy). Julia was widowed in 1898 and later married William George Wiffen, chairman of a chemical company.

Initially educated at King's College School, Wimbledon, he then went to Oundle School. From there he went up to Caius College, Cambridge, where he took his degree in 1913.

He received a commission in the Suffolk Regiment in September 1914 and was promoted to lieutenant in June 1915.

From January to October 1915 he was in the fighting at Ypres and Hooge, after which he was at home for a time, working in the munitions department, rejoining his regiment in April 1916. Having returned to France in May, he was promoted to the rank of captain with effect from 11th July.

A captain wrote: *He had heard a wounded comrade who was lying in a shell hole cry for help, and he at once went to his assistance, the Germans were already on the lookout and wounded Platts in the thigh just as he got to his man. Another officer at once went to Platts' assistance and reached the shell hole in safety.*

The latter officer wrote: *A Lce-Corporal and myself immediately ran out to him. The Lce-Corporal was killed as soon as he reached the hole. I started getting his [Platts'] equipment off... He turned over to let me bandage him, but he was hit again. He fell back without saying a word.*

His commanding officer wrote: *What will always stand out in my memory was Lieut. Platts' irrepressible cheerfulness under difficulties and danger, and it kept everyone else smiling. It means such a lot out here - a cheering smile is sometimes worth a whole Company of Infantry.*

His eldest brother **Reginald Hardy Platts**, Lieutenant, Royal Garrison Artillery, died on 31st May 1918, aged 31. He is buried in grave A.S.836-7 in Wandsworth (Putney Vale) Cemetery.

JOSEPH MASON

Corporal, 15662, 11th Battalion, Suffolk Regiment.

Died on 1st July 1916, aged 34, during the fighting at La Boisselle.

Joseph was one of three children of Thomas (a farmer) and Ann Elizabeth Mason (née Davey) of Burwell, Cambridgeshire.

Following an apprenticeship as a law writer with a firm of Newmarket solicitors, he became a clerk at a local livery stable.

He married Mabel Emily Gaston Morsley on 1st April 1905 and they went on to have a family of five, four sons and one daughter, born between 1906 and 1915. Sometime after the birth of the youngest child, Mabel became unwell and was unable to care for the children. The daughter (Rosie) went to live with Joseph's close friends (George and Emily Bishop) and the boys were split up. The younger two were sent to a family in Bury St Edmunds, whilst the older two spent some time in the Newmarket Union Workhouse before being sent to a family in a nearby village. Mabel spent some time in hospital and was discharged in 1919. The five children never lived with her again as a family but remained close in later years until her death in 1962.

In a letter to Rosie he wrote: *Dada sends his love to you and wants you to be a good little girl and go to school and do all Mrs Bishop tells you. Dada hopes to soon come and see you. Goodnight my darling & God Bless and protect you.*

In a letter to Mr. and Mrs. Bishop dated 23rd June 1916, Joseph thanked them for their letter and a photograph of Rosie which was, *very nice and I think she looks remarkably well*; ending, *Give my love to Rosie and accept my best wishes for you all.*

The company quartermaster sergeant wrote to Joseph's sister, *It pains me very much to have to tell you, and no doubt you will be able to break the news to his wife as I would not care to do it myself… Your brother has been closely associated with me ever since joining, and I liked him very much and appreciated his good qualities.*

In a later letter he added, *…your brother has been with me so long that we had become good friends. I was with the company the night before the attack took place, and had a chat with Joe. I quite expected I should see him again all right, as we did not think for a minute that they would meet with very much resistance. But, as we now know, they were faced by very heavy machine-gun fire. They advanced bravely as if only on parade, and met their deaths like the heroes they were.*

WILLIAM JAMES LOCK

PRIVATE, 24652, 18TH BATTALION, THE KING'S (LIVERPOOL REGIMENT).

Died on 1st July 1916, aged 20, during an attack on Montauban.

William was one of eight children of Joseph (a labourer) and Elizabeth Ruth Lock (née Padden) of Ellesmere Port, Cheshire.

After an education at the Church Schools in Ellesmere Port he became an assistant at the cement works.

He enlisted in Liverpool on 9th January 1915 and went to France on 14th April 1916.

Two friends who served with him wrote: *Your son was loved by all in the platoon, he was a good soldier who did his duty with a smile. His cheery spirits and manner made him exceedingly popular amongst us all and each one of the platoon wish us to convey to you their sympathy. He will be sadly missed in the ranks and his place will never be filled... He suffered no pain, death being instantaneous. He was buried on 3rd July, his burial being witnessed by Private Knight, who has his cap badge, which he will send to you at the first opportunity.* The initial report indicated the burial took place in Trônes Wood Cemetery but the grave was subsequently lost.

A lieutenant wrote: *Although he was comparatively a new member of the company, everybody loved him. He was always so cheery and willing to do anything that was necessary. I shall miss his pleasant face, as I took a great fancy to him, it seems very hard for a mere boy to die as young.*

The captain commanding William's company wrote: *On behalf of the officers and men, I wish to express our sympathy in the loss of your son, killed in action on July 1st. Ever since he joined us he has been liked and respected by all his comrades and he has invariably done his duty on every occasion in the most splendid manner. The company will indeed miss the fine devoted lads who have fallen. In the wonderful charge they made so successfully it was their devotion to duty which won the battle.*

FRANK HOGBEN

SECOND LIEUTENANT, 7TH BATTALION, NORFOLK REGIMENT.

Died on 12th October 1916, aged 24, leading an attack on Bayonet Trench East, to the north of Gueudecourt.

Frank was one of seven children of John (a policeman) and his second wife, Emily Elizabeth Hogben (née Dann), of Northfleet, Kent.

Initially serving as Bombardier 811, Royal Garrison Artillery, he was gazetted as second lieutenant from 8th January 1916.

Three days before he died he wrote his last letter to his fiancée, May Thompson, *I was only thinking last night after reading through your letters, what a down-hearted being I have been, as most of the letters I have written you have been more or less mournful haven't they, but I am quite cheerful now - I am only looking forward to the time when I shall see you again – gosh won't I be bucked. Well dearest now that we know what each other thinks it will be best to let it rest so I'll continue with what little news I have for you… Oh yes I have a photograph of you with me, in fact I have four out here three of which I carry on me and the fourth is in my card case packed away in my valise away back somewhere.*

A chaplain wrote: *He was with a party which was detailed to attack and hold if possible an enemy trench… after gaining a footing in the trench held on in spite of very heavy enemy fire and it was only a few survivors that ultimately managed to regain our trenches. Hogben is said to have been killed during this attack and unfortunately his death could not be verified later as the trench had to be evacuated… His body was never recovered or if recovered was not identified – but very little hope can be drawn from this fact as his body would very possibly be buried by the shells as they ploughed up the ground… None of the officers who were in the Company at the time seem to doubt for a moment that he was killed.*

After the war his fiancée married Frank's older brother, **Frederick George**.

His younger brother, **Sidney Hogben**, Private 534896, 15th Battalion, London Regiment (Prince of Wales's Own Civil Service Rifles), died on 3rd September 1918, aged 19.

He is buried in grave VII.B.37 in Heilly Station Cemetery.

CLAUDE THEODORE CHURCH

SERGEANT, 14082, 8TH BATTALION, NORFOLK REGIMENT.

Died on 2nd July 1916, aged 28, during fighting to the south-west of Montauban.

Claude was one of four children of Herbert (a house painter) and Sarah Church (née Dawson) of Overstrand, Norfolk.

On 3rd January 1911 he became a footman serving in the Royal Mews at Buckingham Palace.

He enlisted at Westminster on 4th September 1914.

A comrade corresponded with the family, and, after a request for more detail, provided the following: *About 7.30am the first wave went over followed in close succession by others, and after some stiff fighting at various points, we took and made good our first objective. It was in this first process that many of our brave comrades fell, including our gallant Captain, B Pitts Ayre*, and the close associate of your dear son Sergt. R Kennedy^, both of whom were shot through the body and succumbed instantly, also our officer was wounded, this leaving Claude in command of the platoon. Having been successful in accomplishing our first objective, we were ordered to take the next... the Regt. made good its second and final objective, this proved to be a straight and very wide trench, a trench that was held at a great cost especially to our company owing to the fact that the enemy were enabled to range so accurately upon it. However, this was not done before all our company officers who commenced had been put hors de combat leaving your beloved son, who was then senior in charge of the company. About six o'clock in the evening of the following day... I was speaking to our late Sergt. at the time and in the course of the conversation he mentioned, that the officer who had then come up to take command, had told him to get some rest observing as we all did that your son was almost exhausted in doing as many duties, all of which I am able to say he did well and with a willing heart. While thus conversing an explosive shell burst almost in the trench and to our horror your dear son received a wound in the back which proved fatal, he dying almost instantly. From the same shell there were three others killed and another buried... Enclosed please find the watch that belonged to your noble son he was wearing same at the time and the glass was broken, his other effects should be delivered to you in due course, by the proper authorities.*

*Captain Bernard Pitts Ayre (one of four cousins from Newfoundland, all of whom died on 1st July), aged 24, is buried in grave D.10 in Carnoy Military Cemetery.

^Sergeant Ralph William Kennedy, 14083, is buried in grave VII.C.1 in Dantzig Alley British Cemetery. Ralph, like Claude, was a footman serving in the Royal Mews.

JOHN BALLS

PRIVATE, 16930, 8TH BATTALION, NORFOLK REGIMENT.

Died on 31st October 1916, aged 27.

John was one of eight children of Samuel (a labourer) and Elizabeth Balls (née Milligan) of Great Yarmouth, Norfolk.

He married Ada Mary A. Osborne in 1914; they lived in Great Yarmouth and had one daughter.

He worked as a potato chip seller for a Mr. Brewer, in Great Yarmouth and enlisted there in November 1914. He went to France on 25th July 1915.

In January 1916 he sent a letter to the *Yarmouth Mercury* which was published under the headline *WHO'LL SEND SOME KIPPERS?* In it he wrote: *We would be very much obliged if some kind person would kindly send us a real box of good old Yarmouth kippers. We have the good old Yarmouth Mercury sent out to us every week, and see other chums have such luxuries sent out to them. I myself have six brothers fighting out here… so I think a little gift like this would help us along, and also a real Yarmouth kipper would help a dry biscuit down.*

He was trained as a sniper and was killed in the area of Regina Trench, near Grandcourt.

His captain* wrote: *Your husband met his death under very sad circumstances. We were in a reserve trench, a mile behind the firing line, when a shell landed on the small dugout in which your husband and another man were sitting and smashed it in. Some of the snipers hearing cries for help went to the spot and succeeded in extricating them but your poor husband's neck had been broken by the weight of a piece of timber… We buried him the same night and marked his grave with a small wooden cross bearing his name and regiment. We left him there with a sad heart for we have known and loved him long. He was a good comrade and a soldier who never shirked his duty and we shall all miss him very much.*

*Captain William Bunting MC, died on 11th August 1917, aged 22. He is buried in grave II.C.20 in The Huts Cemetery.

PIER 2

A

- Suffolk Regiment - **Lance Corporal F. R. Biggins to Private W. Wyatt**
  (completed from Pier and Face 1C)
- Somerset Light Infantry
- West Yorkshire Regiment (Prince of Wales's Own) - **Lieutenant Colonel M. N. Kennard to Lance Corporal W. Lund**
  (continued on Pier and Face 2D)

B

(Blank)

C

- West Yorkshire Regiment (Prince of Wales's Own) - **Private F. W. Taylor to Private A. Younger**
  (completed from Pier and Face 2D)
- East Yorkshire Regiment
- Bedfordshire Regiment
- Leicestershire Regiment - **Lieutenant Colonel J. G. Mignon to Second Lieutenant W. H. Stephens**
  (continued on Pier and Face 3A)

D

- West Yorkshire Regiment (Prince of Wales's Own) - **Lance Corporal J. W. McGrath to Private E. E. Taylor**
  (continued from Pier and Face 2A)
  (continued on Pier and Face 2C)

FRANK DEAN WITHERS MC

SECOND LIEUTENANT, 8TH BATTALION, SOMERSET LIGHT INFANTRY.

Died on 1st July 1916, aged 22, leading his men into action in an attack on Fricourt.

Frank was the youngest of four children of William Patient Withers (a builder) and Sarah Mary Withers (née Knight) of Street, Somerset.

He was educated at Sexey's School, Bruton, and then went to University College, Reading.

Commissioned in the autumn of 1914, he went to France on 6th October 1915.

He won his Military Cross at Armentières, the citation reads, *Temporary Second Lieutenant Frank Dean Withers, 8th Battalion, Somerset Light Infantry. For conspicuous gallantry near Armentières on the night of 15th/16th December 1915. He was in command of the leading party of his battalion in a successful raid on the Germans, and was the first man to jump into their trench. He shot the German sentry and behaved with such cool bravery that the remainder of his party were able to accomplish their task.*

As a result of the action four men were awarded the DCM and one the DSO. Two of those died later in December 1915 and a third died in May 1916.

Speaking of the action Frank said: *It was ticklish work getting over the barbed wire, for the least sound would have been heard by the Germans… I loaded myself up with a range finder, a gas apparatus, and plenty of letters and papers, and finally left a bomb to finish off what was left… we pinched a machine gun, bags of bombs, and killed about 20, including two officers, and took nine prisoners… fine sport while it lasted.*

Frank was notified of the award while still in the field in December 1915. It was gazetted on 21st January 1916. He was formally presented with the medal by HM King George V at Buckingham Palace on 1st April 1916.

ROGER MEYRICK HEATH

SECOND LIEUTENANT, 6TH BATTALION, SOMERSET LIGHT INFANTRY.

Died on 15th September 1916, aged 27, he was killed by a shell just a few hours after reaching the firing line. He was buried near to Delville Wood.

Roger was the only child of Meyrick William (a bank manager) and Katharine Rose Heath, of Clifton, Bristol.

Educated at Lambrook, he then gained a Classical scholarship to Rugby, leaving in 1908 to go to Oriel College, Oxford. He obtained a First Class in Classical Moderations in 1910, and a First Class degree in the Final Classical School in 1912. He was elected Bishop Fraser Scholar in 1912 and in 1913 was awarded the University Diploma in Archaeology, with distinction in Greek epigraphy. He had also been involved in the excavations of an early Minoan settlement in Crete. Appointed to the Craven Fellowship, he went to the British School at Athens.

The following poem, *Memories*, was included in a volume of his poems, *Beginnings*, published in 1913.

Now that the world is dark and grey
Save where the pink clouds far away
Hang over the leafless coppices
Like ghostly blossom on the trees,
We long for the crawling days to bring
The varied colour and scent of spring;
For May to come and the golden hours
When the chestnut-blossoms stand like towers
Each in its land of spreading leaves:
For the hawthorn-bloom, and the sun that weaves
A web of shade on the water's face
Where the shoots of the willow interlace,
Or glows in the leaves of a young beech tree
With an amber light most fair to see;
For early June and a cloudless day
When the winds have scattered the flower of the may,
And the winding stream is carpeted
With petals pink and white and red,
And the small waves set them all aquiver
Where they gather together in bends of the river:

For the cool breeze blowing in wood and hedge,
And the wild-rose tossed at the water's edge,
And the little ripples flickering bright
That catch and mirror the morning light
In crumpled bars of yellow gold
On the face of the river running cold;
For the great perfection and radiant peace
No dream can picture nor thought increase,
The spell that never was caught in rhyme
Of the open fields in the summer time.
But even if we have longed in vain
To see these flowery streams again,
Yet the work of the summer is not lost:
Into our souls those days have tossed
Their floating blossom and shifting shade;
These are the things that shaped and made
Our inmost being, and subtly wrought
The stuff and texture of all our thought.
In the hearts of all that saw aright
With mind undimmed and a true delight,
Those summer waters still shall glide,
Though all the memories shall have died.

When war broke out he returned to England and enlisted in the Public Schools Battalion, Royal Fusiliers gaining promotion to corporal. In May 1915 he was commissioned in the Somerset Light Infantry. Early in 1916 he met with an accident while lecturing as bombing instructor, which resulted in the loss of a great part of his left hand.

Despite his injuries he was keen for active service; his commanding officer was opposed to his going as his hand was still crippled and *he was of very great use* where he was; but eventually he was allowed to go, arriving in France on 8th September 1916.

Dr Geraldine Hodgson, of Oriel College, wrote that he was, *A man of great and rare ability, of deep if silent goodness, he was beloved of his friends for all those best qualities which English people prize, but do not, as a rule, parade. He was esteemed alike by College authorities and by his fellows; and even if, to quote the words of one of those over him, 'he was a mystery to the outer world,' yet, as the same writer observed, 'he was respected and adored for his knowledge and ability, but simply loved for his character'.*

EVELYN HENRY LINTOTT

L<small>IEUTENANT</small>, 15<small>TH</small> B<small>ATTALION</small>, W<small>EST</small> Y<small>ORKSHIRE</small> R<small>EGIMENT</small>
(P<small>RINCE OF</small> W<small>ALES'S</small> O<small>WN</small>).

Died on 1st July 1916, aged 32, during an attack on
Serre.

Evelyn was one of at least five children of Arthur Frederick
(a cattle salesman) and Eleanor Anne Lintott (née Stacey) of
Farncombe, Surrey.

After his secondary education he went to St Luke's
Training College, Exeter, in 1905 and subsequently
became a schoolteacher.

He played football for Plymouth Argyle, Queen's Park Rangers, Bradford City and Leeds
City and was head of the Players' Union (later to become the Professional Footballers'
Association) and edited the *Football Players Magazine*. As an England International he made
seven appearances as a left-half in the 1908/09 season.

He enlisted in Leeds on 14th September 1914 and rose to the rank of sergeant before he
was granted a commission, the first professional footballer so to do. He was part of the
battalion that arrived in Egypt on 21st December 1915 to guard the Suez Canal. In March 1916
the battalion left Egypt and went to France in preparation for the Somme offensive.

A letter published in the *Yorkshire Evening Post* included: *Lieut. Lintott's end was particularly
gallant… He led his men with great dash, and when hit the first time declined to take the count.
Instead, he drew his revolver and called for further effort. Again he was hit and still he struggled on,
but a third shot finally bowled him over. Lieut. Booth*, too, though in sore agony from a shell fragment
which penetrated the shoulder, and must have touched the heart, tried his utmost to go forward, but
pitched forward helplessly after going a few yards. He and Lintott were two gallant sportsmen who
knew how to die – but then, so did all the boys. They went out to almost certain death with just the
cry, 'Now Leeds' on their lips.*

At the time the war broke out Evelyn was a master at Dudley Hill School in Bradford and
the staff and pupils raised the money to have an enlarged picture of him framed and hung in
the school in remembrance.

His brother, **Keith Lintott**, Lance Corporal 8/3675, New Zealand Engineers, died on 23rd
September 1916, aged 21. He is buried in grave D.15 in Thistle Dump Cemetery.

*Second Lieutenant Major William Booth, the Yorkshire cricketer, also died on 1st July 1916,
aged 29. He is buried in grave I.G.14 in Serre Road Cemetery No. 1.

JOHN GILBERT VAUSE

LIEUTENANT, 15TH BATTALION, WEST YORKSHIRE REGIMENT
(PRINCE OF WALES'S OWN).

Died on 1st July 1916, aged 23, during an attack on
Serre.

John was one of five children of Frederick William (a
manufacturer) and Sarah Jane Vause (née Harrison) of
Leeds, Yorkshire.

His education was at Leeds Grammar School and later at
Leeds University. Subsequently, he became an apprentice
with the firm of Messrs. Mortimer and Co., woollen manufacturers, Morley, Yorkshire. During
this time he played for Headingley RFC.

He was part of the battalion that arrived in Egypt on 21st December 1915 to guard the Suez
Canal. This picture shows John (at left) with John Everitt* in the
Egyptian desert. In March 1916 the battalion left Egypt and
went to France in preparation for the Somme offensive.

A wounded private from his platoon reported that John was
first hit in the elbow just as he led his men over the parapet. He
went on, however, and after having his wound bound up
reached the barbed wire entanglements in front of the German
trenches which his platoon had to take. He was hit a second
time in the thigh, and, with the only remaining soldier in his
platoon by his side, he lay in a trench under a terrific
bombardment. The private, who was only rescued thirty six
hours later, continued, *We lay there talking about Leeds and
discussing the possibilities of getting home again. Lieut. Vause told
me that he had been recommended for his third star, and he was very
much "up about it." Some time later the gallant officer was again hit,
first on the chin and then in the back. He made the remark, "This has just about finished me off," and
died shortly afterwards.*

*Second Lieutenant John Paxman Everitt, aged 19, was another casualty on 1st July. He is
also commemorated on Pier and Face 2A.

FREDERICK WILLIAM CROWTHER HININGS

Captain, 3rd Battalion attached to 1st Battalion, East Yorkshire Regiment.

Died on 25th September 1916, aged 28, during an attack on Gueudecourt.

Frederick was one of at least five children of Dr John William and Eugenie Hinings (née Dannatt) of Filey, Yorkshire.

He was educated at Leeds Grammar School and later at Blundell's School, Tiverton, Devon. He was remembered at Blundell's as a fine cricketer (he was captain in 1905 and 1906) and football player. The *Blundellian* referred to him as 'The Genial Giant'.

He played for Yorkshire and was captain of Headingley RFC in 1908 in which year he also played for the Barbarians. A commentator described him as *a splendid full-back, being, without exception, one of the finest tacklers I have ever seen.*

He then went to work in the Malay States, planting rubber at Selangor. In 1910 he joined the Malay States Volunteer Rifles and attained the appointment of lance corporal. He served until September 1914 when he resigned and joined a party of thirteen men who returned to England. It was reported that Frederick's death meant that only one of that party was still alive.

Frederick enlisted in the 3rd Battalion on 6th November 1914 and was subsequently commissioned. He was wounded in May 1915 whilst serving near Ypres, receiving severe shrapnel wounds. It took many months of treatment before he was sufficiently recovered to resume his duties; but even then he was seriously restricted in the use of his right hand.

Promoted to captain on 9th April 1916, he was wounded a further three times and it was not until 25th August that he was able to return to France.

In one of his last letters he had written, *We must all trust in the Lord to pull us through. Some of us must go under. If we do, we will have died doing our duty to our Country, and no one could wish for a finer death.*

An obituary in the *Yorkshire Post* included: *...his powerful physique, coupled with rare football intelligence and initiative, made him one of the finest centre three-quarters who have represented Yorkshire for many years.*

MARK ARMSTRONG

PRIVATE, 1319, 13TH BATTALION, EAST YORKSHIRE REGIMENT.

Died on 13th November 1916, aged 38, during an attack to the north of Serre.

Mark was the son of John Riley Armstrong (a labourer) and Mary Armstrong.

Employed as a lamp lighter, he married Jane Anne Lowther on 24th December 1898, and lived in Hull, Yorkshire. They had eight children born between 1899 and 1914, although one of the younger children died in 1914, aged four.

He enlisted in Hull on 16th November 1914 and went to Egypt on 29th December 1915. The battalion left Egypt at the end of February 1916, arriving in France on 3rd March.

In 1916 Mark and Jane lost a second child, Wilfred, who died aged three.

In a letter from the Front on 8th August Mark wrote: *It was with great pleasure I received your letter it turned to great pain when I read the sad news it contained about poor little Wilfred, god rest his soul, but as you say he will be better off now he has gone to meet his little brother. I don't wonder that your heart is at breaking point, mine is broken already. It seems awful to think I am here facing death everyday for my country, and my little boy dying at home, and what made it worse was having to wait so long for a letter from you… Both my officers and headquarters officers tried their best to get me off. The district headquarters even sent for my regimental number and home address, but I have not heard any more about it and I don't suppose I shall. Now I wish with all my heart that I were with you to share the trouble with you, and also the pain… You remember the words dearest "oh you come to me heavily laden, and I will relieve you". So bear that in mind dear. I can assure you that it has been my hope and prayer and has kept me safe many times while in the trenches, and also remember dear, when your thoughts turn to either of our two little boys that they have gone to the one who loves little children, and they are safe under his mighty arm, and think also they may both be waiting to receive us, when our time comes to follow them.*

HENRY PATRICK CLAUDE BURTON

Captain, 1st Battalion, Bedfordshire Regiment.

Died on 27th July 1916, aged 23 during the capture of Longueval and Delville Wood.

Henry was the eldest of six children of Claude Edward Cole Hamilton Burton (a journalist and newspaper editor known as 'Touchstone') and Katherine Grace Burton (née Dell), of Woking, Surrey.

He was educated at the Dragon School, at Repton and then Wadham College, Oxford. He was a most promising oarsman and was elected captain of the boat club in 1914. During his time at university he was a member of the OTC. He was gazetted as a second lieutenant in the 4th Battalion on 14th August 1914 and went to France on 13th May 1915 attached to the 1st Battalion. A promotion to lieutenant came later that year and a further promotion to the rank of temporary captain followed shortly before his death.

He and his fiancée had planned to marry when he next had home leave.

Having inherited his father's journalistic talents he often wrote for the *Mudlark*, the regimental magazine, using the pen-name of 'Touchstone – Junior'. An article in April 1916 about the loss of 'Henry', a louse that had obviously spent some time residing in the seams of Henry's uniform, concluded, *It was after the company's visit to the Divisional baths that Henry disappeared… Yet, as I turned over to sleep, I felt an inexplicable sense of loss. I tried to ignore it and go to sleep, but still the trouble was there. Slowly it dawned upon me that I had lost an old friend, Henry was with me no longer. With Percy and Archibald, with Ermyntrude and Arabella, I had at least their poor bodies, when they came to an untimely end; but with Henry - not so much as his identity disc. I could only register him mentally as "Missing, believed killed"; there was no grave on which to shed a tear of fond remembrance. How well we knew each other, Henry and I! And now he is gone, and I shall never see him again. Regret for him will follow me to my grave!*

Henry's last article appeared in the December 1916 issue with the footnote that he had, alas, *gone west.*

His company sergeant major wrote: *Throughout the operations he showed wonderful courage, and led us most gallantly in the attack. His last words were to me, requesting me to carry on with the task he had so nobly set out to do. He was loved by all the men under his command, who were very sorry to lose so brave a leader.*

The following is one of a number of poems written by his father after Henry's death.

AN UNKNOWN GRAVE

Somewhere beneath the stars he lies,
Whom Earth has taken to her breast,
Nor ever may our tear-dimmed eyes
Behold where now he takes his rest.
No cross records his well-loved name,
No tomb in days to come shall tell
In golden letters of the fame
That crowned him even as he fell.

Yet he is here with us today;
A thousand things his touch reveal,
Sweet evidence no cumbering clay,
No unknown sepulchre conceal.
In many a heart his grave is green
And sweet with flowers we planted there,
Dear memories of what has been
A wealth of fragrant blossom bear.

What matter if no sign may show
Where rests at last his honoured dust,
Whose life and death have bid us know
The strength of perfect love and trust?
Tis ours to bear before the world
Our part until the goal be won.
The banner that his hands unfurled
Still flies triumphant in the sun!

DAVID WESCOTT BROWN

CAPTAIN, 6TH BATTALION, LEICESTERSHIRE REGIMENT.

Died on 14th July 1916, aged 23, near Bazentin le Petit.

David was one of five children of the Rev. George Gibson Brown and Nelly Brown (née Hardman) of Bedford.

Educated at the Dragon School and at Marlborough College, he then went to Balliol College, Oxford where he took a Second Class in Classical Moderations in March 1914, and was reading for Finals when war broke out. A member of the OTC, he was commissioned in August 1914, gazetted lieutenant two months later and promoted to captain in November 1915. He had been in France since 29th July 1915 and whilst there he wrote a number of poems.

He was last seen going out with a sergeant to reconnoitre. The sergeant was killed and his body recovered but no trace of David could be found. His commanding officer wrote: *After the battalion had taken Bazentin Wood he went forward with a sergeant to reconnoitre. The sergeant was killed, and it is known that your son was wounded. I sent out immediately we heard and brought in the sergeant's body, but your son was not there, and as we were very close to the German lines it is possible he was taken away by them. Your son has done such splendid work with the battalion and was such a gallant and cheery lad, that his loss is a great one to me… Will you please accept from me, on your son's behalf, my very deep appreciation and thanks for the splendid services which he has rendered to the battalion and to his country.*

In May 1916 David had written a letter that was used at his Memorial Service, which included, *I am writing like this because summer is here, and I don't think our present peacefulness can go on much longer. People at home are beginning to wonder what they pay us for; and I think Death must come to many of us, if not to most (I am talking of officers now) before very long; and, if it does come to me, I don't want you to feel it as a shock, and I don't want you or any one to grieve… I don't want to die. I want to live and tell how I was in the War, how I was a fighter in it, not merely a server; but, if I do get killed, I want you and every one to know that I knew of the possibility, that I was ready for it, and facing it, and not shirking and dodging the thought of it. It seems to me that for a man who is, if not ready or willing to die, at least aware of the presence of death, and looking it in the face not caring or wondering what lies beyond, Death has lost its power. When you cease to fear Death you have conquered it, and Death has become only a gate, no harder to pass through than the door of a room.*

LEONARD CRABTREE

PRIVATE, 16/609, 16TH BATTALION, WEST YORKSHIRE
REGIMENT (PRINCE OF WALES'S OWN).

Died on 1st July 1916, aged 25, during an attack on
Serre.

Leonard was one of at least seven children of Walter (a stuff
presser) and Ada Crabtree (née Barrett) of Bradford,

Yorkshire.

He was employed at a local dye works.

The picture shows Leonard and Holly Leach on their wedding
day, 30th November 1915. Leonard left for Egypt the following day.
After his death Holly married Fred Taylor and they had three
children.

In March 1916 the battalion went from Egypt to France. Leonard bought this card in Marseille and at some point in the journey north he
threw it out of the carriage window in the hope that it would find its way to Bradford, which
it did.

The husband of Ivy Leach (Holly's twin sister), **Harry Raistrick**,
Private 36186, 10th Battalion, York and Lancaster Regiment, died
on 18th April 1917, aged 28. He is commemorated on Special
Memorial B9 in Chili Trench
Cemetery.

Leonard's younger and only brother,
Luther Crabtree, also served and
was awarded the Military Medal. He was wounded in 1918 and
subsequently medically discharged.

MAURICE ROBINSON CROWTHER

PRIVATE 15/252, 15TH BATTALION, WEST YORKSHIRE
REGIMENT (PRINCE OF WALES'S OWN).

Died on 1st July 1916, aged 24, during an attack on
Serre.

Maurice was one of two children, both sons, of John (the
local chemist) and Elizabeth Crowther (née Robinson) of
Grassington, Yorkshire.

Educated at Threshfield School, he enlisted in Leeds on
12th September 1914.

He went to Egypt on 22nd December 1915 and then to France early in 1916.

His chaplain wrote that it had been Maurice's
wish to be killed rather than be taken prisoner -
in fact he had vowed never to become a prisoner
himself nor take one - the latter determination
being based upon his experience of the Germans,
whom he stigmatised as *brutes and beasts.*

As well as being the village chemist, his father
was also a well known local antiquarian, historian
and botanist. His book, *Silva Gars,* a guide to
Grassington and Upper Wharfedale, is dedicated
to the memory of eighteen Grassington men who
died in the war.

Maurice was a keen photographer and his
father used a number of his pictures of the area as
illustrations in the book.

His father also erected a cenotaph to
Maurice's memory in the churchyard of St Mary's,
in the nearby village of Conistone which carries
the inscription, *I honour thy memory - Noble Son,
For thy stern duty done, In the Battle of the Somme.*

THOMAS FRANCIS

Private 7898, 1/5th Battalion, West Yorkshire Regiment
(Prince of Wales's Own).

Died on 3rd July 1916, aged 23, during fighting near
Thiepval.

Thomas was one of eight children of Felix (a labourer) and
Elizabeth Francis (née Breare).

He was employed as a weaver at Bankfield Shed,
Barnoldswick, Yorkshire.

He married Gertrude Bird in 1914 and lived in
Barnoldswick.

In November 1914 Thomas enlisted in Keighley, Yorkshire as Private 3/14642, Duke of
Wellington's (West Riding Regiment).

He served in Malta for nine months, during which time he transferred to the West
Yorkshires. He had only been in France about six weeks when he was killed.

In July his wife received a letter from a soldier of the West Riding Regiment enclosing some
of Thomas's personal items. He explained that, *I was out scouting on a piece of 'no man's land' just
after our Battalion had relieved the 1/5th West Yorks from a very hot place when I came across the
dead body of an English soldier in a very lonely spot. As a means of identifying him I searched his
pockets, and I am sorry to say that I am afraid it is your husband, from the pay-book and photos, one
of which I enclose. So gathering his personal belongings together I handed them to the proper quarter
and then proceeded to lay him to rest in a decent grave, just behind the firing line, and may he rest in
peace. My object in writing to you was to let you know the true state of things, for with his pay book,
&c. being on his body when found I thought he might be reported missing, and although I know it is
hard I thought it best for you to know the cruel truth. So please excuse me if I have caused you any
pain. You will at least have the satisfaction of knowing that he is in a decent grave, along with others
who have died doing their duty.*

ALFRED NORMAN SUMMERSCALE

PRIVATE, 15/861, 15TH BATTALION, WEST YORKSHIRE
REGIMENT (PRINCE OF WALES'S OWN).

Died on 1st July 1916, aged 24, during an attack on Serre.

Alfred was one of seven children of James Conyers Summerscale (a leather factor) and Clara Summerscale (née North) of Morecambe, Lancashire.

After an education at Leeds Boys' Modern School, he was apprenticed to Messrs. S. Dixon & Son, Electrical Engineers. He then joined the staff of Messrs. Verity, Electrical Engineers, and was employed in their sales department.

Alfred and his two older brothers enlisted together and subsequently served together in Egypt (from 22nd December 1915) and later in France. All three took part in the attack in which Alfred died, James* was also killed that day while **Frank** was wounded in his legs and feet. Alfred's two younger brothers, **Arthur** and **Alec**, served in the Army Service Corps.

*James Stanley Summerscale, Private 15/862, 15th Battalion, West Yorkshire Regiment (Prince of Wales's Own), died aged 26. He is buried in grave III.B.21 in Mesnil Communal Cemetery Extension.

LEEDS BOYS' MODERN SCHOOL

There are 138 old boys and one master from the school who died in the war. Alfred and fourteen others are commemorated on the Memorial, including these three men who also served as privates in Alfred's battalion and who died on 1st July 1916.

Arthur E. Fillingham
aged 20

Ernest Ingleson
aged 25

John S. Whitehead
aged 20

PIER 3

A
• Leicestershire Regiment - **Second Lieutenant A. B. Taylor to Private S. Yoxon** *(completed from Pier and Face 2C)*   • Royal Irish Regiment   • Yorkshire Regiment - **Captain W. L. Batty to Private J. D. White 16233** *(continued on Pier and Face 3D)*

B
(Blank)

C
• Lancashire Fusiliers - **Private J. A. Mort to Private T. York** *(completed from Pier and Face 3D)*   • Royal Scots Fusiliers   • Cheshire Regiment - **Captain J. L. W. H. Abell to Private W. Tierney** *(continued on Pier and Face 4A)*

D
• Yorkshire Regiment - **Private J. D. White 19628 to Private W. Young** *(completed from Pier and Face 3A)*   • Lancashire Fusiliers - **Major C. W. Merryweather to Private D. Mort** *(continued on Pier and Face 3C)*

ARNOLD BRADLEY TAYLOR

SECOND LIEUTENANT, 9TH BATTALION, LEICESTERSHIRE REGIMENT.

Died on 12th July 1916, aged 22, near Contalmaison.

Arnold was one of seven children of John William (a bellfounder) and his first wife Annie Mary Taylor (née Bardsley), of Loughborough, Leicestershire.

Educated at Shaftesbury and Denstone College, he was in the OTC for two years and then joined the family business.

He was a keen hockey player, a member of the Loughborough Club and played for Leicestershire. He enlisted as Private 3286, 4th Battalion, Royal Fusiliers on 15th September 1914, was gazetted to 9th Battalion, Leicesters on 26th January 1915 and went to France in February 1916.

A fellow officer wrote: *It happened about midday. He had just come back to the trench after helping to bring in wounded when a heavy shell burst nearby, and a piece of it went right through his body. He only lived a few minutes.*

Two of Arnold's three older brothers also died, **John** on 5th September 1916 and **Gerard** on 24th September 1918. All three are commemorated on the **Loughborough Carillon and War Memorial**, which remembers 480 Loughborough men who made the ultimate sacrifice. The carillon contains forty seven bells, all of which were cast at the family's foundry in the town.

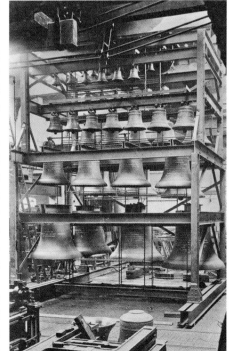

The Denison bell is the largest, weighing over four tons, and carries the inscription: *In proud and loving memory of his three nephews, killed in action in France, John William Taylor, Courcelette, 1916; Gerard Bardsley Taylor, St Quentin, 1918; Arnold Bradley Taylor, Contalmaison, 1916; sons of John William Taylor (1853-1919), grandsons of John William Taylor (1827-1906), Edmund Denison Taylor, the founder of these bells, gives this the largest, 1923.*

In July 1917 the foundry presented the Leicestershire Regiment with a bell in memory of Arnold.

WILLIAM BUCKINGHAM VC

PRIVATE, 6276, 1ST BATTALION, LEICESTERSHIRE REGIMENT.

Died on 15th September 1916, aged 30, in the fighting near Ginchy.

William was a son of William John and Annie Susan Billington (née Bennett) of Bedford. After his father's death his mother married Thomas Henry Buckingham.

At an early age he was looked after in the Cottesthorpe Cottage Homes by Mr. and Mrs. Harrison. After his education he enlisted as a boy soldier, aged 15 years and eight months, in the 17th Foot (Leicestershire Regiment) on 29th November 1901. His service saw him stationed in a number of locations, including Egypt and India. It was from the latter that the battalion returned when war was declared and went to France in October 1914.

The Victoria Cross was awarded: *For conspicuous acts of bravery and devotion to duty in rescuing and rendering aid to the wounded whilst exposed to heavy fire, especially at Neuve-Chapelle on 10th and 12th March 1915.* He was wounded during this time and always contended that his life was saved by a pack of postcards in his left breast pocket that deflected the bullet preventing a mortal wound. He was convalescing with Mr. and Mrs. Harrison when the news of the award first appeared in the morning newspapers. Mr. Harrison saw the name and ran down to where William was staying to learn if the number given corresponded with his, and then the news spread rapidly. William was as surprised as anyone; as he was on leave, he had not been officially notified of the award, as he would have been if he had remained in the trenches. He received his medal from HM King George V at Buckingham Palace on 4th June 1915. He was also presented with other civic awards that reflected local pride in his being the first Victoria Cross to be earned by a Leicestershire man in the war thus far.

He then spent time as part of the recruiting campaign before returning to duty. Before he left he went to a local garden party given for wounded soldiers. It was there that he met a corporal, who told the other guests how he had been one of the men William had carried out of the firing line under heavy fire, thus saving his life. On his return to duty he underwent a period of retraining, during which he was promoted to sergeant. He subsequently relinquished the rank and reverted to private so that he could return to the Front. He then served as a captain's orderly until he was killed by machine gun fire.

A friend wrote: *The thing which struck one most about the Leicester VC...was that the attention and honours lavished upon him left him entirely unspoilt. He remained what in obscurity he had always been - just a quiet, simpleminded soul, to whom the word 'duty' meant a great deal more than obeying military orders, or doing something bravely venturesome on the battlefield.*

ROBERT WILLIAM POPHAM BELL

CAPTAIN, 3RD BATTALION ATTACHED TO 2ND BATTALION, ROYAL IRISH REGIMENT.

Died on 5th July 1916, aged 32, in the Mametz area.

Robert was one of at least three children of the Rev. Robert Popham Bell of Tipperary, Co. Tipperary.

He was educated at The Abbey, Tipperary and afterwards served with the 3rd Battalion, Royal Irish Regiment, rising to the rank of captain.

He left the army and in 1909 went to Ceylon where three years later he was appointed Superintendent of the Woodend Rubber and Tea Company.

He returned from Ceylon in May 1915 and at once applied for a commission in his old battalion. He was gazetted captain and was stationed in Dublin until February 1916, when he was sent to France and attached to the 2nd Battalion.

His commanding officer wrote: *We shall all miss him more than I can say and your grief is shared by the whole Battalion. His men were devoted to him. He died a most gallant death and was killed instantaneously by rifle fire. We recovered his body after the fight and buried him near the place where he fell... Our hearts go out to you and yours and the whole Battalion joins me in the deepest sympathy. Personally I have lost a gallant officer and comrade.*

The Adjutant wrote: *I cannot tell you how grieved we all are to lose such a gallant officer and comrade. He was killed when leading his Company in a most dashing attack against a very strong German position which we afterwards captured...Believe me I feel the loss of a great personal friend and sympathise with you very deeply in your sorrow.*

Both Robert and his father are commemorated on stained glass windows in St Mary's Church in Tipperary.

The loss to the family was heightened as his brother in law, **Lieutenant Colonel William Lyle**, 23rd Battalion, Northumberland Fusiliers, had been killed on 1st July, aged 40. He is buried in grave I.G.1 in Bapaume Post Military Cemetery.

EWART RICHARDSON

Second Lieutenant, 4th Battalion, Yorkshire Regiment.

Died on 27th September 1916, aged 35, during the fighting at Martinpuich.

Ewart was the only son, youngest of six children, of Thomas Henry (an ironworks manager) and Marietta Richardson (née Roberts) of Middlesbrough, Yorkshire.

He received his education at the Royal Masonic School, Wood Green, where he had a good record, passing the Cambridge Senior Local Examination with Honours, and receiving the Canonbury Gold Medal.

He had a literary talent and published several short stories and poems in a number of magazines, including *The Thrush, Pall Mall Magazine* and *The Magpie*. After qualifying as a solicitor in February 1904, he served as secretary to the Middlesbrough Liberal and Labour Association. Commissioned as a second lieutenant in the 4th Battalion on 20th July 1915, he went to France on 28th May 1916.

Later in 1916 his sisters published a book, *War Notes and Sketches,* containing extracts from his diary and letters written between July and September 1916. In one he describes conditions in the trenches: *To be in the trenches is to be in prison. On either side stretch the wretched yellow walls of rotten sandbags or hardened clay beyond the protection of which you may not pass. Even you may not look over the edge, except by means of a mirror through which you see ridiculously as if through a tube stuck through the sandbags. For the rest you must be content with the little tent of blue which prisoners call the sky. In the dug-outs the analogy continues. There is no criminal in England to-day who is condemned to sleep in such a narrow, foul, vermin-infested cell as those in which our soldiers snatch their few hours of broken rest. There is no ventilation. The foul air lies stagnant in these hovels for numberless successions of soldiers to breathe. The little opening of the door is the only ventilation admitted. And the conscious festering of spirit is present also. Men's thoughts grow depressed, even at times despairing. The dull, colourless prospect, the weary waiting for the unknown, the strain of endless watching, imprison and bind the mind, even as the body is enclosed by the sand-bagged walls. It is difficult to read anything but the easiest fiction. To write is almost impossible.*

The book also includes an assessment of him by his captain: *Your son was one of the finest men I have ever met; and the brave and splendid way in which he led the Company at night into action makes everyone of us proud to have known him. His loss to the Company is great, as his judgment and experience in men was invaluable. Few have given their services as nobly and devotedly to their country, and he rests honoured by all who had the privilege to know him.*

MAURICE LESLIE ADAMSON

SECOND LIEUTENANT, ROYAL SCOTS FUSILIERS, ATTACHED TO 10TH BATTALION, ROYAL IRISH RIFLES.

Died on 1st July 1916, aged 23, leading his platoon into action at Thiepval.

Maurice was born in Burma, one of at least three children of Sir Harvey (the Lieutenant Governor of Burma) and Lady Jane Charlotte Adamson (née Leslie).

He was educated at Haileybury, where he was in the OTC, and later at the Faculty of Engineering, King's College, London; and at Pullman College, Washington State, USA.

In 1913, after ranching for one year in western Canada, he entered the service of the Bank of Montreal. In August 1914 he enlisted as Private 17092, British Columbia Regiment and came to England with the regiment.

On 22nd January 1915 he was granted a temporary commission in the 10th Battalion, Royal Irish Rifles and went to the Front in October.

On 22nd May 1916 he was given a permanent commission in the Royal Scots Fusiliers; but at the time of his death he had not taken up the posting and he was killed while still serving with the Royal Irish Rifles.

PHILIP BURNET BASS

LIEUTENANT, 1ST/5TH BATTALION, CHESHIRE REGIMENT.

Died on 1st July 1916, aged 21, during the fighting at Gommecourt.

Born in Jersey, Philip was the eldest of three children, all sons, of Colonel Philip de Salis Bass CMG and Frances Edith Bass (née Craigie). The family later lived in Ealing.

His education at Winton House, Aldershot, was followed by time at The Imperial Services College, Windsor and Pembroke College, Oxford; at both of the latter he was a member of the OTC.

His commission as a second lieutenant was effective from 20th November 1914 and he went to France on 3rd May 1915. A promotion to temporary lieutenant followed on 1st March 1916.

On 1st July 1916 his company was acting in their role as divisional pioneers. They were given the task of producing a strong point near the cemetery at Gommecourt. Philip was supervising the work of making a fire step when a passing party of bombers accidentally dropped one of their bombs, which exploded. The blast wounded Philip in the face and also wounded Private Clifford*. Both were bandaged up by their colleagues but Philip's wounds would not stop bleeding. Private Clifford volunteered to take him back across No Man's Land to a dressing station. They set off but neither was seen again.

His company officer wrote: *He was greatly loved by all ranks, he was so thoroughly brave and conscientious constantly thinking of new schemes for the comfort of his men.*

*John Emmanuel Clifford, Private 1527, 1st/5th Battalion, Cheshire Regiment, died aged 20. He is also commemorated on Pier and Face 3C.

RALPH JOHN HOWELLS

PRIVATE, 244158, 1ST/5TH BATTALION, CHESHIRE REGIMENT.

Died on 8th September 1916, aged 17, during the fighting at Combles.

Ralph was the eldest of six children of Thomas (a colliery labourer) and Blanche Howells (née Evans) of Lydbrook, Gloucestershire.

He was educated at Lydbrook National School and afterwards at the Council Schools before he took employment at Waterloo Colliery.

He enlisted in Hereford as Private 3009, Herefordshire Regiment, on 5th December 1914. This family picture was taken in 1916.

On 27th July 1916 he transferred to the Cheshire Regiment and two days later he went to France, joining the regiment in the field on 7th August.

His platoon commander wrote: *I am deeply grieved having to write & tell you that I firmly believe he has been killed though we never succeeded in finding his body & I feel that you would much rather I told you this than to still live in precious hope. We were out working in the middle of the night when the Hun gave us a very heavy shelling, we were in a communication trench at the start when one fell in the trench & buried five men, we only managed to find three* of them who were quite dead, your son & another man who were last seen with the three we could not find so had to report them missing… I always found him a good lad & it pains me very much losing them.*

*Of the three bodies found, two are buried in Delville Wood Cemetery and the other in Bronfay Farm Military Cemetery. The fifth man, whose body was never found, was **Joseph William Forster**, Private 15653, aged 33, who is also commemorated on Pier and Face 3C.

HARRY MIST

PRIVATE, W/487, 13TH BATTALION, CHESHIRE REGIMENT.

Died on 25th August 1916, aged 25, whilst in trenches at Thiepval Wood.

Harry was one of at least four children of Harry (a general labourer at Lever Bros.) and his first wife, Louisa Mist (née Callnan).

After an education at New Ferry Church Schools, he found employment as a labourer in the Seed Mill Warehouse, Port Sunlight. He played football for Rock Ferry St Paul's AFC.

He married Elizabeth Hatton at Birkenhead on 11th December 1914. Harry never got to see his only child, a daughter, who was born in 1916.

Enlisting at Port Sunlight in August 1914, he went to France on 25th September 1915.

His sergeant wrote that Harry, …*was on sentry duty when a piece of shell hit him and killed him instantly. All the old boys of the battalion miss him very much. He was one of my policemen, and he always did his duty like a soldier.*

His company quartermaster sergeant wrote: *During a very heavy bombardment on our lines…Harry was struck by a fragment of shell and instantly killed. At the time he was on duty at his sentry post, and I hope it will be a consolation to you to know that he died a hero. He was buried in a little cemetery in a valley well behind the firing line with a number of his fallen comrades. The Chaplain conducted a short religious service, and the boys of the regiment made a cross, bearing his name and number and placed it on his grave.*

The burial was reported as being in the south-east corner of Thiepval Wood, but the grave was subsequently lost.

He is also commemorated on the **Port Sunlight War Memorial**, which lists the names of 503 who died from the over 4,000 employees who served. The 13th Battalion was raised in Port Sunlight and contained over 700 of its employees.

FREDERICK CHARLES ROBERT DUNN

LIEUTENANT, 11TH BATTALION, LANCASHIRE FUSILIERS.

Died on 10th July 1916, aged 23, during the fighting at Ovillers.

Frederick was the youngest of eight children of Herbert George (a cabinet maker) and Felicia Dunn (née Harman) of Bromley, Kent.

After an early education at Park View Prep School, South Godstone, he went on to Cranleigh School where, in 1910, he won the Hardy Memorial Music Prize for violin.

After serving three years articled to a chartered accountant in the City, he became secretary to the family firm of H. G. Dunn and Sons Ltd.

Initially he enlisted at Westminster on 2nd September 1914 as a private in the 18th Battalion, Royal Fusiliers. Granted a commission on 14th December he was then posted to the 11th Battalion, Lancashire Fusiliers and went to France on 25th September 1915. He was made second in command of a company in February 1916.

A captain wrote: *I would have written before… I am afraid I rather shirked it because it hurts to write about it. He and I were on the parapet trying to lead some men over and he was hit. He died in my arms, and didn't speak again, or even recognise me. He has been a great friend of mine ever since we were at Boscombe, and I thought an awful lot of him. One seems to have lost all one's friends now.*

His commanding officer wrote: *Your son was killed… whilst gallantly organising the defence of one of our advanced trenches, which was being attacked by the Huns. They had previously succeeded in surrounding and almost annihilating one of our companies, who were holding an isolated trench in front, and were pushing the remnants of the garrison back on to the trench in which your son had his Company. The resistance put up in this trench however, succeeded in stopping and driving back the enemy, and it was during this fighting that your son was killed. He died encouraging his men in difficult situations in a very gallant manner.*

His older brother, **Herbert Harman Dunn**, Lieutenant, 12th Battalion, The King's (Liverpool Regiment), died on 26th September 1916, aged 33. He is buried in grave XXXIII.D.11 in Serre Road Cemetery No. 2.

JOSEPH PATRICK HASTINGS

Company Sergeant Major, 12534, 16th Battalion, Lancashire Fusiliers.

Died on 2nd July 1916, aged 41, during an attack on Thiepval.

Joseph was one of nine children of Michael (a sergeant in the Lancashire Fusiliers) and Margaret Hastings (née O'Shaugnessy) of Bury, Lancashire.

After enlistment on 29th January 1891, he saw service in India, Egypt, Sudan, Crete, Malta and during the Boer War. He was discharged on the expiration of his term on 28th January 1903 but re-enlisted on 24th August and served a further ten years.

In 1913 he was presented to HM King George V during Their Majesties' visit to Bury. The local newspaper reported: *Lord Derby was seen to come out again. He beckoned to Sergeant Joseph Hastings, who was standing almost opposite. He spoke to Hastings, after which both made their way to the Town Hall, Lord Derby leading the way. As Hastings reached the door, His Majesty was seen to come forward and standing on the doorstep shook hands with him and addressed a few remarks to him, evidently congratulating him upon his length of service in the Fusiliers. The King asked him what regiment he had served with, and Hastings replied, "The Lancashire Fusiliers". Next he enquired how long he had been in the service, and Hastings told him 26 years. Sergeant Hastings was wearing five medals earned in many campaign and His Majesty congratulated him upon his record. This recognition of the soldier created the greatest satisfaction, and the crowd cheered lustily.*

Joseph married Mary Ann Kennealy in 1913 and reached the end of his service term on 14th December that year. He returned to the colours on the outbreak of the war and went to France on 23rd November 1915.

A lance corporal wrote: *…whilst going over the top he was wounded in the hand by shrapnel, and whilst he was retiring to the trench he was hit by a bullet in the middle of the back, death taking place immediately… He was a soldier brave, cool, and feared nothing. He died a soldier hero… he was always cheery and bright, and always thought well of the company, and always did his best of the lads.*

His younger brother, **Herbert John Hastings**, Private DM2/096916, Army Service Corps, died on 22nd October 1916, aged 36. He is buried in grave K.P.130.2368 in Bury Cemetery.

JOSEPH ARTHUR KAY

PRIVATE, 9174, 2ND BATTALION, LANCASHIRE FUSILIERS.

Died on 12th October 1916, aged 32, during an attack on Le Transloy.

Joseph was the eldest son, one of twelve children, of Joseph (a life assurance agent) and Elizabeth Alice Kay (née Potter) of Eccles, Lancashire.

After an education at Eccles Parish Church School and Eccles Wesleyan Sunday School, he was employed by the Royal London Insurance Society. He enlisted in Manchester and went to France on 15th July 1915. During his time on active service he had a number of letters published in the local newspaper.

In October 1915 he described a *wild night in the trenches…we commenced a rapid fire just at dusk, and also got our machine guns going. Fritz must have got it into his head that we were coming over the parapet again after his scalp, so he got his artillery going. For four solid hours he kept up a continuous bombardment of our trenches by his big guns. Then we expected Fritz coming for us, so we 'stood to' with bayonets fixed ready for him if he chanced his luck. He would have had a warm time, for there is not a man amongst us who is not anxious to feel his bayonet bite, and bite deep, too. Good Lord what a night that was! The din was awful, one continuous roar and the bursting shells lit up the night, and we were extremely lucky to come out of the trenches safe the next morning. The Germans sent over everything in the firework catalogue except Chinese crackers and pin wheels. When our artillery joined in the display we got a conception of what is meant by the phrase 'Hell with the lid off'. This, however, is a poor description for no one can describe such a night.* He concluded with, *There is no room for swankers in the firing-line, and one's only thought and desire is to do his level best. If he has the ill-luck to go under let it be doing his duty as a soldier and a man. Lloyd George's munition workers will have to work lots of overtime, for Fritz has got to be buried with lead and steel. Once he is on the run he will never stop until he gets to Berlin.*

In January 1916 he wrote: *One begins to think himself a lucky chap to be living out here, after he has seen comrades blown to pieces a few yards away, who only a few minutes before had been joking and laughing. I am glad to think we shall be out of it for a bit, as we are going behind the lines for a rest. We deserve a rest, for we have held one of the worst parts of the line for nearly three months and that has cost us some lives.*

In April 1916 he spent three months in hospital suffering from paralysis caused by shell shock, resumed training in July 1916 and returned to France two months later. His three younger brothers, **Harold**, **Charles**, and **Leonard**, all served and all survived the war. The latter two suffered poor health as a result of the war, Charles succumbing to influenza and pneumonia in February 1919.

JAMES MCLYNN

PRIVATE, 13504, 1ST BATTALION, LANCASHIRE FUSILIERS.

Died on 1st July 1916, aged 32.

James was the youngest son, one of at least nine children, of Michael (an innkeeper) and Thirza McLynn (née Emmerson).

He married Mary Ellen Stevens in 1907 and lived in Rochdale, Lancashire. They had four children, born between 1908 and 1915.

He was employed as a plasterer when he enlisted in Rochdale on 7th January 1915. He served in Gallipoli from 9th August and had to be evacuated suffering from frostbite, after a storm in November. He was treated at Gaza Hospital, Egypt.

He then went to France and was posted as missing after the fighting at Beaumont Hamel.

In response to various enquiries, the British Red Cross wrote in February 1917 with two eyewitness accounts which confirmed that James had been killed by machine gun fire early in the attack. Neither could provide any information as to what had happened to his body.

One stated that they had been in a sunken road: *near Ocean Villas I saw McLynn lying dead. I was quite near him. I saw him laid out. I had to leave him.*

The other stated: *On July 1st 1916 at Jacob's Ladder Trench Beaumont Hamel McLynn was killed outright by machine gun fire when just over the top of our trench during an advance. We retired for three days and I do not know what happened to the body.*

PIER 4

A

- Cheshire Regiment - **Private T. Tipper to Private W. Yates**
  (completed from Pier and Face 3C)
- Royal Welsh Fusiliers
- South Wales Borderers
- King's Own Scottish Borderers - **Captain J. Anderson to Private R. Geddes**
  (continued on Pier and Face 4D)

B

(Blank)

C

- Army Service Corps - **Private H. Stafford to Driver R. Lickers**
  (completed from Pier and Face 5C)
- Royal Army Medical Corps
- Army Veterinary Corps
- Army Chaplains' Department
- Army Ordnance Corps
- General List
- 1st Regiment South African Infantry
- 2nd Regiment South African Infantry
- 3rd Regiment South African Infantry
- 4th Regiment South African Infantry
- West India Regiment

D

- King's Own Scottish Borderers - **Private A. Gibbs to Private J. Young**
  (completed from Pier and Face 4A)
- Cameronians (Scottish Rifles)
- Royal Inniskilling Fusiliers - **Captain E. N. F. Bell VC to Private W. Barnes**
  (continued on Pier and Face 5B)

ADRIAN HAMILTON SILVERTON BARRETT

SECOND LIEUTENANT, 14TH BATTALION, ROYAL WELSH FUSILIERS.

Died on 10th July 1916, aged 20, leading his men in an attack on Mametz Wood.

Born in Paris, Adrian was the only child of Alfred William Wilson Barrett (a magazine editor and publisher) and Ruby Barrett of Stratford-upon-Avon.

He was educated at King Edward VI's School in Stratford-upon-Avon and afterwards joined the family publishing business.

He enlisted as Private 5/1775, Black Watch (Royal Highlanders) on 14th January 1915 and went to France on 10th May. He received his commission in the Royal Welsh Fusiliers five weeks later.

In 1920 his mother visited the area where he was killed. Her experiences were published in the *Stratford-upon-Avon Herald* on 7th May 1920: *At last, after months, even years, I have visited Mametz Wood. I have seen it in my dreams. I have thought of the spot and pictured it to myself – the spot where my son was buried. I wanted to see the French Wood, the scenery last looked upon by the blue eyes of an English boy – and that boy, my son. I have seen it all, and truly it is wonderful it is grand. Nature has done her best to soften the hard marks the war has made… I found four crosses put up in memory of the brave Royal Welch Fusiliers. The first three are to the 11th, 15th and 16th Battalions, and they stand to the south edge of the wood. The fourth one – to the memory of the officers and men of the 13th Royal Welch Fusiliers, July 10th 1916 when my boy fell – seemed to rise as an emblem of peace and rest… I was able to plant my English forget-me-nots and pansies I had brought and as I was planting the flowers from the garden my boy had known, the sun came out after a heavy shower and brightened all the wood. There was a lark singing just near me. No one could believe that once in this lovely spot, there had been so much dreadful battle fire and our dear men had given their lives so bravely…There may be other mothers, like myself, who longed to see the place where their sons had been buried if these lines can comfort any, I hope they will. Mametz Wood is a lovely place… If nature can make lovely marks all made terrible by war how much more can God make man beautiful, all disfigured also by war!… I would gladly see any mother and tell and help her about going out to France to visit her son's grave. Anyone who wants comfort from a broken-hearted mother let her come and see me. For the present I think the poorer mothers better wait, for a little later things will be easier… Oh sons that sleep out there in France, yours was the sacrifice. We owe you – all – our homes, our lives. Let us respect your memory and remember how much we do owe to you.*

DAVID GEORGE HUMPHRIES

PRIVATE, 19362, 16TH BATTALION, ROYAL WELSH FUSILIERS.

Died on 10th July 1916, aged 23, during an attack on Mametz Wood.

David was born in Senghenydd, Glamorgan, one of three children of King Samuel Humphries (a miner) and his first wife, Elizabeth Humphries (née Arthur).

His father, eldest brother and uncle were all killed in the explosion at the Universal Collieries on 14th October 1913. Out of the 950 men working below ground in the three pits, the explosion claimed the lives of 439.

David is one of sixty three men commemorated on the **Senghenydd War Memorial Clock Tower**. At least another two of these men are also commemorated on the Memorial.

Edwin Reginald 'Reg' Lambert, Lance Corporal 20644, 2nd Battalion, York and Lancaster Regiment, died on 25th September 1916, aged 20. He is commemorated on Pier and Face 14B.

Reg, his father and brother all worked at the Universal Collieries but survived the explosion.

Charles Henry George Mayfield, Private 18222, 2nd Battalion, Royal Berkshire Regiment, died on 4th April 1917, aged 21. He is commemorated on Pier and Face 11D.

SIDNEY JOHN WILKINSON DSO

LIEUTENANT COLONEL, 10TH BATTALION, SOUTH WALES
BORDERERS.

Died on 7th July 1916, aged 38, during fighting in
Caterpillar Wood, east of Mametz.

Sidney was one of seven children of Major Henry Chandler
Wilkinson and Eleanor Lydia Grey Wilkinson (née Des
Voeux).

He was educated at Wellington College, Berkshire.

On 10th September 1895 he saved someone from
drowning at Folkestone and in recognition he later received the Testimonial of the Royal
Humane Society.

He married Gladys Mary Rowlands in 1911 and they had one son, born in 1913.

He joined the Militia of the North Staffordshire Regiment on 30th August 1899 and was
commissioned as a second lieutenant in the West Yorkshire Regiment (Prince of Wales's Own),
on 21st April 1900. He served in the Boer War, and was awarded the Queen's Medal with three
clasps. He was promoted to lieutenant on 12th December 1901 and captain on 5th March 1910.

Posted to France on 15th April 1915, he was further promoted to major (1st September
1915) and lieutenant colonel in November 1915. Having been given command of the 19th
Battalion, Welsh Regiment he then transferred, at his own request, to the 10th Battalion, South
Wales Borderers. The award of the DSO was gazetted on 14th January 1916, shortly after he
had been mentioned in despatches.

Another of the regiment's holders of the DSO is also commemorated on Pier and Face 4A.

Alexander Arthur Francis Loch DSO, Captain, 1st Battalion, died
on 22nd July 1916, aged 20.

Born in India, the son of a tea planter, he was educated at
Cheltenham College and Sandhurst and was commissioned as a
second lieutenant on 1st October 1914. Twice mentioned in
despatches, the DSO was awarded on 30th March 1916, *For
conspicuous gallantry and determination. When the enemy had bombed
our grenadiers out of a new post, he led a counter-attack up our sap, and
with a machine gun dispersed some thirty of the enemy who had collected.*
*He was twice wounded and the man at his side was killed, but he hung on till nightfall, and eventually
made the post bullet-proof under very heavy fire.*

FRANCIS HERBERT ZACHARIAS

SECOND LIEUTENANT, 3RD BATTALION ATTACHED TO 1ST
BATTALION, SOUTH WALES BORDERERS.

Died on 25th September 1916, aged 30, between Flers
and Eaucourt l'Abbaye.

Francis was the youngest son, one of five children, of Ernest
Robert (a cotton merchant) and Charlotte Amelia Zacharias
(née Ashley) of Waterloo, Lancashire.

After an education at the Merchant Taylors' School,
Crosby, he studied at Bremen, Germany. Afterwards he was
apprenticed to an American firm of cotton merchants, and worked in the USA for a few years
before returning to England in 1907. Thereafter he was engaged in business in Liverpool and
was an active member of Waterloo RFC.

He was a keen pre war Territorial serving, in the 6th Battalion, Liverpools, and won an
award as the chief recruiter of his company. He was an excellent shot, winning many cups and
other tokens in competition. He had risen to the rank of sergeant at the time of mobilisation
and he was among the first band of Territorials who crossed over to France in February 1915.

In early 1916 he returned to England for training ahead of receiving his commission. He
married Gladys Eastwood on 2nd June 1916 and they had a son, born in 1917. The family lived
in Waterloo. He returned to France on 6th September 1916 as a second lieutenant in the 3rd
Battalion, South Wales Borderers.

He took a group to support men of the 1st Battalion of the Black Watch who had taken part
of a German trench but were having difficulty holding the ground. He immediately rallied the
men and, with a sergeant and two or three others, drove off the enemy. This action allowed
time for the completion of a barricade. He then ordered his men to retire, and while they got
back over the barricade he and the sergeant remained behind to cover their withdrawal.
Francis was shot through the head and killed whilst the sergeant was wounded but made it
back. A comrade wrote: *He died in the way we would have expected of him, and in a manner typical
of his life - utterly unselfish.*

REVEREND FRANCIS HENRY TUKE

CHAPLAIN 4TH CLASS, ARMY CHAPLAINS' DEPARTMENT (AChD), ATTACHED TO 53RD BRIGADE.

Died on 20th July 1916, aged 49, near Bernafay Wood while carrying water to his men.

Francis was one of at least nine children of Henry George (a barrister) and Mary Sarah Tuke of Cheltenham, Gloucestershire.

He married Jane Ellen Francis on 10th February 1897 and they later lived in Hereford. They had two daughters, born in 1903 and 1904.

After an education at Cheltenham College he went to Trinity College, Cambridge and obtained his BA in 1889 and MA in 1893. A keen rower, he was captain of the First Trinity Eight.

Ordained in 1890 by the Bishop of Rochester, he served as a curate at St George's, Camberwell and later at Hatchford, Surrey and Addlestone. He then had time as the vicar of Ripley, Surrey (1896-1902); Hope-under-Dinmore, Herefordshire (1902-1908); and then Holmer, Hereford. During his time in Herefordshire he played cricket for the county team.

He became a Chaplain to the Forces in December 1914. A fellow chaplain wrote: *He was one of the bravest and most fearless men I ever knew…He was admired and loved by all, and the ideal which he set before officers and men, by precept and example, will not easily be forgotten.*

A captain wrote: *As a military chaplain he was splendid. He worked like a Trojan to help the men in every possible way, and I had the greatest admiration for him… He was a true priest of the finest sort… I realized, I think, what a strong sense of duty must have animated him to share voluntarily in all the hardships of active service, being, as he was, above military age, and in view of the fact that there was no obligation, except a moral one, for him to have come forward.*

He is also commemorated on a mural tablet in St Bartholomew's Church, Holmer, and by an inscription on one of the church bells.

Francis is one of two members of the AChD commemorated on the Memorial; the other is **Rupert Edward Inglis**, who, aged 53, was killed by a shell on 18th September 1916 while helping to bring in wounded during the fighting at Ginchy.

The Memorial also commemorates a number of other clergymen who served as officers or other ranks in regiments or corps other than the AChD.

EDWARD TRAVERS BURGES DCM

Major, 1st Regiment, South African Infantry.

Died on 18th July 1916, aged 38, killed by a shell during the fighting in Delville Wood.

Edward was one of at least six children of Daniel Travers Burges (a solicitor) and Alice Sarah Burges (née Travers), of Bristol.

He was the husband of Charlotte Burges, of Clevedon, Somerset.

He was educated at Exmouth and then Winchester, where he was a House Prefect in his last two years. After leaving Winchester he went to South Africa and enlisted in the Cape Mounted Rifles.

During the Boer War he was the regimental sergeant major of the newly formed Border Horse; he won the DCM and his commission for gallantry in action. Later he acted as Assistant Provost Marshal in the Stellenbosch district and raised and trained a special Service Squadron of Colonials. Soon after the conclusion of peace he was appointed to the Cape Police. He saw conspicuous service during the Herero troubles, arresting the ringleader of the rebels with his own hand and subsequently pursuing and shooting him when he tried to escape. He received the thanks of the German Government and a medal from Kaiser Wilhelm II, for succeeding where their officials had failed. In 1913 he was promoted to lieutenant in the South African Mounted Riflemen and appointed a JP; and in the following April he was called to the staff at Pietermaritzburg.

On the outbreak of war he was appointed adjutant and afterwards brigade major of a detachment of the Imperial Light Horse and took part in General Botha's campaign in South-West Africa. At the conclusion of the fighting there he volunteered for the first South African contingent to sail for Europe. He served through the campaign against the Senussi in the western desert of Egypt as adjutant to the 1st South African Infantry, was promoted to major and then went with his battalion to France.

On the day he died his regiment made a successful attack on the German positions in Delville Wood but their position remained insecure. Edward was passing up and down the line urging his men to dig themselves in when he was struck by a shell and instantaneously killed.

He had the distinction of being mentioned in despatches in each of the three theatres of war in which he had served.

His brother, **Lieutenant Colonel Daniel Burges VC DSO,** served in the Gloucestershire Regiment and commanded the 7th Battalion, South Wales Borderers.

ALEXANDER YOUNG VC

LIEUTENANT, 4TH REGIMENT, SOUTH AFRICAN INFANTRY.

Died on 19th October 1916, aged 43, during a German counter-attack at the Butte de Warlencourt.

Alexander was a son of William and Annie Young, of Ballinamana, Co. Galway.

Educated at the Model School, Galway, he joined the Queen's Bays on 22nd May 1890, at Renmore, where his superior horsemanship quickly brought him to notice. He served for a time in India, and became a Riding Instructor. In the Sudanese Campaign, under Kitchener, he first saw active service. A contemporary commented: *He was a wonderful horseman, and had the reputation of being the best rough-rider in the British Army, and also in Egypt; and he was a brave and high-minded man, distinguished by the natural traits of generous, open-hearted good nature, which popularized him with everyone, of every station in life.* He later transferred to the Cape Police as Instructor.

The award of the Victoria Cross was for an action during the Boer War, the citation reads: *Towards the close of the action at Ruiter's Kraal on the 13th August, 1901, Sergeant-Major Young, with a handful of men, rushed some kopjes which were being held by the Boers. Sergeant Major Young then galloped on some 50 yards ahead of his party and closing with the enemy shot one of them and captured Commandant Erasmus, the latter firing at him three times at point blank range before being taken prisoner.*

After the Boer war he returned to his position with the Cape Mounted Police; he left them once more in 1906, for service in the native rebellion, when he was wounded for the second time. For his actions he was awarded a medal by the Kaiser (after the war broke out in 1914 he publicly burned the medal at Capetown). Later he served in the Zululand Rebellion, when he was once more wounded. He then spent four years farming in Natal and was quoted as saying, *After such a life as I have led a man is only good for farming or soldiering.*

In 1914 he was a regimental sergeant major in the Cape Mounted Police and took part in the fighting in German East Africa, ending the campaign as a lieutenant in the 4th South African Mounted Rifles. He was one of the first to come forward as a volunteer for the British forces in France. He was given a commission in the South African Scottish and came to England with them. In July 1916 he was wounded in the arm, but was able a few hours later to rescue a French officer, whose leg was shattered, by crawling from the trenches and dragging him back while subjected to both rifle and shell fire. As a result of the wounds received in the fighting for Delville Wood he was in hospital in England for some time, only returning to the Front in September 1916.

JOHN FRENCH

LANCE SERGEANT, 1803, 4TH REGIMENT, SOUTH AFRICAN
INFANTRY.

Died on 16th July 1916, aged 43, during the fighting at
Delville Wood.

John was one of five children of William (a gardener) and
Elizabeth French (née Lauder) of Peebles.

After leaving school he was employed as a salesman in
the tweed warehouse of Damdale Mill, Peebles, before going
to Glasgow. He had been a member of the 6th Volunteer
Battalion of the Royal Scots, the Glasgow Highlanders, and the Lanarkshire Yeomanry. At the
time of the Boer War he served with the City of London Yeomanry (Sharpshooters). He then
stayed in South Africa and worked as an accountant.

His company commander wrote: *He died as any brave man would prefer, in a fierce fight with
his face to the foe. You have lost a son anyone would be proud of, and the Empire one of her best and
bravest.*

Corporal Adam Neil Malcolm, who, like John, originated from
Peebles, died in Delville Wood the previous day, aged 42. He is
also commemorated on Pier and Face 4C.

Adam was one of at least nine children of Thomas (a joiner)
and Janet Malcolm of Peebles.

Employed as a tailor in Peebles, he then went to South Africa
in 1898. During the Boer War he was a member of the South
African Mounted Police. The husband of May Malcolm, of
Johannesburg, South Africa, they had three children.

When the war broke out, both John and Adam enlisted in the 4th Regiment and came with
them to England in December 1915. They were able to spend a few days in Peebles before
leaving on active service and were involved in Egypt in the Senussi Campaign before being
transferred to France a few months later.

FRANK STUART OLDMAN

PRIVATE, 16071, 10TH BATTALION, CAMERONIANS (SCOTTISH RIFLES).

Died on 15th September 1916, aged 26, during an attack on Martinpuich.

Frank was the only surviving child of Patrick Cheyne Oldman (a schoolteacher) and Nancy Oldman (née Sturges).

He married Alice Hodgson in 1912 and they lived in Burnley, Lancashire.

Employed as an agent of the Pearl Assurance Company, he enlisted in Burnley in November 1914.

After the Battle of Loos he wrote a long letter that was published in the *Burnley Express*. Under the headline, *GALLANT TENTH AT LOOS - BURNLEY SOLDIER'S VIVID DESCRIPTION*, the account included, *Then we got into some bonny scraps in Loos, real hand-to-hand fighting. We brought some 2,400 out of the cellars. I went down one of the cellars, and a German officer was told to bring his men up. He brought three men up, and I was coming up the steps when a shot went by my ear. I turned quickly round, to find a German just about to do for me, but I was a little too quick for him. We then took the hill and dug ourselves in and awaited reinforcements. I shall never forget that Saturday. It was bitterly cold, and I had not had anything to eat since Friday tea-time. I was wet through to the skin. My clothes were torn to shreds, and my equipment had bullet holes galore. To make matters worse we had to retire one hundred yards, and I lost my equipment, but soon got another. I had hardly got it on when I was lifted clean off my feet, and thrown about fifteen yards. It was one of the German shells. I went back to where I was before the shell burst, and found four of the chaps dead, two wounded, and one blind. At that moment I prayed to God for being saved. Later I was sent down to a dressing station by an officer to get something to eat. He said that all the Rifles had been relieved and that I had done my share. I walked four miles over dead and wounded, but I had not been back half an hour before I volunteered to go back with some more chaps to carry rations for the wounded and the chaps in the trenches. I stayed with them in the trenches all Sunday night until Monday morning at 4-30 when we were finally relieved. We marched down the hill, singing as we went, for the gallant 10th had done their duty, and the day was ours.*

His company quartermaster sergeant wrote initially when Frank was posted as missing and wrote again a few days later: *I am very sorry to be the conveyor of the worst news. We have received word that Frank has been buried. It is a great blow to me, as you are aware we were great chums. I cannot make you understand how I feel for you, as he was one of the best men, it has been my pleasure to have with me, and as brave as any. I cannot say how he was killed, as he was lost sight of in the village we took, but word has come from an English regiment that he has been properly buried. I am making full enquiries as to the position of his grave, and you may rest assured I will do all in my power to see it is properly cared for.*

ERIC NORMAN FRANKLAND BELL VC

CAPTAIN, 9TH BATTALION, ROYAL INNISKILLING FUSILIERS, ATTACHED TO 109TH LIGHT TRENCH MORTAR BATTERY.

Died on 1st July 1916, aged 20, during his VC action.

Eric was one of at least four children of Captain Edward Henry and Dora Algeo Bell (née Crowder) of Enniskillen, Co. Fermanagh.

He was educated at Warrington, St Margaret's School, Liverpool and Bedford Road School, Bootle. Later he studied Architecture at Liverpool University, where he proved to be a student of exceptional attainment and several of his large drawings appeared in one of the leading architectural journals. He was an accomplished painter, black-and-white artist, and musician; as well as being fluent in both French and German.

On the outbreak of war he was an assistant to a professor in the School of Architecture, Liverpool University. He was one of the first to volunteer for active service from the university. Gazetted on 22nd September 1914 into the 6th Battalion, he later transferred to the 8th before requesting a posting to the 9th Battalion, where his father served as adjutant. He went to France in October 1915.

One of his men wrote: *I am not ashamed to admit that I cried like a child at the loss I had suffered. I was about a foot and a half from your son when he was shot down by my side. I shall never forget the look he gave me, until my dying day, and I shall cherish his memory through life and eternity - a gentleman every inch of him, and one of the finest officers in the British army. Beloved by all, he fell on the battlefield as you would have wished him to do. I stayed by his side until the last (which wasn't long), and I shall never forget the heaven inspired look he gave me before he died.*

The citation for the award of his Victoria Cross reads: *For most conspicuous bravery. He was in command of a trench mortar battery, and advanced with the infantry in the attack. When our front line was hung up by enfilading machine-gun fire, Captain Bell crept forward and shot the machine gunner. Later, on no less than three occasions, when our bombing parties, which were clearing the enemy's trenches, were unable to advance, he went forward alone and threw trench mortar bombs among the enemy. When he had no more bombs available he stood on the parapet, under intense fire, and used a rifle with great coolness and effect on the enemy advancing to counter-attack. Finally he was killed rallying and reorganising infantry parties which had lost their officers. All this was outside the scope of his normal duties with the battery. He gave his life in his supreme devotion to duty.*

The medal was presented to his father by HM King George V at Buckingham Palace on 29th November 1916.

His father and two brothers served in the same regiment.

ALBERT GOODWILL SPALDING

SECOND LIEUTENANT, 10TH BATTALION, ROYAL INNISKILLING FUSILIERS.

Died on 1st July 1916, aged 25, during an attack on Thiepval.

Born in Chicago, USA, Albert was the son of Albert Goodwill Spalding and his second wife, Elizabeth Minott Spalding (formerly Mayer, née Churchill) of Point Loma, California. His father was a professional baseball player, team manager and co-founder of A. G. Spalding, the sporting goods company.

Educated at the Reja Yoga Academy, Point Loma, he graduated in January 1913. Together with his half-brother he then went on a trip around the world, at the completion of which he stayed on in Europe while his brother returned to America. Albert was in business in Paris at the outbreak of the war, and was obliged to leave there for London.

In London, in late August, he tried to join the Honourable Artillery Company but his American accent was a little too pronounced and the recruiting officer rejected his application. Leaving the recruiting office he was asked by an old sergeant how he had got on, and he told him that he had been refused because he was an American. The Sergeant said: *Man, you only fancy you are an American; you are really a Canadian. The 5th Dragoon Guards are across the way.* He promptly crossed the street and as a 'Canadian' was at once accepted. After serving in Scotland and at Aldershot, he transferred as Private 13808, Coldstream Guards. He went to France, and was promoted to lance corporal, on 27th April 1915. On 8th October 1915 he was in a party of men who recaptured over 200 yards of trench; for his leadership in that action **Lance Corporal Oliver Brookes** won the VC.

Albert was commissioned on 6th December 1915 *for conspicuous bravery and devotion to duty in the field.*

On 1st July he and his men were in the German second line when he was killed. A major wrote: *Lieutenant Spalding had gallantly descended to bomb a German dugout, about eight o'clock in the morning, and, having accomplished his purpose, was coming up again, when he was apparently shot and killed at short range. Several men testify to having seen his dead body in the trench, but unfortunately we were unable to recover the bodies of any of our fallen Officers or men owing to the desperate fighting which went on all day, and to the fact that we were forced to retire to our own lines in the evening.*

It was reported that Albert and the other casualties were eventually buried in the trench where they died. The graves were subsequently lost.

THOMAS THOMPSON

LANCE SERGEANT, 12730, 1ST BATTALION, ROYAL INNISKILLING FUSILIERS.

Died on 1st July 1916, aged 28, during an attack on Beaumont Hamel.

Thomas was one of three children of Edward and his first wife Ann Thompson (née Coulson). There were also five children from Edward's second marriage to Mary Ann Hindmarch.

He married Margaretta Gowland on 25th May 1908. They lived in Pelton, Co. Durham, and had four children, born between 1909 and 1916.

Employed as a coal miner, he enlisted in 1910 at Chester-le-Street, Co. Durham. Initially Private 17186, 1st Border Regiment, he was promoted to lance sergeant on 15th April 1915. He took part in the landing at Suvla Bay on 7th August 1915. Whilst on Gallipoli he wrote letters home; writing paper was scare so at least one of the letters (dated 12th September 1915) was written on the reverse of five labels taken from tins of condensed milk.

Commenting on the unusual paper he wrote: *well Ettie I know you will laugh at the paper but there is a lot of letters written with this sort of paper and they call them views of Turkey.*

He was evacuated from Gallipoli in December 1915 and returned to England before going to France.

Two half-brothers, **John** and **Adam**, both served in the Royal Navy. John (K/40826) died on 2nd December 1918, aged 21, and is buried in grave E.U.150 in the cemetery at Ryton, Co. Durham. His sister's husband, **Alexander Reid**, Private 56759, 7th Battalion, East Yorkshire Regiment, died on 4th November 1918, aged 38. He is buried in grave V.E.5 in Romeries Communal Cemetery Extension.

His wife's brother, **Matthew Gray Gowland**, Corporal 22201, 12th Battalion, Durham Light Infantry, died on 7th October 1916, aged 20. He is commemorated on Pier and Face 14A.

PIER 5

A

- Gloucestershire Regiment - **Private C. W. Giddings to Private A. J. Younger**
  (completed from Pier and Face 5B)
- Worcestershire Regiment - **Major L. Kerwood to Private J. Palmer**
  (continued on Pier and Face 6C)

B

- Royal Inniskilling Fusiliers - **Private G. R. Barrett to Private R. Young**
  (completed from Pier and Face 4D)
- Gloucestershire Regiment- **Major C. H. Hewetson to Private A. J. Giddings**
  (continued on Pier and Face 5A)

C

- Machine Gun Corps (Infantry & Heavy Branch) - **Private F. J. Allchin to Private A. V. Young**
  (completed from Pier and Face 12C)
- Labour Corps
- Machine Gun Corps (Cavalry)
- Machine Gun Corps (Motors)
- Army Service Corps - **Lieutenant C. W. Glenn to Private H. M. Payne**
  (continued on Pier and Face 4C)

D

- The Queen's (Royal West Surrey Regiment) - **Private G. W. Tilley to Private E. Young**
  (completed from Pier and Face 6D)
- The Buffs (East Kent Regiment)
- King's Own (Royal Lancaster Regiment) - **Captain A. D. M. Brown to Private S. Cooper**
  (continued on Pier and Face 12B)

WILFRID EWART DEAKIN

SECOND LIEUTENANT, 1ST BATTALION, WORCESTERSHIRE
REGIMENT.

Died on 4th March 1917, aged 18.

Wilfrid was the eldest of four children of William Henry (a
school attendance officer) and Mary Ann Deakin (née
Genders) of Walsall, Staffordshire.

He was educated at Queen Mary's Grammar School,
Walsall, where he was in the OTC.

In June 1914 he went to London to take up an
appointment at the Post Office Savings Bank at Kensington.

He enlisted as Private PS/6586, Royal Fusiliers on 6th March 1915.

He went to France on 14th November 1915 and spent six months there, which included
time attached to the Royal Engineers on mining and tunnelling work.

After officer training he was commissioned on 24th November 1916 and returned to France
on 5th December.

His commanding officer wrote: …*your son was killed in an attack on the German positions
which was completely successful. His conduct throughout the day until he met his end was of the most
gallant and cool description. When last I saw him he was very cheery over our success and carrying
out his duties of consolidating our captures in the most efficient and soldierly manner. Though he had
only been a short time with us, he had made himself universally liked, and I think his time with us
was a happy one. On the night previous to the attack I had entrusted him with a very important duty,
and this he carried out to my entire satisfaction.*

LAWRENCE JOHN WAREHAM

SECOND LIEUTENANT, 1ST/7TH BATTALION, WORCESTERSHIRE
REGIMENT.

Died on 21st July 1916, aged 20, in the fighting at
Crucifix Corner.

Lawrence was one of six children of Frederick (a school
headmaster) and Harriett Wareham (née Randle) of
Malvern, Worcestershire.

He was educated at Malvern Link CE School and
Worcester Royal Grammar School. He became a student
teacher at Malvern Link CE School and, in September 1914, a student at Saltley Training
College.

Granted a commission in November 1915, he became battalion signalling officer whilst
stationed at Weston-super-Mare. He volunteered for active service and went to France on 17th
May 1916, his twentieth birthday. He had been in the front line for about six weeks when he
was killed.

His eldest brother, **Frederick William Wareham**, Lieutenant,
1st/8th Battalion, Royal Warwickshire Regiment, died on 1st July
1916, aged 25, during an attack on Redan Ridge.

He was also educated at Malvern Link CE School, Worcester
Royal Grammar School and Saltley Training College and was
teaching at a school in Westminster when he enlisted in 1914. He
was commissioned in June 1915.

He is commemorated on Pier and Face 10B.

CHARLES HENRY LOWE

and his older brother,

HARVEY JAMES LOWE

PRIVATE, 2853, 1ST/8TH BATTALION, WORCESTERSHIRE REGIMENT, AGED 24.

PRIVATE, 3190, 1ST/8TH BATTALION, WORCESTERSHIRE REGIMENT, AGED 26.

Both men were killed on 20th July 1916 while working on a communication trench between La Boisselle and Pozières.

They were the only sons of James (a picture frame maker) and Lucy Lowe (née Tombs) of Worcester, who also had one daughter.

Prior to enlisting Harvey was employed as a compositor and Charles worked in the plate shop of an engineering company.

Both enlisted in Worcester and went to France on 1st April 1915. Their platoon commander wrote: *In these two, I have lost two of the best men in my platoon. They were popular with their comrades, always cheerful and fearless, and their loss is deeply felt, both by me and their comrades. We were digging a trench behind the old German front line and they were hit almost simultaneously by German shells. Their death was instantaneous and painless. They died for the old country on a victorious battlefield and although your loss is terrible, it is something to be justly proud of.*

Their company commander wrote: *They were both fine soldiers, and it is a deep sorrow to us to lose two good comrades who have served their Country without fear, so well so long.*

WILLIAM HASTINGS MERRITT

PRIVATE, 4739, 1ST/7TH BATTALION, WORCESTERSHIRE REGIMENT.

Died on 21st August 1916, aged 24, near Ovillers Spur.

William was one of eleven children of Edward John (a labourer) and Isabella Kate Merritt (née Wilson) of Reading, Berkshire.

Educated at Redlands School, he was subsequently employed by a chemist in Reading, which is where he enlisted.

He had only been at the Front about seven weeks when he was killed.

His company commander wrote: *I write to send you the sympathy of myself and everyone in the whole company… On the 22nd August a part of the company was ordered to attack. That part of the company attacked, and afterwards no touch could be gained with them, and we did not know what had happened to them. Therefore it was necessary to find out. One man, therefore, went out over the parapet; he had not gone far before he was wounded. Next another man volunteered and met with the same fate. Finally, your son volunteered and started on his way. He was going successfully when he was badly hit by a shell, from the effects of which he died at once, for by the time the stretcher-bearers could be got to him he was dead. For this most gallant act he has been recommended for the D.C.M. He died a most gallant death far above the ordinary; and I am sure you will be proud to know that, as we all are; and that it will be some small consolation to you in your sorrow. Such a man we are all sorry to lose.*

His platoon commander wrote: *He was in my platoon, and although he had been with me quite a short time I had every confidence in and respect for him. His was a glorious death – a soldier's and a hero's.*

His older brother, **Albert Victor Merritt**, Private 13849, 2nd Battalion, Grenadier Guards, died on 15th September 1916, aged 26, during an attack on Lesboeufs.

He is commemorated on Pier and Face 8D.

LIONEL WATSON MOORE

LIEUTENANT, 1/5TH BATTALION, GLOUCESTERSHIRE REGIMENT.

Died on 27th August 1916, aged 23, during an attack on a German trench near Pozières.

Lionel was the youngest of seven children of Thomas Weaver Moore (an auctioneer) and Ellen Moore (née Watson) of Tewkesbury, Gloucestershire.

He was educated at Tewkesbury Grammar School and King's School, Worcester.

An assistant scoutmaster of the 1st Tewkesbury Scout Troop, he was also a member of the County Territorials. He intended to take up a medical career and enrolled at Guy's Hospital in October 1910; whilst there he was a member of the medical unit of the London University OTC.

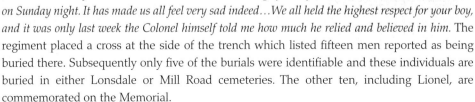

On the outbreak of war he enlisted as Private 2736, Gloucestershire Regiment and was quickly granted a commission. He went to France in March 1915 and was promoted to lieutenant the day after his brother's death.

The chaplain wrote: *I buried your splendid son this morning at 4 am in the very trench which he and his men took magnificently on Sunday night. It has made us all feel very sad indeed…We all held the highest respect for your boy, and it was only last week the Colonel himself told me how much he relied and believed in him.* The regiment placed a cross at the side of the trench which listed fifteen men reported as being buried there. Subsequently only five of the burials were identifiable and these individuals are buried in either Lonsdale or Mill Road cemeteries. The other ten, including Lionel, are commemorated on the Memorial.

His older brother, **Thomas Harold Moore**, Lieutenant, 1/5th Battalion, Gloucestershire Regiment, died on 27th September 1915, aged 32.

He is commemorated on a Special Memorial in Serre Road Cemetery No. 1.

CYRIL VINCENT NOEL PUCKRIDGE

SECOND LIEUTENANT, 1/5TH BATTALION, GLOUCESTERSHIRE REGIMENT.

Died on 21st July 1916, aged 21, near Pozières.

Cyril was the only son and youngest of three children of the Rev. Jonathan Samuel and Elizabeth Helen Puckridge (née Owen) of Welbourn, Lincolnshire.

He was educated at St John's School, Leatherhead, Surrey, where he served as a lance corporal in the OTC. He had been granted a place at Wadham College, Oxford in 1914.

He enlisted in Lincoln as Private 3136, Royal Fusiliers, on 4th September 1914.

In October, while still a private, he sent his mother this postcard of part of his company taken just before a parade.

He received his commission on 21st February 1915 and went to France on 27th May.

On 1st June 1916 he wrote to his sister, Vera: *We had a sixteen mile march due west yesterday so that we are a long way back from the front line now, we started out at 4 a.m. and got here about 11.30 having an hour's halt for breakfast at 8 a.m. although we had something before we started. It was a lovely morning for marching and a nice breeze which kept the temperature down. We are in a very small village now but we have got ripping bedrooms, sheets and everything; we couldn't find a room to mess in so as we were only two of us we deposited ourselves in the Oxford Headquarters and asked them to feed us after having had lunch at Brigade! You want a little cheek sometimes in this life and you get on well!!... There is a little single line railway runs past the village and it is quite a change to hear it whistling and panting at night.*

He contributed to the regimental magazine and the July 1916 issue included one of his poems *On Leaving*, together with a note that he was posted as missing a few days after it was written.

RALPH LOUIS DAVIS

LANCE SERGEANT, 15679, 10TH BATTALION,
GLOUCESTERSHIRE REGIMENT.

Died on 23rd July 1916, aged 21, during a failed attack on
the Switch Line, south-west of Martinpuich.

Ralph was one of ten children of John (a chair maker) and
Rosanna Davis (née Thompson) of High Wycombe,
Buckinghamshire.

He was also employed as a chair maker and enlisted in
High Wycombe in September 1914. He went to France on
9th August 1915.

His officer wrote: *Your son was a good soldier, and was by me for a good part of the night on which he was missed. It is just possible that he was taken prisoner, and I can but hope that is the case. If he has had to 'answer the call,' you may be sure he did so nobly, with his face to the enemy. Allow me to express my deep sympathy with you and your family, and if any information comes in you may be sure we shall let you know at once.*

His company sergeant major wrote: *I spoke to him as we were getting the men out of the trench to attack, and he was all right then. He was seen within about fifty yards of the German line, and was not seen afterwards by any of his men nor myself. We are very sorry indeed to lose him, as he was liked by everyone of us. We always found him capable and willing. It is possible he may have been taken prisoner. But after the attack we were unable to bring all the wounded in.*

His younger brother, **Victor Job Davis,** Private 2977, 1st/1st Bucks Battalion, Ox & Bucks Light Infantry, died on 23rd August 1916, aged 19. He is commemorated on Pier and Face 10A.

He was an apprentice cabinet maker, enlisted in Aylesbury, Buckinghamshire in October 1914 and went to France on 25th June 1915.

His captain wrote: *He was going forward bravely with the rest of his platoon, and was shot through the head. He died instantly, and suffered no pain. Davis was an awfully good lad, did his work well, and was always cheery. All his mates liked him greatly. Just before the battle I asked him what he would do if he got a German prisoner, and he replied in his usual joking way, that it would depend on the size of his prisoner.*

THE GREAT WESTERN RAILWAY (GWR)

The GWR war memorial on Paddington Station in London was unveiled in November 1922 and commemorates over 2,500 of the staff who died during the war.

During the war, the monthly staff magazine featured many letters from those serving as well as recording many of the deaths with pictures and obituaries. The pages of the magazine record at least 110 men commemorated on the Memorial.

At least eight of those served in the Gloucestershire Regiment and are commemorated on Pier and Face 5B.

John Yeatman	Thomas J. Bayliss	Charles Farndell	William G. Weaver
Sergeant	Lance Corporal	Lance Corporal	Lance Corporal
Signal Dept	mechanic's labourer	labourer	engine cleaner
22nd August 1916, 33	18th November 1916, 27	30th July 1916, 35	21st December 1916, 19

Charles N. Andrews	William Banning	Albert H. Collins	Alfred Gentle
Private	Private	Private	Private
labourer	packer	porter	goods clerk
21st July 1916, 20	20th August 1916, 28	9th September 1916, 21	17th August 1916, 20

CHARLES JOHN HARVEY

Private, 5369, 64th Company, Machine Gun Corps (Infantry).

Died on 1st July 1916, aged 19, during an attack towards Fricourt.

Charles was the eldest of four children of Charles William (a labourer) and Caroline Emma Harvey (née Croxson) of Plaistow, Essex.

Employed as a barman, he enlisted in Canning Town on 27th August 1914 in the 5th Battalion, King's Royal Rifle Corps; but was discharged on 24th November 1914.

He then re-enlisted as Private G/17766, Middlesex Regiment and later transferred to the Machine Gun Corps.

Having just celebrated his nineteenth birthday he wrote home on 27th June 1916: *i have just got your letter with the birthday cards and i thank you very much for them they both have very good tokens on them and are very pritty i will look after them and each time i look at them will remind me of the first Birthday i have ever had away from my home but i am living in great hope the by the time i am 20 that will be next June 1917 i will be with you all at home and enjoying myself...i must say that i am getting on with the life well i think i shall soon be a regular pipe smoker which will be better for my chest as you know i am very short winded and it's a great truble to me out here i would be glad if i could get my wind back again...i think i done wrong when i joined up the second time but all being well and with Gods help i will soon be with you all again.*

Charles ended the letter with:

> *A Loving heart but far away*
> *but thinks of home every day*
> *though the war may last long*
> *I hope to come home well and strong*

GEORGE MUNRO MANN

PRIVATE, 40019, MACHINE GUN CORPS (HEAVY BRANCH).

Died on 16th September 1916, aged 22, south of Flers when his tank **D14** was hit by artillery fire.

George was a son of Christina Mann of Avoch, Ross.

He gained a Royal Highland Society bursary to study as a chartered engineer at Glasgow University.

He later lived in Manchester and enlisted there in April 1916.

The other members of the tank crew of **D14** were:

- **Gordon Frederick Court** - Second Lieutenant, aged 27

- **Robert Baden Pebody** - Sergeant, 206118, aged 21

- **Laurence William Upton** - Lance Corporal, M2/178194, aged 23

- **Thomas Cromack** - Lance Corporal, 206153, aged 37

- **William Henty Barber** - Private, 206178 (38184), aged 35

- **Joseph Elliott Crowe** - Private, 206160, aged 19

- **Andrew Charles Lawson** - Private, 20616, aged 21

After the tank was forced to stop Pebody and Upton got out to see how they could avoid the obstacle. The tank was then hit by a shell, fatally wounding both men and killing the rest of the crew.

Robert Pebody and **Laurence Upton** are buried in A.I.F. Burial Ground, the other crew members are commemorated on either Pier and Face 5C or 12C.

JOHN EDWIN SUNDERLAND

PRIVATE, 6253, 18TH COMPANY, MACHINE GUN CORPS (INFANTRY).

Died on 27th September 1916, aged 18, killed in trenches near Lesboeufs.

John was one of five children of John Edwin and Mary Parker Sunderland (née Robinson) of Burnley, Lancashire.

He was educated at St Stephen's School in Burnley.

When the war broke out he immediately enlisted in Burnley as Private 6549, East Lancashire Regiment; and some time later transferred to the Machine Gun Corps.

A comrade wrote: *As soon as Jack came to this company, I took to him, and made him my chum. Jack died straight away, as the shell burst between two of them. Your son was one of the best, and the lads keep saying 'Poor Jack, we miss his songs and his Lancashire talk, and it will be a long time before we get a lad like Jack again.' All the section officers are downhearted about him. He was more than a brother to me as we were always together in the trenches and in billets. He was buried behind the firing line and I promise I will look after his grave whilst I am around this position.*

A corporal wrote: *We all miss him very much indeed as he was a jolly fine lad in and out of the trenches, and he kept us happy for he was always singing…your son was with me in the trenches when he got killed. A shell fell on top of our trench killing Jack and another young fellow, and wounding two more. I was left with only two men and the gun, and it was marvellous how any of us in the team were left. When it got dark we buried him near the village that was captured the day before. I shall always remember Jack.*

His lieutenant wrote: *We had been all day in some captured trenches, under heavy shell fire, and in spite of the terrible strain on our nerves Private Sunderland was cheerful. He was singing when the shell killed him. He lived about one minute after being struck, and even then he lay on the trench floor and smiled. He died as he lived, brave and cheerful. I never knew a man better loved by men and officers alike. I saw to it that he was laid in a decent grave. Your son was a great favourite of mine, and his life and death were something for you to be proud of.*

ALBERT VICTOR YOUNG

PRIVATE, 10304, 27TH COMPANY, MACHINE GUN CORPS
(INFANTRY).

Died on 25th October 1916, aged 33.

Albert was the youngest son, one of six children of John James (an hotelier) and Caroline Young of Thame, Oxfordshire.

He enlisted in Oxford and served for seven years as a pre war Regular in the Royal Irish Rifles; he then joined the Reserve.

At the start of the war he re-enlisted as Private 10097, Ox & Bucks Light Infantry. He was wounded in November 1915 and then transferred to the Machine Gun Corps. He returned to France in April 1916.

In August 1916 he had a letter published in the *Thame Gazette* which included: *We went into action on the 1st of July, and after seven days stiff fighting came back to the large guns for three days rest, went back again for another week, and then three days more rest and at it again for another week; so we had three weeks stiff fighting. We suffered heavily, but the Germans suffered double and more than us… The Germans had some tremendous dug-outs built in the bank of a trench about 20 feet below ground and quite safe from shell-fire; they came in very handy for us as we advanced. We are out for a good rest and to get reinforced; we do not know for how long, or where we are for (perhaps the best). We had several machine-guns knocked out by a shell-fire, so I had plenty of work keeping the teams going, as I am armourer and artificer to this machine-gun company. The enemy are nearly all Bavarians, and good fighters, and the ground is chalky, so you can tell how the trenches were when it rained, and the wood-work used for dug-outs were fur trees just cut down through the centre (no paring), so you see the strength; no wonder our shell-fire would not pierce the dug-outs… We are having some grand weather now, and I hope it is improving the crops at home. The crops out here are looking well; I passed some bearded wheat in the field yesterday, and I measured it, some of it being six feet long, which I thought a good length. The women work hard on the land out here, and cows are milked by women.*

His corporal wrote: *…your son Albert met his death out here on the morning of 26th October, by shell-fire. On behalf of myself and his comrades, I must say he was a soldier that was much admired by his company. He was well liked, trustful, and a most willing and intelligent worker…after your son met his death his body was brought in by his comrades and was laid to rest beside one of our own men who had fallen a few days before. Everything was done for him that could have been done, but I am sorry to say there was no hope whatever, as death must have been instantaneous.*

HORACE PAUL CATH

PRIVATE, G/11317, 7TH BATTALION, THE BUFFS (EAST KENT REGIMENT).

Died on 18th November 1916, aged 36, during an attack on the German trenches near Grandcourt.

Born in Geneva, Switzerland, Horace was the eldest of three children, all sons, of Horace and Marie Stephanie 'Berthe' Cath (née Scherzinger). The family returned to England shortly after Horace's birth and lived in Penge, Kent.

After an education at Rutlish Science School, Merton, Surrey, he went to Canada in 1904 and spent time working on a farm but the unsatisfactory working conditions forced his return. He then worked as a cashier for a Swiss watch and clock maker in London's Hatton Garden.

He married Daisy Ethel Eastwood on 31st August 1907 and they lived in Surrey. They had four children, born between 1909 and 1917, the youngest born four months after his death.

He attested on 1st December 1915, was mobilised on 13th June 1916 and went to France on 11th October, joining his battalion in the field ten days later.

On 28th October 1916 he wrote: *I am well and still cheerful and smiling though I must admit the life out here is such that no pen can ever adequately describe the conditions although I am hopeful someday of giving you some idea of them. Devastation and mud hold sway in all directions. I am hopeful that I shall be able to send you a few lines again soon, in several days perhaps and until then I guess my occupation will not be quite like anything pleasant, however I have got to come out of it alright.*

On 10th November 1916 he wrote: *I may not say where I have been or what I have been doing but I must say that I shall not forget and in due course I hope to give you my impressions of life at the Front. For the present I must keep you cheery and let the goings on here look after themselves. In spite of everything my cheerfulness sticks to me like a good pal just as it does with practically everybody this side of the Bosch's trenches… I have not received your parcel yet but am looking forward to it with joyful anticipation just as any schoolboy might… I do not expect to be home for Xmas worse luck. With regard to the knitted articles the helmet and muffler will be very acceptable if it will not put you to too much trouble and expense… Have been all the afternoon scraping the mud off my clothes with a knife and have succeeded in getting myself a little less like a "mudded oaf".*

His younger brother, **Sidney Heinrich Cath**, served in the Army Service Corps and died in 1923 as a result of malaria contracted whilst on active service.

JOHN THOMAS MILLER

Private, G/4907, 6th Battalion, The Buffs (East Kent Regiment).

Died on 7th October 1916, aged 37, during an attack on Rainbow Trench. He was trying to bring in his wounded officer when he was hit by shrapnel.

John was one of at least three children of William (a general labourer) and Hannah Miller of Ashford, Kent.

He married Miriam Nicholls in 1905 and they also lived in Ashford, Kent. They had at least one son, born in 1909.

Between 1896 and 1905 he served in the Royal Marine Light Infantry, Plymouth Division, which included service in South Africa. He also spent some time at the depot in the Military Police.

On returning to civilian life he worked as a general dealer. After the start of the war he tried to rejoin the Marines but was rejected. He therefore enlisted in The Buffs in Ashford, Kent on 3rd December 1914 and went to France on 1st June 1915.

An officer wrote: *Your husband was killed at my side… He was struck by shrapnel, and his death must have been instantaneous and painless. He was one of the finest and bravest soldiers I knew, and during the time that he was my servant, he showed great devotion… On the 7th, he was left in the trench, in charge of the officers' mess basket. He evidently heard that I had been hit, and strolled over 'no man's land,' with a pair of field glasses in his hand to look for me. He found me, and re-arranged my bandages. I told him to get under cover in the shell hole, but just as he was going to do so he was killed. He was the most popular man in the company, and I am sure all the survivors join with me in the deepest sympathy… While I was in France, your husband always behaved to me as a friend, a gentleman, and a sportsman. His advice to me was very good, and I often followed it.*

CHARLES CHRISTOPHER MACWALTER DCM

SECOND LIEUTENANT, 1ST BATTALION, KING'S OWN (ROYAL LANCASTER REGIMENT).

Died on 1st July 1916, aged 23, at Redan Ridge.

Charles was one of four children of Robert and Fanny Louisa MacWalter (née Iggulden) of Dover, Kent. Robert was a captain in the 12th Lancers and 13th Hussars and had served in India and South Africa.

Educated at Dover Boys' Grammar School, he then enlisted in the band of The Buffs (East Kent Regiment) and completed a course in euphonium and viola at Kneller Hall, the Royal Military School of Music. He went to France on 7th September 1914 as Corporal 8669, 1st Battalion, and was later promoted to sergeant.

In December 1914 he was involved in the 'Christmas Truce'; he told his father of the experience in a letter that was published in the local newspaper: *On Christmas Eve, the Germans and British were singing carols, and not firing. I was out in front of our trenches when I heard a German shouting. 'Englishman! Englishman! I wish to have an English paper,' so I shouted out that if he would not shoot or take me prisoner, I would bring him one. I collected a few and in company with a corporal I strolled out, and when I saw the German in front of his trench with his hands up I put my rifle down and walked up to him with my hands up. When I reached him he shook hands with me, calling me 'comrade,' and about 30 others came out. Most could talk English, and all French… After getting some cigarettes, cigars, etc., from them I came back again. The officer offered me all sorts of stuff to eat and drink, but not knowing what it really was, I refused. I told a German corporal my name, and after getting back he kept on calling out, 'Macwalter, come back.' They seemed quite a decent lot of fellows… I managed to get a little information from them, which was what I was after, but they told me nothing much…the funny part was that none of them wanted any information from me. After 'chinning' for half-an-hour the German officer told me to return to my own trench, and ordered his own men back, so I came back, picking up my rifle on the way, and here we are again, scrapping away at each other again.*

He was mentioned in despatches in May 1915 for actions during January, February, March and April 1915. The award of the Distinguished Conduct Medal was gazetted on 30th June 1915 whilst he was a lance sergeant: *For conduct in performing hazardous reconnaissances of the enemy's lines, for which he was always ready to volunteer. On the last occasion he undertook this duty he was severely wounded.*

He was commissioned in the King's Own with effect from 7th November 1915.

ROBERT FRANCIS POSTLETHWAITE

LANCE CORPORAL, 201675 (5003), 1ST/4TH BATTALION,
KING'S OWN (ROYAL LANCASTER REGIMENT).

Died on 28th September 1916, aged 29, in the area of
Gird and Gird Support trenches, east of Eaucourt
l'Abbaye.

Robert was one of five children of Robert Walter (a mason
and builder) and Mary Postlethwaite (née Sedgwick) of
Skerton, Lancaster.

He was educated at the Boys' National School and was a
keen member of St Mary's Football Club.

He married Margaret Baldwin in 1911, they lived in Lancaster and had one son born in
1914.

Employed as a labourer in the St George's Paint Works, he enlisted in Lancaster on 8th
September 1914, was mobilised on 25th June 1915 and promoted to acting lance corporal
(unpaid). His promotion to lance corporal (paid) was effective from 26th August.

Posted to the 5th Battalion of the King's Own on 1st July 1916 he went to France on 11th
August. He was then transferred to 4th Battalion and joined them in the field on 20th August.

His brother, John*, enlisted and served alongside Robert. It was he who broke the news to
Margaret that Robert was missing after taking part in a bombing raid on German trenches.
John said that he missed Robert during the action and had been unable to find a trace of him
since.

Official notification of his death did not come through until January 1917.

*John Edmund Sedgewick Postlethwaite, Corporal 201677 (5005), 1st/4th Battalion, King's
Own (Royal Lancaster Regiment) died on 31st July 1917, aged 27. He is commemorated on the
Menin Gate Memorial.

PIER 6

A

- Duke of Wellington's (West Riding Regiment) - **Private H. Beaumont to Private J. W. Yates**
  (completed from Pier and Face 6B)
- Border Regiment - **Captain A. E. Corbett to Private G. Pearson**
  (continued on Pier and Face 7C)

B

- East Surrey Regiment - **Private H. G. Churcher to Private F. Yirrell**
  (completed from Pier and Face 6C)
- Duke of Cornwall's Light Infantry
- Duke of Wellington's (West Riding Regiment) - **Captain G. S. Edwards to Private A. Beardsell**
  (continued on Pier and Face 6A)

C

- Worcestershire Regiment - **Private J. Parker to Private J. A. Young**
  (completed from Pier and Face 5A)
- East Lancashire Regiment
- East Surrey Regiment - **Captain J. L. Buckman to Private J. H. Church**
  (continued on Pier and Face 6B)

D

- Royal Scots - **Private G. Forbes to Private T. Yuill**
  (completed from Pier and Face 7D)
- The Queen's (Royal West Surrey Regiment) - **Captain M. Bessell to Private E. Tickner**
  (continued on Pier and Face 5D)

FRED BENSON

PRIVATE, 13694, 10TH BATTALION, DUKE OF WELLINGTON'S (WEST RIDING REGIMENT).

Died on 11th July 1916, aged 25, during the fighting at Contalmaison.

Fred was one of at least four children of William and Ann Benson (née Thompson) of Cowling, near Keighley, Yorkshire.

He was employed as a weaver at Messrs. J. Binns & Sons Ltd, Carr Mills.

One of eighteen local lads who enlisted in August 1914, he went to France on 26th August 1915.

A corporal, also from Cowling, wrote: *On Monday afternoon a part of our brigade attacked a village for which there had previously been heavy fighting by other brigades. We were in support, and as dusk fell we moved out through a heavy barrage of fire to reinforce and to consolidate the position… During the evening Fred and another lad went on listening post duty a little in front of the trench where we had dug ourselves in. A little later they gave the alarm and turned round to get back into the trench, but before they had gone a yard they were both hit by the Germans. A small enemy patrol had crept up within a short distance unobserved till quite close. Both staggered back somehow into the trench. A minute or two later when the alarm was over, I and two others got them out and did what we could, but it was to no avail, for he must have been bleeding internally. He was in some pain for a minute or two during which he said four times "Take me", he then drifted into unconsciousness and a few minutes later passed quietly and gently away. He was hit in the back just above the left hipbone and the bullet passed through and out at the right groin. I was supporting his head when he died. We were relieved a few minutes later and had reluctantly to leave him there with his waterproof sheet over him. We went to get a stretcher to carry him out, but none were available. He will probably have been buried by now by the salvage Corp. We were all so upset…he was a cheerful, willing comrade. We shall all miss him very much. He was in great spirits, as were we all because of our successes of the past few days. We were all much affected by his and the other chap's death.*

Three months later his sister, **Adelaide**, drowned herself in a local reservoir on her twenty ninth birthday. At the inquest her mother said she had taken Fred's death very much to heart, and would talk about very little else, and had become very much depressed. After hearing the other evidence the jury concluded that her death was the result of …*suicide by drowning, whilst temporarily insane, brought about by grief at the loss of her brother in the war.*

CARL STEPHEN MOULDING

PRIVATE, 12750, 9TH BATTALION, DUKE OF WELLINGTON'S (WEST RIDING REGIMENT).

Died on 3rd August 1916, aged 22, while trying to save a wounded comrade during the fighting at Delville Wood.

Carl was the only surviving child of William Charles (a schoolmaster) and Christina Moulding of Lazonby, Cumberland.

After home schooling he won a scholarship and was educated at Worksop. He then got a position as a booking clerk with the Midland Railway at Addingham, Yorkshire. He enlisted in Ilkley, Yorkshire, in September 1914.

A number of his letters were published in the local newspaper.

September 1915: *Thanks for parcel… We are all in the best of spirits and taking things as they come. We are at present in the firing line doing as much damage as we can to the Germans opposed to us, but whom we very rarely see. It is rather a dangerous business popping your head up during the day time to see if you can see any of them. Their snipers are generally on the look-out for such a target, just the same as ours, so it pays to keep down and, if you want to see what is going on at the other side, use your periscope.*

June 1916: *We are out of the trenches now and are back in the country. We had a good four days march to get here, not very pleasant, the weather being scorching hot… We do not spend the whole day doing nothing out here; we get a lot of manoeuvring and such like, but we are out of danger and able to have a good night's sleep, which is a big consideration… I have had 10 days in hospital with German measles, but I feel all right again.*

Initially letters from comrades indicated that he was reported wounded, one said: *…but where he is I cannot say, as he must have got to one of the Field Ambulance dressing stations, and sent from there to hospital.*

His death was confirmed in a letter from another private: *He was found and buried, we are officially informed, by a Regiment of the Yorkshire Light Infantry. Dear old Carl, how we miss him, one of the old hands! He lost his life in helping to save a wounded comrade. What an awful time we had that week! But Carl was a brave lad, and I well remember him on the 19th December, and again on the 2nd March. Yes, in every big 'do' we have had he always proved himself a gallant lad, and we shall never forget him and our deepest sympathy is extended to his parents.*

JOSEPH ALBERT PLUMBLEY

PRIVATE, 12353, 2ND BATTALION, DUKE OF WELLINGTON'S (WEST RIDING REGIMENT).

Died on 12th October 1916, aged 22, in the fighting near Lesboeufs.

Joseph was the eldest of five children of Henry (a gas meter inspector) and Mary Ann Plumbley (née Fletcher) of Barnoldswick, Yorkshire.

Employed as a cotton weaver at Messrs. W. Bailey's Ltd., Wellhouse Mill, he enlisted in Keighley, Yorkshire in November 1914.

He went to France on 27th January 1915 and was able to enjoy some home leave in November.

During the fighting on 1st July 1916, he helped bring in the wounded commanding officer of the Royal Warwickshire Regiment. In recognition of his actions the adjutant wrote: *...on the night of July 1st, you volunteered to assist to bring in the Commanding Officer. I wish to make you some acknowledgment of the good work you did under trying circumstances.*

In November 1916 Joseph's parents received a letter from a private in the Lancashire Fusiliers, who was being treated in a Dewsbury hospital: *I beg to inform you that Pte. J. A. Plumbley, of the Duke of Wellington's, was killed by the same shell which wounded me on the 11th Oct. I did not know the young fellow, but he dropped at my feet in the German front line trench. He had his hip and left leg blown off. He went over the top the same time as us, and died about ten minutes after being wounded. The reason I got to know him was that an officer dropped close to him, and when the stretcher bearers came to take the latter away he saw your son, and said 'That is Plumbley, dead.' So I thought of the name ever since.*

In a later letter the same private wrote: *Your son only spoke to me once during the charge. He said, 'Here are some Germans coming' and as we saw them we both got over the trench to meet them when a shell hit him full in the hip...I bandaged him up as well as I could, using all the stuff I had, but it was such a funny place. I could not carry him to a place of safety as there was hand-to-hand fighting going on all around us, and I had all my work on to get back to our own lines. He had his senses, and died with a smile on his face.*

A packet containing a bible, letters, photos, etc. was found on the battlefield by another soldier who was subsequently wounded and treated in England. The items were eventually returned to Joseph's family by the soldier's parents with the comment, *We sincerely hope the young man to whom they belonged is safe and well.*

ALFRED JAMES GUY

PRIVATE, 20177, 1ST BATTALION, BORDER REGIMENT.

Died on 1st July 1916, aged 17 years and nine months, during an attack to the south of Beaumont Hamel.

Alfred was one of seven children of James (a farmer) and Ellen Guy (née Barton) of Lancaster, Lancashire.

Educated at Greaves Council School, he then won a scholarship to Lancaster Grammar School. Afterwards he worked as an ironmonger at Fenton's and Co.

He enlisted in Kendal, Westmoreland, on 11th April 1915 into the 3rd Battalion, Border Regiment. On his enlistment he stated his age as 19 years and 14 days, overstated by 2½ years.

He was posted to the 1st Battalion on 11th August and went to the Middle East on 14th September. He was one of the last soldiers to leave Gallipoli. He then went to France on 11th March 1916.

For over a year his mother, by then a widow, petitioned for his return to England on account of his age and her cause was supported by Sir Norval Helme, Lancaster's MP.

Although Alfred's real age was eventually accepted, the military authorities judged that, by that time, he was over 17 and was of a standard that passed him fit, which meant that the likelihood was that he would remain on active service. Eventually it was agreed that he would be returned to England, ...*if he is willing*, but by then he had already been posted as missing.

GEORGE LEONARD JENKINS

Private, 31187, 13th Battalion, East Surrey Regiment.

Died on 24th April 1917, aged 26.

George was one of three children of George (a manager to a metal merchant) and Alice Jenkins of Clapham, Surrey.

He married Marjorie Phyllis Watson on 5th January 1917. They had a very short honeymoon; just before midnight on the 8th he was in Dover. He was stationed there for basic training until he was sent to France around 12th March.

During his training, and whilst in France, he wrote many letters home.

April 1917: *I am at present sleeping in an empty barn and writing this round a camp fire, and I can tell you I wish I was miles from here, in dear old Blighty, near my darling. I am always thinking*

of you dear. It is now snowing and our "roof" is "rather" leaky".

9th April 1917: *I am not in the firing line yet but in the rest huts, and we are crowded in like sardines, it's worse than the tent at the base. We had a march to here on Good Friday night, and if I come home safe & sound I shall never forget it as long as I live… I can't imagine this being Easter Monday. I wonder what you have been doing. What a difference to last year. Do you remember we went to Kew Gardens & the Theatre in the evening. How I wish I was there now. I would give anything to be able to come to you now my own dear… The mud here is worse than awful, and also the "livestock", Everyone gets them here it can't be helped.*

George and his comrades were out at night digging trenches between the lines when they were spotted by the Germans. A friend wrote: *…it was only 3.30 in the morning and day-break was near; the shells lit up the field, choked us with fumes etc., but George was following me when eight of us all fell together, only two of us being wounded, and I shouted to George, but had no reply. I crawled as near as possible to see him, but failed… I saw him lying down with his rifle still in his hand.*

ROY DUNCANSON

SECOND LIEUTENANT, 3RD BATTALION ATTACHED TO 9TH BATTALION, DUKE OF WELLINGTON'S (WEST RIDING REGIMENT).

Died on 7th July 1916, aged 26, in the fighting at Contalmaison.

Roy was one of nine children of James (a farmer) and Annie Ferguson Duncanson of Langley, Kent. In this family group, taken in 1911, Roy is at the right of the back row.

Educated at the Maidstone Grammar School, he enlisted in the 19th Battalion, Royal Fusiliers, in September 1914, later earning his commission.

His brother **Ian Ferguson Duncanson**, Second Lieutenant, 8th Battalion, Argyll and Sutherland Highlanders, died on 12th October 1917, aged 21. He is buried in grave III.D.1 in Poelcapelle British Cemetery.

Three of his sisters served in the Voluntary Aid Detachment. The eldest, **Una Marguerite Duncanson**, died on 31st December 1917, aged 25. She was one of eight nurses and 201 others who were lost when the Transport Ship *Osmanieh* (which was taking troops and some nursing staff to Egypt) struck a mine in Alexandria harbour. She is buried in grave B.41 in Alexandria (Hadra) War Memorial Cemetery.

FREDERICK GREEN DCM

COMPANY SERGEANT MAJOR, 13314, 9TH BATTALION, DUKE OF WELLINGTON'S (WEST RIDING REGIMENT).

Died on 7th July 1916, aged 30. Though wounded himself, he was assisting another Barnoldswick comrade* to the dressing station when he was struck by a piece of shell.

Frederick was one of at least three children of John (a cotton warp dresser) and his first wife Catherine Green (née Holmes) of Barnoldswick, Yorkshire. After Catherine's death John married Charlotte Dolby and had at least five more children.

He enlisted in Skipton, Yorkshire, and went to France on 15th July 1915. He was promoted to CSM whilst serving in the Ypres sector, having previously been mentioned in despatches.

The award of the Distinguished Conduct Medal was gazetted on 20th March 1916: *For conspicuous gallantry and ability during operations. He rendered great assistance to his company officers, and by his courage and example kept the men in good spirits.*

Shortly after the award was announced he wrote to his brother: *Well, I have got the D.C.M. all right, and am wearing the ribbon; but I expect to wait some time before I get the medal - most likely when some big General comes around when we are out for a rest. The weather is mending up beautifully and it is quite like summertime…[censored] is a very big place and in some parts not much damaged by shellfire. Many of the residents are still here and there are some big shops open where we can buy anything - but they often forget to make us pay.*

*Sam Woodhead, Private 13197, recovered from his wounds and returned to duty. He was killed eleven months later, on 9th June 1917, aged 36. He is buried in grave XIV.H.4 in Lijssenthoek Military Cemetery.

HERBERT 'BERT' WATSON ATKINSON

Sergeant, 11427, 8th Battalion, Duke of Wellington's (West Riding Regiment).

Died on 14th September 1916, aged 44, during fighting at Thiepval.

Bert was one of six children of William Hodgson Atkinson (a railway carriage builder) and Emma Atkinson (née Watson) of York.

He married Caroline Reynolds in 1895, they had a son and three daughters born between 1897 and 1901.

As a highly skilled coach builder, he followed his trade across the country, working for a number of companies in rapid succession. At one time he was a traveller for the United Electric Car Company, Halifax, Yorkshire.

He volunteered for service in the Boer War, and did some training, but was not allowed to go to South Africa, much to his disappointment, because he was the father of a young family.

When war was declared he volunteered immediately and went to France on 30th November 1914 with the 2nd Battalion. In 1915, he was gassed at Hill 60, and was evacuated to England to recuperate. Subsequently he was sent to the Dardanelles, where he joined the 8th Battalion, and then to Egypt and later to France.

Bert was granted a field commission but the promotion had not been gazetted at the time of his death. A chaplain wrote that he had ...*died a hero's death in a noble cause.*

After his death he was initially posted as 'absent without leave' and subsequently as 'deserted.' The War Office eventually acknowledged its mistake but only after considerable pressure from his widow.

His son, **George William 'Bill' Atkinson,** enlisted when only 17 and served in France as a signaller with The Loyal North Lancashire Regiment. Not long before Bert was killed the two were able to spend three days close to each other behind the lines.

JOHN WALDRON WILDE

PRIVATE, 23337, 3RD BATTALION, WORCESTERSHIRE
REGIMENT.

Died on 16th July 1916, aged 25, killed by a shell at
Contalmaison.

John was one of ten children of John (a shopkeeper) and
Mary Lucy Wilde (née Waldron) of Castleford, Yorkshire.

He was employed as a mechanic and electrician at
Wheldale colliery in Castleford. He was a member of the
Castleford Harriers and won many prizes for running.

He was used to horses, could ride and shoot, so he enlisted into the Dragoon Guards on
7th September 1914. Later he was transferred to the Worcestershire Regiment and became part
of the machine gun section. He went to France on 14th July 1915.

In a letter to his brother he wrote: *I am going on all right just now, we are out for a few days
rest, then we go back in the trenches again, the hardest part about it is walking to, and from the
trenches, about 8 or 10 miles, with all our luggage to carry, the last time I went to the trenches, they
saw us going, so they started to drop a few shells about us, 3 at a time, 3 dropped about 20 yds from me but there
was a bit of a slope, and we were walking half down this slope at the time, so we dropped down, so we were
safe, you can guess we get a bit of excitement when they dropped near us.*

"Somewhere in France"

A comrade wrote: *I had a great deal of experience with him and he was a
daring fellow and a man highly respected by us all. We very much miss his good comradeship. He died
from exhaustion and loss of blood and was in no pain whatever. He asked for a smoke and went to
sleep. All officers and men of our company join you in your sorrow.*

HENRY DAVISON RILEY

CAPTAIN, 11TH BATTALION, EAST LANCASHIRE REGIMENT.

Died on 1st July 1916, aged 34, during an attack towards Serre.

Henry was the only son, one of two children, of William John (a cotton manufacturer) and Annie Eliza Riley of Burnley, Lancashire.

Educated at Shrewsbury School, he was keen on cricket, football and especially rowing.

He became a member of the firm of Messrs. W. & A. Riley, fancy cloth manufacturers, Colne, Lancashire, and was also a director of the firm of Messrs. R. J. Elliott & Co. (Ltd.), cigar manufacturers, of Huddersfield and Leicester. He was a well known and popular figure on the Manchester Exchange and was appointed as a county magistrate in 1912.

He was credited with making a major contribution towards improving the life of the young men of Burnley in the period before the war, particularly the creation of the Burnley Lads' Club. He was also a member of a number of other local organisations involved in education and welfare.

He was one of the main instigators in the formation of the Burnley Pals Company which became part of the 11th Battalion, East Lancashire Regiment. Around seventy members of the Lads' Club followed him. He was first gazetted a lieutenant and his promotion to captain followed quickly. He went on active service in December 1915, first going to Egypt and then went with the battalion to France on 8th March 1916.

Writing in the *Manchester Guardian* a friend recalled that Henry hated war and all that stood for war, but he had said: *How can I let my lads go and not go myself?*

BURNLEY LADS' CLUB

By the time Henry Riley died, some 600 members of the Club were serving in the Forces. The Club's Roll of Honour lists 123 who had lost their lives by the time the war ended.

There are at least ten members commemorated on the Memorial. Seven were in the East Lancashire Regiment and are also commemorated on Pier and Face 6C. A number of those were in Henry's battalion and died with him on 1st July 1916.

FRANCIS THOMAS NIGHTINGALE

Lance Corporal, 5480, 1st Battalion, East Lancashire Regiment.

Died on 1st July 1916, aged 21, during an attack on Redan Ridge.

Francis was the only son of Joseph (a carter) and Ann Nightingale of Burnley, Lancashire.

His education was mainly at Pickup Croft School. When he was only 12 years of age he jumped into the canal and rescued another boy who was in difficulties.

He was employed by an iron broker and was a member of the reserve. After being mobilised on the outbreak of war he went to France on 30th September 1914.

While having a four day rest in a cottage a shell came and blew it up; *We just got a few scratches with falling bricks,* he commented in a letter.

On another occasion he was one of twenty five men ordered to silence a gun in a farmhouse that was causing havoc. During the advance the captain commanding the group was shot in the arm and neck, dying from his wounds an hour later. The men silenced the gun but on the way back a shell killed them all with the exception of Francis and one other. His rifle and bayonet were smashed in two by the force of the explosion.

He had a reputation for bravery and being a volunteer for dangerous and difficult tasks. On July 29th 1915 he was commended for bravery. On the 10th October he received another commendation card, which stated: *These two men on July 6th at Pilkem carried messages from the firing line to battalion headquarters and back throughout the action. The communication trenches were badly knocked about and consequently their task was a very perilous one. Both of them were buried by a shell, but they continued at their duty, and were directly responsible for the excellence of the communications throughout the day.* This action gained him his lance corporal's stripe. He had previously twice refused to have any stripes, saying that he preferred to earn one.

In April 1917 the War Office officially presumed his death to have taken place on 1st July 1916; but his mother always felt that he was alive. A newspaper report in 1919, which had referred to a Thomas Nightingale winning a medal, gave her renewed hope that he had somehow survived, but it proved to be unfounded.

FRANCIS WILLIAM HALLIDAY MM

CORPORAL, 2487, 9TH BATTALION, EAST SURREY REGIMENT.

Died on 16th August 1916, aged 22, during the fighting at Guillemont whilst attending to a wounded soldier.

Francis was the only surviving son of four children of George Henry (a hairdresser and tobacconist) and Susan Halliday of South Norwood, London.

Educated at Sydenham Road School, Croydon, he later became a hairdresser.

He enlisted in September 1914. As a chief stretcher bearer he was recommended for the Distinguished Conduct Medal during the Battle of Loos and again in June 1916; he was awarded the Military Medal for the latter action on 21st June 1916.

An officer wrote: *He was our chief stretcher bearer, and I don't think there is a man in the battalion who does not feel sad about it. The doctor is broken-hearted, and could not prevent himself from breaking into tears. The doctor of course, had seen many sad cases that day, but Corpl. Halliday was one in a million, and I don't think we shall ever find a man to replace him. I know the other bearers, who had been doing splendid work up till then, fell all to pieces, and felt helpless when they lost their Corporal. His death was really as wonderful as the work he always did. He was hit through the stomach. Most other places a man can stand it, but through the stomach means agony. The Corporal was more than equal to it, making not the least complaint, and speaking in his usual quiet way until he died. He was truly a wonderful example of what a man can do, and you can perhaps understand there were lumps in many throats when we had news of his death.*

His former headmaster wrote: *As a scholar he was very bright, both in work and play, and he was never lacking in friends. The manner of his death only emphasises the self-sacrificing traits he showed as a school boy. During his last visit home he called at the school...he was determined he said, to try to secure the V.C... The irony of the case is marked. Corporal Halliday had fired never a shot during the whole time he had been at the front. His activities were directed to saving life, and in carrying out his work he sacrificed himself. His old school is proud of him.*

WILLIAM GSCHWIND

PRIVATE, 29480, 15TH BATTALION, ROYAL SCOTS.

Died on 1st July 1916, aged 27, during an attack at La Boisselle.

William was the eldest of three children of William Gabriel (a Swiss-born shipping merchant) and Bertha Maria J. Gschwind (née Troxler) of Didsbury, Lancashire.

Educated at the National School, Didsbury, he enlisted in Manchester on 27th November 1915 into the 18th Battalion.

He went to France on 5th May 1916 and joined the 15th Battalion in the field on 23rd May.

The commanding officer wrote: *I am unable to give definite information regarding the fate of Pte. W. Gschwind. As you stated, he was slightly wounded by a piece of shrapnel in the leg on June 21st. He went over with the battalion on July 1st & nothing further has been heard of him. Our orderly presumes that he was killed, but there is a faint hope that he may be a prisoner of war.*

Given the uncertainty over William's fate the family followed the example of other families and included appeals in the local newspaper. This was in the hope that a comrade on leave, or recovering in hospital could supply some small piece of information which might help resolve the mystery of why someone was still missing.

The family also appealed through the Queen Victoria Jubilee Fund Association in Switzerland.

No trace of William after 1st July 1916 was ever discovered.

QUEEN VICTORIA JUBILEE FUND ASSOCIATION

The Association, from its offices in Switzerland, circulated information on the missing in the hope that soldiers in German hospitals or prison camps could provide some additional information.

This is an example of the card which families received from the Association to confirm that their relative's details would be included in a forthcoming circular. This relates to **Bernard Locker**, who was reported missing on 7th November 1916, aged 19. Bernard was never found and he is commemorated on Pier and Face 2C.

Circular no XXXXV (date unknown) included **William Gschwind's** details. Of the thirty men pictured in the circular sixteen (including William) are commemorated on the Memorial. Another twelve are either commemorated on other memorials or have a marked grave. Only two appear to have survived the war.

BENJAMIN EASTLAKE LEADER

CAPTAIN, 3RD BATTALION, THE QUEEN'S (ROYAL WEST
SURREY REGIMENT), ATTACHED TO 2ND BATTALION, DUKE OF
WELLINGTON'S (WEST RIDING REGIMENT).

Died on 12th October 1916, aged 39, during an attack on
Spectrum Trench near Lesboeufs.

Benjamin was the eldest of six children of Benjamin Williams
Leader (an artist) and Mary Leader (née Eastlake) of
Gomshall, Surrey.

He was educated at Charterhouse and Trinity College,
Cambridge, and matriculated in 1896. On leaving university he studied as a landscape painter
under Sir Hubert von Herkomer, and later at Newlyn, Cornwall.

He married Isabella Anderson in Glasgow on 8th September 1910. They later lived in St
Buryan, Penzance, Cornwall and had a son* in 1914 and a daughter in 1916.

He was a member of the
Artists' Colony at Lamorna,
near Penzance, and for five
years was a well known
exhibitor at the Royal
Academy. This landscape *A
Common near Guildford* was
painted in 1901.

He volunteered his
services after the outbreak of
war and was gazetted a
second lieutenant in the West
Surreys on 25th September
1914. Promoted to lieutenant
on 20th November, he went
to France on 14th January 1915 and achieved his captaincy on 22nd May.

Benjamin's only brother, **Edward Eastlake Leader** was a member of the British Olympic
Athletics team at the 1908 Games. During the war he served as a lieutenant in the Royal Naval
Volunteer Reserve.

*Benjamin's only son, **Benjamin John Leader**, Pilot Officer 116403, Royal Air Force Volunteer
Reserve, died on 4th August 1942, aged 28. He is buried in Bude Haven (St Michael)
Churchyard.

HENRY LLOYD MARTIN

Captain, 7th Battalion, The Queen's (Royal West Surrey Regiment).

Died on 28th September 1916, aged 36, killed by a shell whilst leading his company in their ultimately successful attack on the Schwaben Redoubt.

Henry was the only surviving son, one of seven children, of James (a stockbroker) and Mary Ellen Martin (née Noakes) of Limpsfield, Surrey.

Educated privately in Sevenoaks, he then went to Tonbridge School. Afterwards he joined the office of his father's firm, Messrs Martin & Hilder, and later became a partner in the firm of A. Brampton & Co. At school he had been a member of the Cadet Corps and later joined the Artists' Rifles for a time. In the years immediately prior to the war he had devoted his spare time to the Boy Scout movement. As well as being a local Scoutmaster he had served as District Scoutmaster for the East Surrey Association.

He applied for a commission immediately after the outbreak of war and was gazetted as lieutenant in the West Surreys on 23rd September 1914, promoted to captain on 13th March 1915 and went to France on 27th July. Whist there he served as intelligence officer, commanded the snipers, and afterwards had command of B Company. He was slightly wounded twice, on 25th May 1916 by an accidental explosion of bombs behind the trenches, and on 13th July in the attack on Trônes Wood.

In a letter addressed to Scouts he had written: *I am writing this on the eve of my departure. God only knows whether I am to return or not… Remember, boys, that each one of you brings an influence on your fellows either for good or bad…be just simple, straightforward, honest, kind-hearted, pure-minded boys, and you will turn out to be men well worthy of glorious England and all her noble traditions.*

The Chief Scout, Lord Baden-Powell wrote: *To the Scouts his memory and the message which he left for them will be a real inspiration in carrying on their duty at the present time.*

His major wrote of him as a man for whom he, *had the highest respect and the greatest affection*, and added, *I saw him a few minutes before he moved off, and he was quite cheery and calm. As he neared the enemy a shell pitched almost at his feet, killing him instantly.*

His commanding officer wrote: *Henry was a very fine character, and one of the soundest officers that a C.O. has ever been blessed with. He was wonderfully cool and gallant under fire, and I always knew that anything that I asked him to do would be done in the best way possible, and that he would never fail me however tight the corner.*

WILLIAM HENRY BRIGHT GROSS

SECOND LIEUTENANT, 1ST BATTALION, THE QUEEN'S (ROYAL WEST SURREY REGIMENT).

Died on 3rd November 1916, aged 26, during an attack on Boritska Trench, near Lesboeufs.

William was one of eight children of George (a stationary engine driver) and Emma Eliza Gross (née Lines) of Barrow-in-Furness, Lancashire.

Educated at Barrow Grammar School, he later went to Westminster Training College. At the time the war broke out he was a teacher at Vickerstown School, Barrow-in-Furness.

He enlisted as Private PS/2733, 21st Battalion, Royal Fusiliers, and went to France on 14th November 1915. In March 1916 he returned to England for officer training and was commissioned into the West Surreys on 6th July.

A letter he had written on 17th September 1916 was published in the school magazine. It ended: *There seem to be endless nationalities of troops here now – English, Highlanders, Australians, Indian cavalry Zouaves, Turcos – all ready, as far as one can see, in every detail. But I think the day of wild optimism is long past, and there's simply steadfast determination instead. I don't know whether to think it surprising or not, but the men are full of cheerfulness – brimming over with fun and good spirits. Growl? Yes, but the right kind of grouse.*

William is one of 20 members of the **Fell & Rock Climbing Club** of the English Lake District who died in the war. They are commemorated on a memorial near the summit of Great Gable, where a service is conducted each year on Remembrance Sunday.

In 1923 the Club gifted 3,000 acres of land above the 1,500 foot contour to the National Trust as a memorial to its members who died in the war. The land included the peaks of Great Gable, Green Gable, Brandreth, Grey Knotts, Base Brown, Seathwaite Fell, Glaramara, Allen Craggs, Kirkfell, Great End, Broad Cragg and Lingmell.

PIER 7

A

- South Lancashire Regiment - **Second Lieutenant A. Leighton to Private J. Wright**
  (completed from Pier and Face 7B)
- Welsh Regiment - **Major P. Anthony to Private T. A. Savory**
  (continued on Pier and Face 10A)

B

- Hampshire Regiment - **Private H. D. Kearns to Private H. S. Young**
  (completed from Pier and Face 7C)
- South Staffordshire Regiment
- Dorsetshire Regiment
- South Lancashire Regiment - **Lieutenant Colonel H. T. Cotton to Second Lieutenant R. Jones**
  (continued on Pier and Face 7A)

C

- Border Regiment - **Private C. T. Perrin to Private H. Young**
  (completed from Pier and Face 6A)
- Royal Sussex Regiment
- Hampshire Regiment - **Captain D. C. Arnell to Private E. B. Kay**
  (continued on Pier and Face 7B)

D

- Coldstream Guards - **Private F. Collacott to Private T. L. Young**
  (completed from Pier and Face 8D)
- Scots Guards
- Irish Guards
- Welsh Guards
- Royal Scots - **Major J. R. Bruce to Private A. Forbes**
  (continued on Pier and Face 6D)

FRANK CHANDLER

PRIVATE, 3018, 2ND BATTALION, SOUTH LANCASHIRE
REGIMENT.

Died on 3rd July 1916, aged 44, attempting to rescue his
officer during an attack south of Thiepval.

Frank was one of at least five children of William Henry (a
photographer) and Ellen Ruth Chandler (née Shirley).

He married Ruth Rowbottom in 1902 and lived in
Seedley, Lancashire. They had a son in 1905 and a daughter
in 1908.

He enlisted as Private 2352, 3rd Battalion, South Lancashire Regiment in Manchester on
7th January 1890. He then served in India and Egypt and through the Boer War. After leaving
the Army he was employed as a postman in the Pendleton district but re-enlisted on the
outbreak of war. He went to France on 5th December 1914.

After he was posted as missing Ruth made enquiries through the British Red Cross and
received a reply in late August which included the following information: *I think you may like
to receive the following account of the great gallantry and self-devotion which caused your husband's
death. Pte. John McGrath (now in Mill-road Hospital, Liverpool) tells the following story: – 'at
[censored] Lieut. Beven* was seen lying wounded outside, and Pte. Chandler called for volunteers to
get him in. Three men went with him, and Pte. Chandler gave Lieut. Beven first aid. Then the four men
tried to get the officer in on their rifles, as there was no stretcher, just as they reached the trench a shell
struck. It struck Pte. Chandler full and killed him instantly, killed Lieut. Beven and one of the men, and
wounded the other. The fourth man…escaped unhurt. Please allow me to express my admiration as
well as my feeling at your great loss.*

*Second Lieutenant Thomas Beven was aged 19 and from Brighton. He is commemorated
on Pier and Face 7B. Unfortunately, the identity of the other man killed is not given but the
likelihood is that he is commemorated with Frank on Pier and Face 7A. Of the other seventy
five privates from the 2nd Battalion who died on 3rd July only nineteen have a marked grave
and the others are on the Memorial.

Two Rugby Internationals are commemorated here, the first from the League and the other from the Union code.

WILLIAM GEORGE THOMAS

PRIVATE, 15041, 8TH BATTALION, SOUTH LANCASHIRE REGIMENT.

Died on 3rd July 1916, aged 35, during the fighting south of Thiepval.

William was one of fourteen children of William (a coal hewer) and Sarah Ann Thomas of Caerphilly, Glamorganshire. He married Ethel Mary Williams on 13th August 1901; they lived in Warrington, Cheshire, and had one son. He worked as a miner and while living in Wales played Rugby Union for two clubs. He later played Rugby League for Warrington, scoring a total of 537 points in 385 appearances. He played in four Challenge Cup finals, and was on the winning side in two. He set a club record (which stood until 2000) when he scored 33 points in a match in 1909. George played in the first ever international Rugby League match for Wales against the New Zealand 'All Golds' on 1st January 1908. A few weeks later he also played for Great Britain against New Zealand to become Warrington's first Test player. He enlisted in Warrington on 6th October 1914 and went to France on 28th September 1915.

RICHARD THOMAS

COMPANY SERGEANT MAJOR, 24093, 16TH BATTALION, WELSH REGIMENT.

Died on 7th July 1916, aged 35, during the fighting at Mametz Wood.

Richard was the only son, one of five children, of Joseph (a coal miner) and Mary Ann Thomas (formerly Robling, née Jones) of Llanwonno, Glamorganshire.

A member of the Glamorganshire Constabulary and a keen sportsman, he was a well known boxer but his main interest was rugby. He played for a number of clubs as well as the Police. He was also a Welsh International, playing for his country four times (between 1906 and 1909). He was unable to get away from his police duties to enlist until 16th January 1915; but still was one of the earliest Welsh Rugby Internationals to join the colours. He went to France on 4th December 1915 and gained his promotion to company sergeant major in March 1916.

PERCIVAL ANTHONY

Major, 15th Battalion, Welsh Regiment.

Died on 10th July 1916, aged 36, during the fighting at Mametz Wood.

Percival was the youngest son, one of six children, of Charles (an author, journalist and newspaper proprietor) and Elizabeth Anthony (née Warrington). He was a cousin of Lord Baden-Powell and Anthony Wilding, the champion tennis player.

He was educated at Dulwich College where he was a keen sportsman. Afterwards he played cricket for Herefordshire, in 1900, being top of the averages with 47.14; and was invited to qualify for Surrey and Worcestershire but his military career took precedence.

He served in the Boer War as a lieutenant in the Herefordshire Volunteer Company, attached to the 2nd Battalion, Shropshire Light Infantry, and was awarded the Queen's Medal with five clasps. He returned to South Africa after the war and settled in Johannesburg. His sporting career continued and included being captain of the Wanderers Cricket Club and playing rugby for the Transvaal. Some years later he went to the Malay States and took up rubber planting at Batu Gajah.

In October 1914 be resigned his appointment and on his arrival home was gazetted captain in the 15th Battalion, Welsh Regiment. He went to France on 4th December 1915 and was promoted to major in April 1916.

His commanding officer wrote: *It is very difficult indeed to say how much we all miss him. He was far and away the best and most painstaking company commander I had, and was universally respected and beloved. He met his death leading his men most gallantly in an attack on a position that was held by a most determined and resourceful enemy, and which we eventually captured and held.*

Someone who had served as a sergeant under him wrote: *Major Anthony never had an enemy of any kind, his disposition, being too fine, and his heart too large and open for that to be possible.*

THOMAS COLLINS

PRIVATE, 17572, 14TH BATTALION, WELSH REGIMENT.

Died on 22nd June 1916, aged 22 as a result of a tunnel collapse.

Thomas was one of seven children of John (a dock labourer) and Rachel Collins (née Balling) of Swansea.

He enlisted in Swansea and went to France on 2nd December 1915.

A chum wrote: *He was the nicest fellow anyone wished to meet, and was thought a great deal of by both officers and men.*

Thomas was working with a number of men from 254th Tunnelling Company, Royal Engineers, driving a tunnel in the Givenchy area. At 2.50 am a German mine blew in a section of the tunnel, trapping five men. After two days a rescue tunnel reached the men and three were rescued. Thomas was seriously injured and Sapper William Hackett* refused to leave him saying, *I am a tunneller, I must look after the others first.* Later that day the gallery collapsed again and entombed both men. Rescue attempts continued but after a further two days they had to be abandoned.

*Sapper William Hackett VC, aged 43, is commemorated on the Ploegsteert Memorial. The award of his VC for this action was gazetted on 4th August 1916.

Both men are also commemorated on the **Tunnellers' Memorial** near Givenchy which was unveiled in June 2010.

ALFRED EDWARD FLAXMAN

Second Lieutenant, 1st/6th Battalion, South
Staffordshire Regiment.

Died on 1st July 1916, aged 36, during the attack on
Gommecourt.

Alfred was the elder of two children, both sons, of the Rev.
Alfred Edward and Harriet Jecks Flaxman (née Reeve), of
Bournemouth, Dorset.

An accomplished boxer and gymnast he was also a
talented violinist and artist. Noted for being extremely
strong, he was able to bend a horseshoe or tear a pack of playing cards in two.

As a member of the 1908 Olympic team he competed in hammer throwing, standing high

jump, pole vault, discus and javelin. He featured in the
Amateur Athletics Association hammer competition for
ten years (1905 to 1914) and was Champion in 1910.

His adjutant wrote: *At the "Bull Ring" at Etaples, when he
first arrived in France, he caused consternation by hurling a
bomb well over seventy-five yards. On one occasion, when the
Boche blew up a mine in front of the South Staffordshire's
position and occupied the crater, Flaxman spent the whole night
alone on the lip above, bombing the lurking Huns beneath until
he was forced to rejoin his unit in the front line trench at
daybreak. On the night that preceded the first advance on the
Somme on July 1st, 1916, Flaxman was at Gommecourt, when
he spent the whole of the waiting hours detonating bombs in
order that his men might snatch what rest they could. When the advance was made he went forward
with the rest; he was struck by a bullet and died between the German lines and our own. When his
brother* searched for him after the battle he could find no trace; this is accounted for by the fact that
the Germans were observed burying our dead after the attack had failed.*

*His brother, **Samuel Christopher Reeve Flaxman**, was a captain in the Royal Army Medical
Corps.

FRANCIS TIPTON BYTHEWAY MC DCM

COMPANY SERGEANT MAJOR, 8860, 1ST BATTALION, SOUTH STAFFORDSHIRE REGIMENT.

Died on 14th July 1916, aged 29.

Francis was one of six children of Thomas Samuel and Lydia E. Bytheway (née Wright) of Walsall, Staffordshire.

After an education at Palfrey Infants and Palfrey (Boys) Junior School, he was employed as an office boy and later worked at the Alma Works in Walsall as a tube tester.

Joined the Militia in 1904 and in 1910 he enlisted in the 1st Battalion, South Staffordshire Regiment. He served in Gibraltar (1911 to 1913) and South Africa (1913 to 1914). He only returned to England in September 1914 but was in Belgium by the following month.

He was awarded the DCM and Russian Cross of the Order of St George for actions during the First Battle of Ypres. The DCM citation reads: *For conspicuous devotion to duty on 29th October 1914, near Kruiseik during a counter attack, when he personally carried a machine gun in the firing line for three quarters of a mile and only ceased firing when his ammunition was exhausted, he then continued to carry the gun till the end of the attack.*

He was wounded by shrapnel in the arm and shoulder at Loos in September 1915 and was treated in hospital in the UK. Whilst still on sick leave he was presented with both medals at a public ceremony on The Bridge in Walsall. When he was able to return to duty he spent time training recruits but then volunteered to return to the Front. He was offered a commission but declined.

TAKE UP THE SWORD OF JUSTICE

The award of the Military Cross was earned during the capture of Mametz on 1st July 1916. The citation reads: *For conspicuous gallantry when assisting his company commander to rally and lead on his men. When the company commander became a casualty he took command, and was conspicuous in the successful assault of an enemy position.*

He was reported to have been shot through the head while leading his men in the battalion's attack on High Wood. He had taken command of the men when their officer was killed in earlier fighting.

BEDE LIDDELL FENTON

Major, 1st Battalion, Dorsetshire Regiment.

Died on 15th July 1916, aged 33, whilst searching for an officer.

Bede was the only son, one of two children, of the Rev. Enos and Margaret Fenton (née Hinde) of Coleford, Gloucestershire.

He was educated at Lancing College and Keble College, Oxford, where he gained his BA in 1908 and MA in 1912.

He was an assistant master at the King's School, Worcester and later became house tutor at School House. At Worcester he was the first commanding officer of the school OTC, which he organised and raised to a high degree of efficiency. He then took up the post of headmaster at the State School at Johore Bahru, Singapore, on a five year contract. On the outbreak of war he sought permission to return to England but this was refused. He therefore broke his contract and arrived home early in 1915 and took up a commission. He was promoted to lieutenant on 4th April and captain on 15th November.

He went to France on 26th May 1916 and was promoted to major on 2nd July. His last letter to his father was dated two days before his death: *I cannot remember when last I had my clothes, or even boots, off, or when I washed my hands or shaved, but it seems a long way back… I see the "Daily Mail" talks about fighting from house to house and street to street. The only signs of a village, however, are parts of the E. and W. walls of the church and a few heaps of bricks. Not a sign of a street or road, nothing but trenches and craters…we passed heaps of dead bodies of both our fellows and the Huns… I saw a head and a hand just beside it – probably all that remained of some poor chap.*

He was killed near Ovillers whilst searching for **Lieutenant William Coley***, who had been reported wounded.

A fellow major wrote: *His body was found beside that of one of his men, not 15 yards away from the German trenches…his conduct under fire was an example to all near him…he had since been buried in a small cemetery…the whole regiment mourn with you in your great loss.*

His father was also vicar at Shotton Colliery, Co. Durham and commemorated Bede's death in a stained glass window in St Saviour's Church.

*William's body was subsequently found and buried in grave I.E.3 in Bouzincourt Communal Cemetery Extension.

JOHN HAROLD RYLE JONES

SECOND LIEUTENANT, 7TH BATTALION, SOUTH LANCASHIRE REGIMENT.

Died on 4th July 1916, aged 29, during an attack to the east of La Boisselle.

John was the youngest of three children of the Rev. John Roger and Jane Jones of Great Sankey, Warrington, Cheshire.

He was educated at Boteler Grammar School, Warrington, Liverpool College, and Jesus College, Oxford, where he matriculated in 1906.

In his early days in Warrington he played for Stockton Heath. At Oxford he served as a sergeant in the OTC and was a prominent athlete, winning many trophies in 1908 and 1909. He also represented his college at rowing and as a member of the football and rifle-shooting teams.

He had thought of entering the Church but decided to follow a different path. After spending time as a language teacher in Cologne and Grenoble he went to Canada in 1911. There he worked as a railway surveyor for the Canadian Pacific Railway. He was working in a remote part of Alberta when news came of the outbreak of war. He then walked seventy miles to the town of Athabasca in order to get transportation back to a city.

He enlisted on 23rd September 1914 as Private 19211, 101st Edmonton Fusiliers and came to England with the First Canadian Contingent.

Commissioned later in 1914, he went to France in 1915 and was slightly wounded in February 1916.

His adjutant wrote: *Both officers and men say that your son fought and led his men splendidly, and with great courage. His company gained their line and were consolidating their position. Your son was walking across the open to get some wire when he was shot through the head (probably by a sniper) and died instantaneously. Your son was very popular with officers and men.*

JOSEPH ARTHUR HULME

CORPORAL, G/4581, 7TH BATTALION, ROYAL SUSSEX
REGIMENT.

Died on 3rd October 1916, aged 38, during fighting at
Gueudecourt.

Joseph was one of six children of Samuel (a silk picker) and
Hannah Hulme of Leek, Staffordshire.

He was employed as a silk gimper.

He played football for local teams and joined Lincoln
City in 1897. At the end of the season his contract was not
renewed, so he moved to Gravesend United. Again he was released after a year and spent the
next two seasons at Wellingborough and Bristol Rovers respectively.

For the 1902/03 season he joined Brighton and Hove Albion and stayed with them until
1909. He captained the side in the 1905/06 season. He retired at the end of the 1908/09 season,
having played for the team in 174 matches and scored seven goals.

He returned to Leek and became the trainer of a local team. Enlisting in Leek, he decided
to join the Sussex Regiment rather than a Staffordshire Regiment.

He went to France on 18th May 1915.

An officer wrote: *I am writing to send you the sympathy of all who knew him 'out here'. He was
one of the most popular men in the Company and a very good N.C.O., and while we were being
heavily shelled he set an excellent example by his coolness. He was killed instantaneously and was
buried in a field behind our trenches by the men of his platoon, who also erected a cross over the grave.*

RICHARD WILLIAM PARRIS

CORPORAL, G/8402, 9TH BATTALION, ROYAL SUSSEX REGIMENT.

Died on 18th August 1916, aged 32, during an attack on Guillemont.

Richard was one of seven children of Alfred Albert (a brewer's drayman) and Mary Parris (née Reed).

He married Ada Sophia Portch on 27th October 1909 and had a son, born in 1912. He was employed as a telegraph messenger and postman when he enlisted in Maidstone on 25th November 1915. He was promoted to lance corporal on 19th February 1916, went to France on 1st June and was promoted to corporal later that month.

On 14th July 1916 he wrote to Ada: *...we have quite a smart dugout a fire and we have got plenty of candles and I have rigged up a table, so we sit round quite in style, yesterday I found some rice so I boiled it and served it out with peach jam, as we had no sugar, it was quite a relish, am making some more today for the remainder of the men.*

In another letter to Ada he wrote: *I met Bert Blackman, who is in the 1st Life Guards the other evening he looks very old and fed up, and is looking forward to the time when it is all over, he has been out here 2 years now. Dear Ada the time slips by very quickly fancy 2 months gone by, we have had only one of our draft killed but several have been wounded, the noise of the guns at this place is terrible at night, its one continual roar, our people are simply pouring shells into the Huns, you would not think it possible for anything to live through it.*

His last letter to Ada was dated six days before he was killed. In it he wrote: *...thanks so much for the cigs I must tell you they were most welcome, as we are stuck in this place, miles from anywhere and I have not got a smoke left, and I do not know how long we will be here, we are holding this place, which is a short distance behind the front line, the ground we hold has been captured from the Germans and by jove, it is a wreck, villages blown to atoms, we passed a church yesterday, with only one wall standing, and a statue of the Virgin quite undamaged, but the Huns dug-outs are splendid, they go down a great depth, and some of them, the officers especially, have every comfort, such as table, chairs, mirrors etc but I expect they find a great difference now that we keep pushing them back...but do not worry, if you don't hear sometimes quite as regular as usual, as I do not always get the opportunity to write, excuse paper and envelope dear as I had to borrow it, now with kisses to you both.*

His captain wrote: *...my most sincere sympathy in the death of your son. He was a fine Soldier and I am glad to say that I recognised his merit soon after he joined us and was instrumental in getting him promotion had he been spared I should have promoted him further. He however died as every brave soldier wishes to die on the field of battle fighting for his beloved country.*

JOHN HENRY MAWER

PRIVATE, G/15088, 12TH BATTALION, ROYAL SUSSEX
REGIMENT.

Died on 17th October 1916, aged 20, during the fighting
around the Schwaben Redoubt.

John was the eldest of five children of John (a goods guard
on the Midland Railway) and Annie Maria Mawer (née
Cooper) of Coalville, Leicestershire.

He initially enlisted in Loughborough as Private 4611,
5th Battalion, Leicestershire Regiment and transferred to the
Royal Sussex Regiment in 1916.

In response to a query from the family his commanding officer wrote: *I know no more,
probably you can find out by writing to War Office. Once we evacuate wounded from trenches we
don't know where they go to. Anything I can do for my men or relatives then I am only too glad to
do… Poor chaps we have to get them out as best as we can and have no time to find out any details.
I did not know him & his company commander was wounded on the same day.*

The family continued to make enquiries through the Red Cross and in January 1917 this
resulted in some information from a wounded comrade: *We had just left the Schwaben Redoubt,
and were making our way to the communication trench…and Mawer was in front of me, when he was
wounded in the back by a shell. As we were being heavily shelled we had to go on. The stretcher bearers
may have reached him.* An official of the Red Cross added: *What we fear has happened is that your
son has been hit a second time as he lay wounded, so was never brought in by the stretcher bearers.
Had he been taken a prisoner of war, his name would have reached us by now… All this makes us
very anxious about him, and it leads us to fear that your boy has lost his life.*

Another eyewitness account was forwarded in March 1917, which included: *We were being
relieved at Schwaben Redoubt…when a shell came over, and I saw Mawer was very badly wounded.
Stretcher bearers were in attendance when I had to pass on.* This time the Red Cross official added:
*This account tells us a little more than we knew before, that is to say, that your son was attended to
by stretcher bearers after he was wounded. But I am afraid we can have no hope that he survived.*

The Army Record Office wrote in July 1917 that John was now officially presumed dead. In
April 1918 the War Office wrote that his grave was reported as being *at a point North West of
Thiepval;* but no grave was ever identified by the Graves Registration Unit.

ALAN VICTOR CAIN

SECOND LIEUTENANT, 3RD BATTALION ATTACHED TO 2ND
BATTALION, HAMPSHIRE REGIMENT.

Died on 18th October 1916, aged 24, during an attack on
Grease Trench, near Gueudecourt.

Alan was one of six children of Henry Frederic (a solicitor)
and Edith Lucy Underwood Cain (née Soundy) of Hove,
Sussex.
He was educated at Herne Bay College, where he gained
his colours both for cricket and football.

In 1913 he became a Professional Associate of the Surveyors' Institution, a member of the
Land Agents' Society and held a post with Hampshire County Council at The Castle,
Winchester.

Immediately after the outbreak of war he enlisted in the Hampshire Yeomanry and served
with them until February 1915. He then received a commission and was attached to the
Hampshire Regiment and went to Gallipoli. While there he also acted for some time as an
observer in the Royal Naval Air Service. He was invalided home after being incapacitated by
frostbite and rheumatism.

On recovery he went to France in July 1916 and served with the 2nd Battalion, Hampshire
Regiment.

In recording his dying wishes he had written to his father: *I have tried to do my Duty and
have given all that one is able to give in the service of his Country. I have died a glorious death.
Remember, I am well content.*

The day before he fell he wrote in reference to the attack planned for the next day, and with
a premonition of his coming end, asked those dear to him not to grieve, adding, *I am only doing
what thousands of other fellows are doing and my only anxiety is that I may not fail at the critical
moment, as so many other lives depend on my steadiness.*

An officer wrote: *We shall all of us miss him very much indeed. He was universally liked by both
Officers and men, and was always a most capable Officer. He was present at a Celebration of the Holy
Communion held in the trenches the day before he was killed, and he was buried just behind our
trenches.*

JAMES HENDRIE

PRIVATE, 13043, 1ST BATTALION, SCOTS GUARDS.

Died on 15th September 1916, aged 28, during an attack on Lesboeufs.

James was the eldest of eight children of David (a farmer) and Jeanie Hendrie of Galston, Ayrshire.

He was educated at Galston Public School until 1904, when the family moved to Durisdeer, Dumfriesshire. It was here that he became friendly with John Boyle (the local schoolmaster) and for four years attended his winter continuation classes whilst also working on the family's farm. He was very interested in the political questions of the day and his interest and knowledge meant that he was in demand as a public speaker. In 1913 he was part of a delegation from Dumfriesshire that went to Ulster to discuss the question of Home Rule. He was then offered a place as a student in the Agricultural Department of Edinburgh University.

He went to France on 1st January 1916 and throughout his time in training and in France he regularly wrote to his friend John Boyle. A volume containing those letters and a number of tributes to James was published after the war under the title *Letters of a Durisdeer Soldier.*

His last letter, written while he was in Albert and dated 10th September 1916, mentioned two local lads* who had died and also that he had met up with his brother, David, who was *...looking exceptionally well.* The letter ended: *My writing of this was interrupted by having to pack up, as we were to move forward, and just now the light is hardly sufficient to allow me to see. We stand on the brink. When the plunge will come I know not. I have borne in mind the injunction contained in your last letter.*

Unfortunately **David Hendrie**, Corporal S/16893, 6th Battalion, Cameron Highlanders, died five weeks after James on 22nd October 1916, aged 20. He is buried in grave I.Y.2 in Bécourt Military Cemetery.

*Privates **James Laidlaw**, S/16483, aged 30 and **John McLellan**, S/22210, aged 27, were both in the 6th Battalion, Cameron Highlanders. They died on 24th August 1916 and are commemorated on Pier and Face 15B.

CHARLES FRANCIS PURCELL

Lieutenant, 2nd Battalion, Irish Guards, attached to
Machine Gun Corps (Infantry).

Died on 15th September 1916, aged 25, during the attack
on Ginchy.

Charles was one of at least four children of Matthew John
and Anna Mary Purcell (née Daly) of Buttevant, Co. Cork.

He was educated at Beaumont College, Windsor,
Stonyhurst College and then Balliol College, Oxford. While
at Oxford he helped to start the St Patrick's Society, and was
full of enthusiasm for a movement which should unite parties in Ireland and bring over to a
reasonable Irish nationalism the young men like himself ...*who used to be Unionists.* He got a
degree in History in 1913 and joined the Inner Temple.

He went to France on 31st October 1914 as a driver with the Red Cross and also as a
despatch rider. On 6th March 1915 he obtained a special reserve commission in the Irish
Guards and was back in France in August. He was promoted to lieutenant after the battle of
Loos, and was made machine gun officer. His cheery temper won him the nickname of 'Sunny'
among his men.

His orderly wrote: ...*as we advanced over the German lines he was shot, and died immediately.
The Machine Gun Section of the Irish Guards deeply deplores his loss, as he was a brave soldier and
a gentleman to his men, as he always saw to their wants. If he had lived he would, I am certain, have
made a great name for himself.*

A survivor of the Machine Gun Company wrote: *'Sunny' was hit early in the advance, but his
men went on and did splendidly, as they would do, for he had trained them well. They were all very
fond of him; he was of their own country and understood them.*

An artillery officer wrote: *He was such a good chap, so manly, and always so bright. He was the
life and soul of his mess, and was just loved by all his men, who miss him very keenly. As practically
all his brother officers were also killed, it is difficult to get a good account as to how he met his death.
I have learned that it came early in the attack, not long after he had leapt from our trenches with his
men. He received a clean wound which killed him instantly. His men say he was slightly wounded first
and refused to stop or go back, but went on with them - and I can quite believe it of him.*

A colonel in the Irish Guards wrote: *He was a real good soldier and was universally loved. I
have heard nothing but good of him since he came into the regiment.*

A prominent Irish MP wrote: *He seemed to me precisely the type of young Irishman who ought
to have had a splendid career hereafter in the service of Ireland.*

GEORGE HERIOT'S SCHOOL ROLL OF HONOUR

The Roll of Honour of this Edinburgh school indicates that over 2,600 men, staff and former pupils, served in the Forces and 459 died. At least thirty five of those are commemorated on the Memorial. These thirteen men are all from the Royal Scots and their names appear on Pier and Face 7D.

John A. Henry
Captain
14th July 1916, 19

Herbert G. Eagar
Sergeant
23rd July 1916, 23

Robert Brown
Corporal
1st July 1916, 23

James M. S. Calderhead
Corporal
1st July 1916, 23

James R. Crowe
Lance Corporal
1st July 1916, 20

Thomas C. Moffatt
Lance Corporal
1st July 1916, 33

Peter Spowart
Lance Corporal
1st July 1916, 21

Hew E. Browne
Private
1st July 1916, 21

John Colthart
Private
4th August 1916, 22

Thomas Cowan
Private
1st July 1916, 20

James W. Duguid
Private
21st October 1916, 21

George W. English
Private
1st July 1916, 20

Alexander J. Falconer
Private
30th July 1916, 30

ERNEST EDGAR ELLIS

PRIVATE, 19009, 16TH BATTALION, ROYAL SCOTS.

Died on 1st July 1916, aged 30, during the attack on Contalmaison.

Ernest was one of seven children of Harry William (a boot maker) and Maria Ellis (née Taylor) of Norwich, Norfolk.

He was the husband of Isobel Ellis. They lived in Edinburgh and had one daughter.

Having played football for Norwich City, he transferred to the Heart of Midlothian in the summer of 1914, where he played in the second team. In this team picture Ernest is the player in the back row, second from the right.

He enlisted in Edinburgh on 25th November 1914 and went to France on 8th January 1916.

His body was found and buried but the grave was subsequently lost.

HEART OF MIDLOTHIAN

At least thirty men from the club served during the war and seven of those died. Four, all from the Royal Scots, are commemorated on the Memorial. Three, including Ernest, are on Pier and Face 7D; and one, Henry Wattie, is on Pier and Face 6D.

Duncan Currie
Sergeant
1st July 1916, 23

James Boyd
Private
3rd August 1916, 21

Henry Wattie
Private
1st July 1916, 24

PIER 8

A

- Royal Horse and Royal Field Artillery - **Gunner R. Bentham to Driver H. Winter**
  (completed from Pier and Face 1A)
- Royal Garrison Artillery
- Honourable Artillery Company
- Royal Engineers - **Lieutenant G. L. B. Fayle to Sapper P. Owen**
  (continued on Pier and Face 8D)

B

- The King's (Liverpool Regiment) - **Lance Sergeant W. Fidler to Private J. Livesey**
  (continued from Pier and Face 8C)
  (continued on Pier and Face 1D)

C

- Royal Fusiliers - **Private H. Ibbotson to Private T. R. Young**
  (completed from Pier and Face 16A)
- The King's (Liverpool Regiment) - **Lieutenant Colonel C. E. Goff to Lance Sergeant J. S. Ferris**
  (continued on Pier and Face 8B)

D

- Royal Engineers - **Sapper L. Pantling to Pioneer H. Woolf**
  (completed from Pier and Face 8A)
- Grenadier Guards
- Coldstream Guards - **Captain H. P. Meakin to Private W. T. Colgate**
  (continued on Pier and Face 7D)

WILFRED CUBITT SPELMAN

LANCE CORPORAL, 4177, 1ST BATTALION, HONOURABLE ARTILLERY COMPANY.

Died on 13th November 1916, aged 31, during an attack on Beaucourt.

Wilfred was the eldest of five children of William (an insurance clerk) and Ellen Mary Spelman (née Cubitt) of Lavender Hill, London.

He was educated at Felix College, St John's Hill, and at Clark's College. He then joined Parr's Bank and played football and cricket for the bank, he also played football for the London Bank Association. He enlisted at Armoury House on 9th August 1915 and was posted to 1st Battalion on 7th January 1916. He went to France the following day and joined the battalion in the field on 21st January. He was promoted to lance corporal (unpaid) just a week before he died.

His 1916 diary, which is still held within the family, records a short note on most days. A few of the entries are given here:

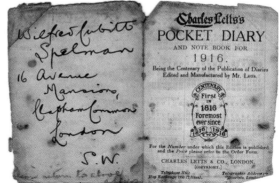

8th January: *Had the morning off. My friend White and I had quite a musical morning at a teashop, he singing and charming the ladies while I occasionally broke in at the piano. Paraded at 2pm for march off to docks. Eventually left docks at 5o/c. rather choppy passage several ill fortunately not I. Reached Rouen at 7.30am Sunday.*

9th August: *Today is a red letter (or black letter?) day. It is exactly one year since I in my innocence toddled up to Armoury House in City road & took the oath, which led to several – yes you guess what I am about to write – so enough!! Suffice to say that I am glad to have gone through it, but like a million and one others sincerely trust it will not be necessary again. Also an equally earnest hope that it is nearer the end than the beginning.*

16th August: *On arrival in the firing trench last night I (with two others) got the job of riflemen in an advanced trench (known as a sap) only some 25 yards from the Hun similar sap. Each rifleman has a bomber with him & the pair work together through the night (one hour on guard & 2 off) & it is advisable to keep low & quiet. Even then you get plenty of bullets over.*

The last entry, on 15th October, reads, *Spent the day in the transport field – a day of rest.*

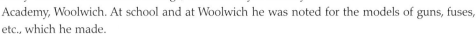

CYRIL EDWARD BRIETZCKE DEAN

Second Lieutenant, 121st Heavy Battery, Royal
Garrison Artillery.

Died on 15th September 1916, aged 19, during the
fighting at High Wood.

Cyril was the eldest of eight children of Cyril Charles
Stephen (a solicitor) and Georgina Dean (née Wilson) of
London.

He was educated at St Benedict's College, Ealing, the
Army Class at Wimbledon College, and the Royal Military
Academy, Woolwich. At school and at Woolwich he was noted for the models of guns, fuses,
etc., which he made.

Gazetted second lieutenant on 22nd April 1915, he went to France on 20th August where
he was posted to the 121st Heavy Battery.

In June 1916 he was mentioned in despatches and his commanding officer wrote: *Their
billet was shelled, causing several casualties, including one officer killed. Your son, being the only other
officer there at the time, took charge, got the men out of their billet in the short interval between the
shells, and himself remained behind with a dying man, who could not be moved… His conduct has
been splendid… He was the most lovable boy, with the most charming manners, that I have ever met.*

Later he also wrote: *Your son was instantaneously killed by a shell while doing liaison work with
the infantry during the big attack of 15 Sept. He had done this important and dangerous, work on
behalf of our group of batteries during other attacks, always in the most efficient and plucky way and
the Colonel decided that he was to do it, again in this big attack, as he was the best subaltern in the
group for the work. He was following up the infantry with two telephonists, and had laid out his wire
to the German switch trench which had just been captured, when a shell fell behind him, killing him
and a telephonist instantaneously… He has been buried where he fell, and a cross put on his grave
with his name, battery and date when he was killed in action… He was my observation officer during
the six months I have commanded the battery, and I never hope to have a better one. We have been in
many hot corners together, and a pluckier or cheerier companion it is impossible to imagine. Everyone
who knew him loved him, myself, I think, the most.*

Although he was buried in a marked grave, the location was subsequently lost.

ERIC CAUTY ANDREWS

Second Lieutenant, 9th Field Company, Royal Engineers.

Died on 12th October 1916, aged 21.

Born in the Transvaal, South Africa, Eric was the eldest son of George Frederick and Isabel Gertrude Andrews (née Cauty) of Rosettenville near Johannesburg.

He was educated in England at Dunstable Grammar School and then in Natal at Michael House, Balgowan. At the age of 16 he matriculated in the second class. He then proceeded to the School of Mines in Johannesburg to study civil engineering. After his third year course he fought through the German South West Africa Campaign (September 1914 to July 1915) as a private in the Rand Rifles. He then returned to the School of Mines and passed the final examination for the Civil Engineering Diploma.

He was a keen footballer and tennis player and in his last year at the mining school he won both the singles and the doubles tennis championship.

He then obtained a commission in the Royal Engineers and landed in England on 31st December 1915; after training in north Wales he went to France in June 1916.

His commanding officer wrote: *He was a very gallant Officer beloved by his men and in the mess. He and I went out together last night with half the Company to consolidate some ground won and he unfortunately was shot through the heart by a bullet just after his work was done and he had set his men on to work. He was the cheery boy of the Mess and I, personally, feel his loss very much as although the youngest Officer of the Company he was one of the best I had.*

Another senior officer wrote: *Knowing him you will realise how great his loss is to us. He was always so cheery, stout hearted and a splendid companion. His men buried him where he fell and erected a cross over his grave which lies amidst the waste and ruin of the greatest battlefield the world has ever seen.*

Although buried in a marked grave on the battlefield the grave was subsequently lost.

WILLIAM CLEWLEY MM

SAPPER, 97432, 156TH FIELD COMPANY, ROYAL ENGINEERS.

Died on 9th September 1916, aged 28, during an attack on Ginchy.

William was the only son, one of two children, of Alfred (a coal miner) and Mary Ann Emma Clewley (née Tipping).

He married Maria Madelaine Nocetti in 1914 and lived in Hanley, Staffordshire. They had a son born later that year.

Employed as a pipe fitter at the Deep Pit, Hanley, he enlisted in Stoke-on-Trent on 29th April 1915 and went to France on 19th December. He was promoted to sapper on 21st January 1916 on attainment of proficiency as a platelayer.

The award of the Military Medal was gazetted on 14th September 1916; the citation reads: *In the field on March 26th, 1916, Sapper Clewley was with a party of R.E. sent up to consolidate a mine crater blown up by the enemy. The explosion had damaged our front line severely, burying many of the infantry garrison. Sapper Clewley, with Sergeant Normanton and Sapper Thomas, carried out the work of digging out the buried men and removing them to a place of safety. This work was done under heavy fire from rifle grenades, trench mortars, and machine guns, and several lives were saved. In the field on April 29th, 1916, the enemy made a gas attack, accompanied by intense bombardment. During the bombardment the billets occupied by the company were damaged, and one house collapsed, burying ten men. Sapper Clewley was at once on the spot, and displayed great coolness and energy in extricating the buried men. By the prompt action of the party several lives were saved. This work was carried out under heavy shell fire, and was witnessed by his company commander.* For the earlier action he also received a personal letter on parchment complimenting him on his bravery. The Military Medal was publically presented to his widow in May 1917.

His lieutenant wrote: *He came along with myself and the rest of the section in operations which succeeded in capturing a strong enemy village. His behaviour throughout the action was splendid, and indeed I never came across a braver man. He was quite cheerful, even when hit, and no one was more surprised than myself when he died shortly afterwards from the gunshot wound in his leg. He was a general favourite with the company, and his loss is felt by us all. It will be some consolation to you to know that he died cheerfully doing his duty.*

CHARLES DAVENPORT

LANCE CORPORAL, 3215, 1ST/5TH BATTALION, THE KING'S (LIVERPOOL REGIMENT).

Died on 25th September 1916, aged 22, during an attack on the Gird Lines near Gueudecourt.

Charles was one of eleven children of Charles William (a builder and contractor) and Kate Davenport (née Isherwood) of Stockton Heath, Cheshire.

Educated at the local Grammar School, he was an accomplished athlete and held the school's silver championship trophy for swimming.

He married Olive Bradshaw in 1913 and lived in Rock Ferry, Cheshire; they had a son, born later that year.

He was working in the family building and contracting business when he enlisted in Liverpool on 4th December 1914. He went to France on 21st February 1915 and was promoted to lance corporal on 14th August 1916.

He took part in the fighting at Neuve Chapelle, Ypres, Loos, Festubert and Guillemont and had a number of narrow escapes. Writing to his mother he said: *I have been buried three times last week, the second time under three or four men who had been killed. I had difficulty in digging myself out.*

On another occasion he was buried but a bomb, that had been lying in the trench, exploded practically beneath him and blew him out. He sustained severe burns and scorches, but was otherwise uninjured, commenting that he was *...not downhearted yet.*

He distinguished himself as a sharpshooter, at sniping work and on dangerous sentry duties.

The *Warrington Examiner* reported the following exchange between a family friend and a lieutenant of the Liverpools that took place over lunch in a Liverpool cafe one day. Talking of Warrington the officer said: *Do you know a family name Davenport in Stockton Heath?* the friend replied, *'Very well.' 'Do you know a young fellow named Charles Davenport?' 'Yes, I knew him from his youth.' 'Well,'* said the officer, *'he has gone through a terrible time from the first. He is the finest man I have got in my regiment, and was the first man on top of the crest at Guillemont.'*

JOHN DYKES HOLT

LANCE CORPORAL, 22415, 20TH BATTALION, THE KING'S
(LIVERPOOL REGIMENT).

Died on 12th July 1916, aged 22, during an attack on the
German section of Maltz Horn Trench, near Trônes
Wood.

John was one of nine children of John (a foreman
shipwright) and Mary Holt (née Dykes) of Runcorn,
Cheshire.

He was one of the secretaries of the Brunswick Sunday
School and correspondent for the Brunswick Wesleyan magazine.

Employed as a clerk, he enlisted in Liverpool on 10th November 1914. He went to France
on 7th November 1915 and was promoted to lance corporal on 2nd July 1916.

While on active service he was in demand as a letter writer for those wounded soldiers who
could not write home. He also provided comfort by reading the Bible to them and praying for
them.

During his time in the trenches he had a number of narrow escapes and was nicknamed
'the lucky Pal'.

On 16th June 1916 John and three other men volunteered to carry in a number of soldiers
from the South Lancashire Regiment who had been wounded by German shelling. They
performed the task under fire and through a communication trench full of twists and turns,
which hampered the movement of the stretchers. Two days later the four men were called to
their orderly room and commended for their gallant and distinguished conduct. In thanking
them, the South Lancashires said that they were ...*a credit to their battalion.*

His sergeant wrote to John's brother: *He was hit this morning as he was being relieved, and
died about an hour afterwards in a French dressing station... Every man in the company feels he has
lost a real comrade. He was undoubtedly one of our best men, and we shall miss him more that I can
tell. He will be buried to-day in a small but steadily growing cemetery behind the line among some of
our best and our Ally's army who have been called upon to make the great sacrifice, and the locality
of which I will tell you later on, as we are not allowed to make known the place at present.*

GEORGE HENRY COCKAYNE

PRIVATE, 6307, 13TH BATTALION, THE KING'S (LIVERPOOL REGIMENT).

Died on 16th August 1916, aged 23, during an attack on the German lines south of Guillemont.

George was one of four children of Samuel (a cashier) and Louisa Harriet Cockayne (née Hickman) of Bootle, Lancashire.

Educated at Christ Church Higher Grade School and Bootle Municipal Technical School, afterwards he was employed by the National Provincial Bank of England, and worked as a clerk in the branches at Liverpool and Blackburn.

He enlisted in Bootle on 30th November 1915 and was mobilised on 16th February 1916. He went to France on 14th July and joined the battalion twelve days later.

A comrade wrote: *We were in a charge on the 16th, and poor George was not with us afterwards when we left the trenches for a short rest. I did not see him as we went over, but know fellows who actually saw him hit and fall. Naturally, in the confusion, he may have got down to the rear and away with the wounded, but I fear the worst. He was hit in the head, and fell almost immediately we got over the top… It broke me up altogether, for he was such a good old pal… You must not give up all hope yet, and I am making every enquiry and shall communicate with you as soon as I am sure. For myself I fear the worst, and shall be overjoyed to find some reassuring news. If the worst is a fact, I do not need to tell you he went over smiling like a hero – in fact all the lads did. It was grand to see them, and yet awful to see the good lads falling. I shall never be able to forget my experiences.*

The same comrade dedicated a poem in George's memory, which was published in the *Waterloo and Crosby Times* on 6th October 1916, it included the verse:

> *He was dearly beloved by all whom he knew,*
> *Of him no man could speak ill,*
> *And though 'neath the soil out in France here he lies,*
> *He lives in our memory still.*

It was later reported that George had been buried north-west of Guillemont and east of Albert.

FRANK FOSTER HARPER

PRIVATE, 15896, 17TH BATTALION, THE KING'S (LIVERPOOL REGIMENT).

Died on 30th July 1916, aged 22, during an attack on Guillemont Farm.

Frank was the only child of Thomas Harwood Harper (a marine insurance underwriter) and Florence Harper (née Foster) of Birkenhead, Cheshire.

Educated at Birkenhead School, he then joined the Liverpool & London & Globe Insurance Company. By the time the war began he was an assistant surveyor in the fire branch. He enlisted in Liverpool on 31st August 1914 and went to France on 7th November 1915.

Wounded by gunshots to his back and neck on 27th June 1916, he was treated at the 21st Casualty Clearing Station and was able to return to his unit two days later.

He was in the machine gun section, and during the advance they waited in a shell hole for an opportunity to proceed. A German gas shell exploded killing, practically the whole section.

In memory of Frank his father founded two prizes, the Frank Harper Memorial Prizes, to be awarded at Birkenhead School for French.

BIRKENHEAD SCHOOL

The School's Roll of Honour remembers ninety six former pupils who died during the war. Frank and at least three others are commemorated on the Memorial.

THOMAS FRANCIS PHILLIPS

Private, E/438, 17th Battalion, Royal Fusiliers, attached to 5th Light Trench Mortar Battery.

Died on 2nd September 1916, aged 29, killed by a shell whilst in the trenches between Beaumont Hamel and Serre.

Thomas was one of four children of Charles John (an electrical engineer) and Emily Bertha Phillips (née Collbran) of Orpington, Kent.

Educated at the Whitgift Middle School, Croydon, Surrey, he then went to Northampton Polytechnic Institute, St John Street, London. He became a student of the Institution of Electrical Engineers in 1910 and an associate member in 1914. During this time he held a number of positions and in 1912 he joined the engineering staff of the newly created General Post Office. In July 1913 he resigned and joined the staff of Gill & Cook, Consulting Engineers. The following year he was posted to Constantinople in order to prepare plans for the extension of the telephone system in the Turkish capital.

With the prospect of war looming he returned home in July 1914, journeying through Germany (via Berlin) by the last train permitted by the German military authorities to cross the frontier into Holland a few days prior to the declaration of war.

He enlisted in the Fusiliers on 30th August 1914 and went to France on 17th November 1915. He was selected for a course at the Trench Mortar School at St Pol, Pas de Calais, and on the completion of this course, he was posted to the 5th Light Trench Mortar Battery.

His battery commander wrote: *I write to inform you of the death of your son which took place at 11.30 p.m. on Saturday, Sept. 2nd. Your boy was killed at his post by the explosion of an enemy shell and you will doubtless be proud to hear that he died while doing his duty as a soldier and Englishman. He was actually engaged in firing at the enemy when the unfortunate occurrence happened. It will perhaps be a relief to you to know that he suffered no pain, his death being absolutely instantaneous… I cannot speak too highly of the courage and devotion to duty which always characterized your son. He was beloved by officers and men alike, and his loss and that of his fellow soldier, who was on duty with him at the time, has cast quite a gloom over the Battery.*

WILLIAM NORMAN PODMORE

PRIVATE, 10567, 9TH BATTALION, ROYAL FUSILIERS.

Died on 7th October 1916, aged 36, during an attack on Bayonet Trench, near Gueudecourt.

William was one of eight children of James (an estate agent's clerk) and Emma Podmore (née Conyers) of Dewsbury, Yorkshire.

On leaving school he joined the Co-operative Laundry in Dewsbury, where he worked until he moved to Wallsend, Northumberland, as manager of the English Laundry.

He enlisted on 13th April 1916; although in a protected occupation he had agreed to join up, a proposal acceptable to the local Tribunal, in order that his cashier, who had the care of a widowed mother, might remain behind. Later he joined the battalion's Lewis gun detachment.

He was slightly wounded on 2nd October but remained on duty.

A comrade wrote: *I am sorry to say that up to now I cannot give you any information as to what really did happen to poor Willie, only one of his gun crew told us that he himself was hit within twenty yards of the German lines, and that he saw Willie still going forward carrying the gun. He asked us what became of him. He was a generous kind-hearted old soul. He seemed like a brother to me. You can imagine how I miss him. He always tried to look after my welfare before his own.*

An officer wrote: *He took part in an attack made by this battalion and did some very brave work. I cannot tell you how sorry I am to have lost him from my section, as he was always very good with the Lewis gun, and did his duty well.*

JOSEPH EDWIN SUNDERLAND

PRIVATE, 5720, 20TH BATTALION, ROYAL FUSILIERS.

Died on 20th July 1916, aged 21, during an attack on High Wood.

Joseph was the elder of two children of John William (a florist's manager) and Susannah Sunderland (née Jowett) of Todmorden, Yorkshire.

He was educated at Roomfield Council and Todmorden Secondary Schools.

After enlisting in Manchester in January 1915 in a Public Schools Battalion of the Royal Fusiliers he went to France on 15th November.

His sergeant* wrote: *In the absence of really definite information, it is a matter of considerable difficulty to know what to say about Joe…we have hoped against hope that some sort of news would come through…none had been forthcoming so far, and I am afraid that the only news we have is of the worst kind… I think we knew each other better than ever during those first four days in the woods. And then came that awful fifth day. What was left of my little platoon had advanced across the flat in front of the place we were attacking, quite untouched amidst all the shells which were coming over, when…a shell burst very close and hit two or three of my fellows… I could not tell how many had been hit, and all I could do was to take all that was left of my platoon forward with the rest of the fellows… I was extremely sorry to find that poor Joe was missing from my party. It was fearful that morning, and few of us who were in the wood ever thought that they would get out alive… Joe was incapable of a selfish deed or action, and was one of the best fellows in a company of good fellows. His loss is a personal one… I hope to go over to see you when I get home on leave, and then I can describe more fully all that I know of him. There is just the faintest chance that he was taken away wounded…but surely news would have reached us by this time if that had been the case.*

The following week a number of photographs, of Joseph's fiancée and other family members, were returned to his parents. They had been found on Joseph's body and, by an indirect route, had been sent to a family friend in the hope that someone could identify them. A letter that accompanied the photographs indicated that his body had been buried. The grave was subsequently lost.

*Sergeant Ernest Airlie Holden was commissioned as a second lieutenant in The Loyal North Lancashire Regiment on 3rd October 1916. He was killed two weeks later, aged 23, and is buried in grave II.A.21 in Contay British Cemetery.

JOHN THEODORE ST CLAIR TISDALL

SECOND LIEUTENANT, 1ST BATTALION ATTACHED TO 11TH
BATTALION, THE KING'S (LIVERPOOL REGIMENT).

Died on 8th August 1916, aged 22, leading his company
during fighting at Guillemont.

John was born in Ispahan, Persia, one of nine children of the
Rev. William and his second wife Marian Louisa St Clair
Tisdall (née Gray), of Deal, Kent.

Educated at Bedford School, where he was a member of
the OTC, and Peterhouse, Cambridge (Classical School and Bell University Scholar). He was a
keen athlete and was in the First XV at Bedford, played rugby for the East Midlands, and at
Peterhouse played football and rowed for his college.

He joined King Edward's Horse in 1913. When the war broke out he applied for a
commission and was gazetted a second lieutenant in the 1st Liverpools on 7th October 1914.
He spent time at Sandhurst then went to France on 27th September 1915, being wounded two
weeks later. Invalided home, he only returned to the Front in February 1916.

A senior officer wrote: *Tisdall took command of B. Company. He…is the most gallant officer I
have ever seen in action. He was a typical V.C. hero – a wonderfully fine man.*

Another officer wrote: *We were together through that awful show in Delville Wood just before
the attack on Guillemont, and those of us who are left still talk of Tisdall, his fun and his fearlessness.
As one of the men said, 'The very looks of him put confidence in you'.*

His older brother, **Arthur Walderne St Clair Tisdall VC**, Sub-
Lieutenant, Anson Battalion, Royal Naval Division, RNVR, died on
6th May 1915, aged 24. He is commemorated on the Helles
Memorial. The award of the Victoria Cross was gazetted on 31st
March 1916: *During the landing from the SS* River Clyde *at V Beach,
in the Gallipoli Peninsula, on the 25th April, 1915, Sub-Lieutenant
Tisdall, hearing wounded men on the beach calling for assistance,
jumped into the water, and, pushing a boat in front of him, went to their
rescue…In all, Sub-Lieutenant Tisdall made four or five trips between
the ship and the shore, and was thus responsible for rescuing several wounded men under heavy and
accurate fire.*

PERCIVAL GEORGE WAINE

SAPPER, 137675, 178TH TUNNELLING COMPANY, ROYAL ENGINEERS.

Died on 21st December 1915, aged 27.

Percival was the eldest of five children of George (a farm labourer) and Susan Waine (née Humphries) of Garsington, Oxfordshire.

Employed as a labourer, he enlisted on 28th September 1914 as Private 3362, 1/4th Battalion, Ox & Bucks Light Infantry.

He went to France on 29th March 1915 and transferred to the Royal Engineers in the field on 10th November as a Tunneller's Mate.

He was one of fourteen men killed when the Germans exploded two large mines at the Tambour Duclos, near Fricourt. The blasts wrecked thirty yards of trench and collapsed several shafts and galleries. The bodies of Percival and six other men were never recovered and their names are commemorated on the Memorial.

- **Llewelyn Morris**, 2nd Corporal, 102836

- **Christopher Barlow**, Sapper, 112688

- Henry Halton*, Sapper, 137670

- **William Hemingway**, Sapper, 102867

- **Alexander McDougal**, Sapper, 102844

- **Arthur Weston**, Sapper, 112691

Like Percival, Arthur Weston's name is on Pier and Face 8D, while the other names are all on Pier and Face 8A.

The bodies of the other seven men were recovered and are buried side by side in graves I.C.24 to 30 in Norfolk Cemetery.

*Henry Arthur James Halton was the younger of two children of James (a cowman) and Annie Halton. He worked as a miner and enlisted as Private 3162, 1st/8th Battalion, Worcestershire Regiment on 29th September 1914 and went to France on 1st April 1915. On 14th October he transferred, in the field, to the Royal Engineers as a Tunneller's Mate.

FREDERICK HAVELOCK PETERS TREGIDGO

PIONEER, 86972, 82ND FIELD COMPANY, ROYAL ENGINEERS.

Died on 29th July 1916, aged 30.

Frederick was one of eight children of Thomas Henry Pitts Tregidgo (a ship's carpenter) and Sarah Jane Tregidgo (née Tregaskis) of Falmouth, Cornwall.

He married Mary A. Bryan in 1915 and later lived in Coddington, Nottinghamshire.

His major wrote: *He was killed instantaneously on the night of 29th July, while working with his section on some work prior to an attack on the enemy, at about 200 yards away from the enemy's trenches… Everyone misses him very much, as he was such a splendid fellow, and a brave soldier. He never gave any trouble at all, and was always willing to volunteer for any job that had to be done. He is a very great loss to us.*

The British Official History, in a footnote, states: *No. 3 Section…was engaged under fire in building strong points in front of Bazentin le Petit village during the night of the 29th/30th July. The infantry assisting the section was withdrawn to prepare for an attack next day, but the sappers volunteered to go on with the work and did so, until nine were killed and nearly all the others wounded.*

A memorial at Bazentin-le-Petit commemorates these 'Nine Brave Men.'

Frederick and six others: Pioneer **William Haviland** and Sappers **Richard Frank Choat**, **James Joiner**, **Charles William Vernon**, **Ambrose Robotham**, and **Thomas Blakely** have no known grave and are commemorated on the Memorial.

Of the other two, **Sapper Charles Douglas Ellison** is commemorated on a Special Memorial in Caterpillar Valley Cemetery, while **Sapper John Higgins** is buried in grave I.P.9 in Bécourt Military Cemetery.

THE HON. RICHARD PHILIP STANHOPE

CAPTAIN, 3RD BATTALION, GRENADIER GUARDS.

Died on 16th September 1916, aged 31, during the fighting at Lesboeufs.

Richard was the youngest of four children of Arthur Philip (the 6th Earl) and Evelyn Henrietta Stanhope (née Pennefather) of Revesby Abbey, Lincolnshire.

He was educated at Eton and Magdalen College, Oxford. At both he was a keen rower and gained his Blue rowing in the winning Oxford Eight in the 1908 University Boat Race. He took his BA in 1907.

After inheriting Revesby he was actively involved in the management of the estate as well as playing a full part in county and other local affairs.

On 13th May 1914 he married Lady Beryl Franziska Kathleen Bianca Le Poer Trench, only daughter of the Earl of Clancarty. They had just returned from their honeymoon when war broke out. Lady Beryl gave birth to a stillborn son on the day that Richard was killed.

When he was mobilised he held the rank of lieutenant in the Lincolnshire Yeomanry. He was keen to get into action so, in August 1915, he transferred to the Grenadier Guards. Promoted to captain, he went to France on 9th October.

A private wrote: *Captain Stanhope was shot whilst in the open between the German first and second lines of trenches and in getting back to the dressing station he was shot again. This was told to me by his runner. I saw his dead body in the shell hole where I was sheltering.*

A memorial service was held in Revesby Church on 3rd October 1916, at which the vicar said: *He was destined at a very early age to discharge the responsible duties of the Revesby estate… His desire was to win his way into the affections of his people, with what success this remarkable gathering shows, for here are met representatives of the numerous bodies of Committees, Councils, both local and national, magisterial, educational, diocesan, and local Churches. To one and all he gave of his best with no unsparing hand, his one ambition being the uplifting of his fellowmen… The call came: it was a call of duty, and it met a ready response. To leave that charming bride required a supernatural power, for they were so profoundly devoted to each other…they were always cheerful and hopeful of the future, and none more so than the Captain himself. When the sad news came it struck us as a bomb… Revesby and neighbourhood has lost its squire, its elder brother.*

On the 15th September 1918 another service in the church saw the dedication of the south windows and a memorial tablet in his memory.

HARRY BILSBURY

PRIVATE, 21539, 2ND BATTALION, GRENADIER GUARDS.

Died on 15th September 1916, aged 25, during an attack from Ginchy to Lesboeufs.

Harry was the youngest of thirteen children of William (an insurance agent) and Nancy Bilsbury (née Isherwood) of Leigh, Lancashire.

He was a large man and a keen sportsman, starting on the athletics field where he progressed from jumping to running. Despite his size he won prizes in local events staged over 100 to 440 yards. He also played for Leigh FC, where his reach and stride earned him the nickname of 'Long Span'.

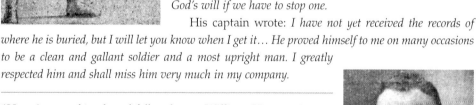

In late 1913 he was persuaded to take up boxing and was successful in a number of contests over the years. He was also a sparring partner for Bombardier Billy Wells, the British and Empire Heavyweight Champion.

He was employed at the Albion Foundry when he enlisted in November 1914; he went to France on 27th October 1915. Harry continued to box while in the Army

Writing to his own parents a comrade said: *No doubt you will have heard about W. Harvey* and H. Bilsbury being killed. It is very hard lines. I might say we have had some narrow shaves - too near to be nice - but I suppose it is our luck. It is God's will if we have to stop one.*

His captain wrote: *I have not yet received the records of where he is buried, but I will let you know when I get it… He proved himself to me on many occasions to be a clean and gallant soldier and a most upright man. I greatly respected him and shall miss him very much in my company.*

*Harry's great friend, and fellow boxer, **William Harvey**, Private 20566, 4th Battalion, Grenadier Guards, died on 12th September 1916. He is buried in grave IV.L.6 in Delville Wood Cemetery.

PIER 9

A

- Royal Warwickshire Regiment - **Private S. Jackson to Private R. Yoxall**
  (completed from Pier and Face 9B)
- Royal Fusiliers - **Lieutenant Colonel G. S. Guyon to Sergeant H. Goodfellow**
  (continued on Pier and Face 16A)

B

- Royal Warwickshire Regiment - **Lance Sergeant E. A. Etheridge to Private P. T. Jackson**
  (continued from Pier and Face 10B)
  (continued on Pier and Face 9A)

C

- 8th Bn. London Regiment (Post Office Rifles) - **Rifleman F. Eames to Rifleman F. Winter**
  (completed from Pier and Face 9D)
- 9th Bn. London Regiment (Queen Victoria's Rifles)
- 10th Bn. London Regiment (Hackney)
- 11th Bn. London Regiment (Finsbury Rifles)
- 12th Bn. London Regiment (Rangers)
- 13th Bn. London Regiment (Kensington Bn.)
- 14th Bn. London Regiment (London Scottish) - **Major F. H. Lindsay to Private D. J. McIntyre**
  (continued on Pier and Face 13C)

D

- 3rd Bn. London Regiment (Royal Fusiliers)
- 4th Bn. London Regiment (Royal Fusiliers)
- 5th Bn. London Regiment (London Rifle Brigade)
- 6th Bn. London Regiment (City of London Rifles)
- 7th Bn. London Regiment
- 8th Bn. London Regiment (Post Office Rifles) - **Second Lieutenant G. E. Stirling to Rifleman W. C. Dunn**
  (continued on Pier and Face 9C)

HERBERT CHARLES OSBORNE

PRIVATE, 240589, 1ST/6TH BATTALION, ROYAL WARWICKSHIRE REGIMENT.

Died on 1st July 1916, aged 24, during an attack on the Quadrilateral.

Herbert was the youngest of four children, and only son, of Abner (a gardener) and Emma Osborne (née Perrin) of Bishop's Stortford, Hertfordshire.

He worked as a gardener with his father before moving to Hallingbury Place and later to Highbury, Birmingham, where he worked in a fruit garden.

He enlisted in Birmingham in September 1914 and went to France in February 1915.

In February 1917 the British Red Cross Society wrote: *I wish we had any reassuring news to send you concerning Private Osborne, who has been missing for so many months. We have been making every effort to find out what has happened to him, when he was wounded, as I understand from your letter he was seen going to the dressing station, and what we fear happened is that he was hit a second time before he could reach the dressing station. Private Nash tells us he saw Osborne wounded in the hand at [censored], but this does not add much to what you already know. Had this gallant soldier been a prisoner his name would have been on the official lists of prisoners we regularly receive from Germany, but so far, I regret to say, it has not appeared on any of them. This long silence without any news of him leads us to fear that Private Osborne has given his life for his King and Country like so many other brave men. Should we hear anything further rest assured we will let you know. Please accept our sympathy in your trouble.*

WILLIAM THORNE

PRIVATE, 96, 16TH BATTALION, ROYAL WARWICKSHIRE REGIMENT.

Died on 25th September 1916, aged 30, during fighting at Morval.

William was one of four children of Thomas (a police constable) and Ann Thorne.

He worked as a collector in the meter inspector's department of the Birmingham City Gas Department and was well known in local athletic and football circles. He enlisted in Birmingham in September 1914 and went to France on 21st November 1915.

While he was in France he had a number of letters published in the staff magazine describing his life in and out of the trenches. One, in the July 1916 magazine, included some lines of thanks: *We have just received a gift of a gramophone from the employees of the City of Birmingham Water Department, a gift that will be well appreciated by our fellows, and we are looking forward to spending a few enjoyable evenings while out of the trenches for a rest. All this helps to take the monotony of trench warfare away from our minds.*

William was killed, together with **Albert Edward Whittingham**, also a former Gas Department employee, when they tried to take a wounded soldier, **Private Walter Wright**, to a dressing station.

ALBERT EDWARD WHITTINGHAM

PRIVATE, 243, 16TH BATTALION, ROYAL WARWICKSHIRE REGIMENT.

Died on 25th September 1916, aged 24, during fighting at Morval.

Albert was one of six children, all sons, of William (a Chief Inspector of Police) and Annie Whittingham (née Perks) of Small Heath, Birmingham.

He was employed as works chemist at the Nechells Gas Works. He also enlisted in Birmingham and went to France on 21st November 1915.

The staff magazine said in his obituary that he *possessed a good knowledge of analytical chemistry, and had he been spared to take up his duties again with the Department after the War, he would no doubt have had a very successful future. He had a cheerful disposition and singular charm of manner, and will be greatly missed by those who knew him.*

After Private Wright was wounded there was no stretcher immediately available to take him to the dressing station. William and Albert volunteered to carry him down even though the area was under fire from enemy artillery. They had almost achieved their task when they were both killed. A corporal described their last moments: …*two men of another battalion came past carrying a stretcher. They placed the stretcher a few yards behind our trench and came up to ask us the way down to the dressing station. We were directing them when a shell came and exploded between them, killing both instantly and wounding two or three of our chaps. We buried them side by side in a garden in the village.*

The wounded man they were carrying, **Walter Wright**, survived and afterwards wrote to Albert's parents: *Bert was one of the best, and was respected by all who knew him. It was through Bert that I got down to the dressing station so quickly. When I got wounded I could not walk, and no stretchers were available, so Bert at once volunteered to carry me down on his back. Seeing I was so heavy for him, 'Billy' Thorne said he would give him a hand. Bert carried me half way through the village, where they got a stretcher, and I was soon at the dressing station. Had it not been for Bert I might have lain there for hours, and something else might have happened for we were subject to a rather heavy bombardment, and I think had it not been for Bert I might not have seen England again. It was Bert all over. If anyone was in difficulties he was always the first to give a helping hand.*

As well as being connected through their employer and their fathers' profession William and Albert were also both in Platoon IV of A Company, 16th Battalion.

Of the fifty seven men in this platoon picture, six died during the course of the war; of those William, Albert and one other (**Private Horace Steele**) are commemorated on Pier and Face 9A.

NORMAN JAMES RICHARD LITTLE

LIEUTENANT, 11TH BATTALION, ROYAL FUSILIERS.

Died on 13th March 1917, aged 33, while commanding his company, the Officer Commanding having been wounded earlier in the day.

Norman was one of two children, both sons, of James (a bank clerk) and Mary Ann Little (née Wheeler) of London.

Educated at the City of London School, where he studied to be an artist, he then went to the Royal Academy Schools, where he won the £40 prize for the best design for Mural Decoration.

He married Beatrice Winifred Paddon on 12th July 1910. They lived in Folkestone, Kent and had at least one child, born in 1912.

He was an actor and reciter of considerable ability. As an exhibitor at the Royal Academy he was responsible for a number of portraits and murals. He also designed and painted many book illustrations such as this example from *The Gateway to Tennyson*. A critic observed: *Mr. Norman Little, the Artist, has shown a rare skill in design and the use of colour, and his future work will be watched with interest.* Whilst in France he drew the designs for the 1916 Christmas cards for his battalion and the brigade.

He had served in the Honourable Artillery Company and early in 1915 he joined the Inns of Court OTC before being commissioned in the Royal Fusiliers in July. He went to France in May 1916 and was promoted to lieutenant in September.

His commanding officer wrote: *He was killed by a bullet last night about 10 p.m. whilst commanding his Company, holding a front line trench which we had taken that day from the enemy… Your son was a great favourite with us all, and we shall miss him a great deal… I knew your son personally quite well, as he was a member of the Head Quarters' Mess, and he was so popular with us all.*

A comrade wrote: *He was very popular with us and we all miss him terribly. He was always so keen about everything, and though he hated the war and all to do with it more than most people, no one could have been more thorough or energetic about everything he had to do.*

He was mentioned in despatches on 4th January 1917.

STUART MILNER RAWSON

LIEUTENANT, 20TH BATTALION, ROYAL FUSILIERS.

Died on 20th July 1916, aged 24, during fighting at High Wood, when a tiny fragment of shell pierced his heart.

Stuart was the youngest of three children, all sons, of Edward Creswell Rawson (a member of the Madras Civil Service) and Marion Emma Rawson (née Duffield) of Blackheath.

Educated at Blackheath and Eastbourne, he then went to Tonbridge School, where he was a member of the OTC. From there he went to the City and Guild Technical College, South Kensington to study electrical engineering, receiving his diploma in 1912.

In October 1912 he started his practical training as a pupil with a firm in Westminster and in May 1913 he was apprenticed to The British Thomson-Houston Company, at their works in Rugby. After the war broke out, the company agreed to end his apprenticeship and he enlisted in September 1914 and was posted to the 3rd Public Schools Battalion, which in due course became the 20th Battalion, Royal Fusiliers.

Commissioned on 20th March 1915, he went to France in September. He was promoted to lieutenant on 24th January 1916. Whilst in the Army he continued his interest in sport and games, and was also a keen musician, composing and setting to music many of the battalion's marching songs.

His company commander wrote: *Nothing has affected me so much as losing dear old Stuart, who had been with me so long. You do not need me to tell you of his unfailing cheeriness and generosity… There was no need to give him detailed instructions nor to worry how the work was being done. One merely indicated one's desires to him and the thing was done promptly and efficiently and with the greatest good humour… Before the attack Rawson was the cheeriest of the lot, and went into action with full confidence of success and full of jests. In the wood he did wonders in rallying the men and consolidating the position. About mid-day he came to my dug-out to tell me that he was holding the line with a handful of men and that the enemy looked as though they were going to attack… Rawson treated the whole affair lightly and yet gave me an exact account of how matters stood. I promised him reinforcements and asked him to stay down in my dug-out until the shelling had slackened down, but in his usual cheery way he said, 'No thanks, I must get along back to the men. We'll pull through all right. Cheery-O, old man.' Then, just as he got to the top of the steps he was hit by an exploding shell.*

WILLIAM JOHN 'JAKE' ASBURY

PRIVATE, 503, 14TH BATTALION, ROYAL WARWICKSHIRE REGIMENT.

Died on 23rd July 1916, aged 27, during the fighting near High Wood.

Jake was the stepson of Arthur Edward (a tobacconist and commercial traveller) and Annie Asbury (formerly Hollins, née Morgan) of Small Heath, Birmingham. The picture shows William's half-sister (at left) and a friend at the family shop.

Employed as a stockbroker's clerk, he enlisted in Birmingham in August 1914 and went to France in December 1915. Shortly after arriving he wrote about the journey from the port, the many stops they had made, and the marching (which amounted to around seventy miles) in between, before they had their first experience of the trenches: *The next night we were in the front line of the trenches.*

Mind you, right in the firing line with live bullets and shells flaying about, the men seemed to take it just as a matter of course… For myself I did not feel a wee bit funky and managed to find a hole in the trench and got into it and slept for about five hours, only waking with the cold…we had to stay in the trenches for four days and nights, no water to wash, very little to drink. At the end of the four days every man was dead beat. I could hardly march to the camp…we were here for three nights and then back to the firing line…the last turn in the trenches lasted 3 days and we came out on Saturday night and marched to where we are now… We expect to go back again on Xmas night for 4 days…I do not care much about it. Too much marching and work. Everybody is fed up – the Germans just as much as ourselves, if not a bit more… It seems fairly safe in the trenches providing you take care of yourself and keep your head well down. The Germans have darn good snipers. One man we had killed was shot through the head when he was firing over the trench, all in the space of 4 seconds.

His officer* wrote: *…your dear Son was killed instantaneously without any pain at all and I am glad to say he was decently buried behind our trench by some of his friends… We indeed miss him very much for he was always a most faithful and devoted Soldier and Servant unto his life's end… It was great grief to me to lose Asbury but still I like to think of him as being safe in the Arms of the Lord.*

*The officer, **Second Lieutenant Alfred Stanhope O'Dwyer,** was killed just a few days later, on 29th July 1916. He is commemorated on Pier and Face 10B.

GEORGE EDWARD 'TED' BERRY

PRIVATE, 1229, 15TH BATTALION, ROYAL WARWICKSHIRE REGIMENT.

Died on 23rd July 1916, aged 21, during the fighting near High Wood.

Ted was one of six children of George Russell Berry (a farmer) and Emma Jane Berry (née Kembery) of Erdington, Birmingham.

He enlisted in Birmingham and went to France on 21st November 1915.

The following are extracts from some of the letters Ted wrote to his older sister Norah.

3rd December 1915: *We have marched some 50 miles since arriving, & the roads are something terrible just now. We are billeted in barns or old empty houses at the places we stop at. We have had some very decent billets, others have been rotten. We are in a fair one to-night. The trenches are quite close here, expect we shall soon be in them. The French people taken on a whole don't seem to appreciate the English soldiers at all, they think the war ought to be fought in England… Wines are the chief drink of the people here, & they make some excellent coffee, which I go in for. We get pretty well of food, bacon, bully beef cheese and biscuits & jam compose the menu.*

13th January 1916: *…have done several turns in the trenches, & am pleased to say our casualties were very small. We have been shelled rather heavily several times, but with scant success to the enemy. The conditions are the worst thing we have to contend with, they are terrible. Have been in mud and water nearly up to my waist, & two days is quite enough in the trenches at a time.*

23rd February 1916: *Well am still getting on all right don't know when we shall be going in again. Hope the weather will have improved by the time we do, as it is bitterly cold here at present. We went for a big march yesterday about thirteen miles. Was a bit tired when I finished but soon felt all right. Have been out doing six hours digging a day so you can see we are doing "some" work. The battalion is starting leave this week, so hope my turn will come soon.*

10th June 1916: *Well am still going on alright. The batt have had rather a rough time lately, but thank goodness I have come through it all safely. We are out of the trenches on rest just now, we do eighteen days up at the trenches and six days out on rest. Can't see any signs of my leave coming yet, do wish I could as it is over six months since we left England. Suppose I must be patient like others & wait… Poor old Jack's army career was short wasn't it. They should never have passed him, hope he won't be called up again.*

GEORGE WILLIAM COLLETT

PRIVATE, 3279, 1ST/8TH BATTALION, ROYAL WARWICKSHIRE REGIMENT.

Died on 18th July 1916, aged 16½, whilst in the front line near Ovillers.

George was born on 1st December 1899, the eldest of six children of Joseph (a tailor) and Elizabeth Collett (née Combes). The family lived in Newark until 1914 and then moved to Erdington, Birmingham.

After an education at the Mount School he gained a scholarship at Magnus Grammar School, Newark.

He was employed by the General Electric Co. at their Witton works when he enlisted in Aston in November 1914. Although not yet 15, he stood 5 ft. 9 ins. and looked much older. Indeed he declared himself to be 19½ and one of the doctors passed him with the comment that he was ...*a well developed man for his age.*

He went to France on 22nd March 1915; although his true age was subsequently discovered and an application lodged for his return, he was unwilling to leave his company.

The official Army response was that he had been *medically examined and found physically fit to bear the strain of active service, and as he has expressed the wish to remain with his unit in the Expeditionary Force he is being retained.*

In a letter to a friend he wrote: *Now I am going to tell you the reason I have never mentioned anything in reply to the news of Dad trying to get me back. He had written to my C.O. about the matter and I have been medically examined by the best medical officer in the Division. He said I was in perfectly good health and the life out here was not harming me in any way at all. Therefore I think it is my duty to stop out here. I assure you that the wet muddy trenches are no attraction – it is no delight to sit in two foot of water all night long. Nevertheless, why are we all sticking it so? Supposing all us chaps were to give in, then the Boches would get through. We have seen and heard what the Germans did to the peasants when they advanced in the early part of the war, and we know they would do their work just as well on the English civilians provided they get through and overrun England. That is the reason we have got to hold out. So you can see the reason why I am sticking it; there are plenty of chaps not much older than me doing the same.*

THE GENERAL ELECTRIC COMPANY ROLL OF HONOUR

The Roll of Honour indicates that 2,150 men, from a workforce of some 10,000, enlisted in the Forces and 255 lost their lives. Of these, at least twenty eight are commemorated on the Memorial.

FRITZ JAMES COX

PRIVATE, 15/1661, 15TH BATTALION, ROYAL WARWICKSHIRE REGIMENT.

Died on 23rd July 1916, aged 23, during the fighting near High Wood.

Fritz was the only son, one of three children, of John (a publican) and Rebecca Cox (née Penn) of Kidderminster, Worcestershire.

Employed as a solicitor's clerk, he enlisted in Birmingham in 1915.

His platoon sergeant wrote: *It is with the deepest regret that I have to inform you that your son has been reported missing. You must excuse me for not writing before, as I have been waiting to hear of any information regarding him. Our Battalion was engaged in an attack on the enemy's trenches on the night of July 22nd and your son took part in the assault and did his duty as a true Briton always does. It may be consoling if I tell you that there is every hope of your son being a prisoner of war, as the Huns were out in the early part of the morning, collecting our wounded who were lying near their lines. All the boys in my platoon express their sympathy also. I am sending you his watch which we received some time ago. Several parcels we have received and these I have divided among his comrades.*

His lieutenant wrote: *I am extremely sorry to inform you that your brother was reported missing after our attack on the German trenches. We have been waiting for information regarding him. The Platoon Sergeant, after making enquiries has, I understand, written to you stating all he knew. Your brother was certainly one of the most popular men in the Company and his loss is most keenly felt by all ranks.*

Originally posted as missing, his death was officially confirmed on 19th February 1917.

ROBERT FINDEN DAVIES

CAPTAIN, 1ST/9TH BATTALION, LONDON REGIMENT (QUEEN VICTORIA'S RIFLES).

Died on 9th September 1916, aged 39, during an attack on Bouleaux Wood.

Robert was the eldest of four children of Frederick Herbert (a member of the Stock Exchange) and Blanche Josephine Davies (née Haines) of St Marylebone, London.

He was educated at Marlborough College and became a member of the Stock Exchange in 1898.

He married Helena Lucy Atkins in 1906.

He served in the Boer War, attached to the King's Royal Rifle Corps and was awarded the Queen's Medal with four clasps, and gazetted an Honorary Captain. On his return to England he was made the battalion's musketry instructor. He was a member of the Territorial Force Reserve from October 1908.

He was an excellent shot. At the Bisley Meeting in 1906 he won a number of events, including the King's Prize and gold medal with a then record score of 324. The picture shows him being 'chaired' around the camp in the time honoured tradition. He had reached the final stages on four previous occasions. In an interview he said: *You may say that I regard rifle shooting as not only an important thing from the point of view of Imperial defence, but a healthy and agreeable pastime.*

He shot for England in 1910 and 1911 at Bisley and, as a member of the British Men's Shooting Team, took part in the 600m free rifle and 300m military rifle events at the 1912 Olympic Games in Stockholm.

He rejoined the London Regiment on the outbreak of the war and was placed in command of the regimental depot, subsequently transferring to a battalion, with which he served as a temporary major. He had been at the Front less than two months, and died leading his company.

EDWARD WILLIAM HATCHER

LANCE CORPORAL, 390914 (3442), 1ST/9TH BATTALION,
LONDON REGIMENT (QUEEN VICTORIA'S RIFLES).

Died on 1st July 1916, aged 28, during the fighting at
Gommecourt.

Edward was the youngest of four children of Edward William
(a carpenter and joiner) and Emily Augusta Hatcher (née
Merifield) of Milton, Portsmouth, Hampshire.

Educated at Portsmouth Boys' Secondary School, he then
served his apprenticeship as a pupil teacher in one of the
Portsmouth schools. Later, he went to Winchester Training College, becoming a member of the
College Company of the Hampshire Volunteer Rifles. At the end of two years' residence he
gained the Teacher's Certificate with additional qualifications. In August 1908 he was
appointed as an Assistant Master at St Gabriel's Church School, Westminster.

He was an ardent swimmer and the holder of the Royal Humane Society's Life Saving
Certificate.

When the war broke out he was on holiday in Switzerland and had, like many others, some
difficulty in getting home. In November 1914 he enlisted and went to France on 29th March
1915. He was involved in the fighting at Hill 60, St Julien, and the Second Battle of Ypres. He
was promoted to lance corporal early in 1916.

A comrade, who was a prisoner of war, reported that he had seen him, severely wounded
in the back, lying quite still in an exposed position and where it was quite impossible to render
any assistance. No more definite information ever reached his relatives.

Another former pupil of Portsmouth Boy's Secondary School is
also commemorated on Pier and Face 9C. **Herbert Thomas
Scarbrough** was a pupil from 1906 to 1911; and he too became a
teacher after training at Westminster. He enlisted in the 14th
Battalion, London Regiment (London Scottish) in September 1915
and held the rank of sergeant when he was killed by a sniper at
Bouleaux Wood on 9th September 1916, aged 22.

SHIEL RONALD BARRY

Second Lieutenant, 11th Battalion, London Regiment (Finsbury Rifles), attached to 1st/12th Battalion, London Regiment (The Rangers).

Died on 7th October 1916, aged 36, during a failed attack on Dewdrop Trench, near Lesboeufs.

Shiel was one of at least eight children of Andrew Dion Shiel Barry (an actor) and Rachel Harriett Barry (née Pocock).

He married Dorothy Scott in April 1907; they had at least one daughter, born in 1908.

He and Dorothy were both actors; Dorothy used the stage name of Dorothy Minto.

He began his stage career as a 'call boy' at the Lyceum, made his first appearance in Berlin in 1899 and appeared in London in 1904. He joined the actor-manager Lewis Waller at the beginning of 1906, and remained with him until 1909, during which time he appeared in practically every production with which Mr. Waller was associated. This postcard shows Shiel in his role of *Abdulla* in *The Fires of Fate*. He joined the Liverpool Repertory Company in 1913. He never played a leading role on the London stage, which meant that he was perhaps better known to provincial audiences. He experimented with his portrayal of characters and was reported to have said, in private, that he was tired of always playing the same part in the same way.

He enlisted in the Inns of Court OTC in January 1915 and was gazetted to the Royal Fusiliers in October. He transferred to the 11th Londons in the hope that he would be sent to the Dardanelles.

He returned from Egypt on sick leave in July 1916, and received his papers to return there in September. He volunteered for service in France with the 12th Londons and had been there about a month when he was killed.

Shiel is one of over 200 actors, musicians, writers and stage workers who died in the war, all of whom are commemorated on a plaque in the Theatre Royal, Drury Lane, London.

FRANCIS HOWARD LINDSAY

MAJOR, 1ST/14TH BATTALION, LONDON REGIMENT (LONDON SCOTTISH).

Died on 1st July 1916, aged 40, during an attack on Gommecourt.

Francis was one of eight children of William Alexander (a barrister) and Lady Harriet Lindsay (née Hamilton-Gordon).

Educated at Malvern College, he went up to Clare College, Cambridge, graduating BA in 1898. Afterwards he became an Examiner in the Scottish Education Department.

He married Helen Margaret MacDougall on 14th April 1910 and lived in South Kensington, London. They had three children born between 1910 and 1915, one of whom died in infancy.

A pre war Territorial, he was promoted to captain on 27th November 1905. In 1914 he volunteered for foreign service, and was severely wounded in the head by shrapnel at Messines on 14th November. Promoted to temporary major on 14th January 1916, he was only declared fit for service in April 1916 and rejoined his battalion at the end of the month. He was mentioned in despatches for the action in which he was killed: *This officer, having gallantly led his company to its objective under very heavy fire, by his personal bravery, example and devotion, organised his bombing and blocking parties, and as far as possible consolidated the position. Though the artillery, machine gun and sniping fire was very heavy, he at all times exposed himself fearlessly and by his splendid example and courage held the position until killed.*

A chaplain recalled talking with Francis on the eve of the attack: *He spoke of his wife and child and told me of the joy he had in his little boy's faith and of the wonder of his childish prayers. He lay bare to me something of the intense happiness of his home life, and went on to say how confident he felt he would come through safely. 'The faith of my little boy is so real. He prays every night for my safety. God could not disappoint a faith like that'.*

The regimental magazine recorded: *At 2.30 p.m. Major F. H. was killed by a sniper, who had been gradually creeping up and had already laid out about six of our chaps. We laid F.H. along the bottom of the trench and covered him over with a waterproof sheet, and I am sure he got a decent burial, for the Huns opposite us played the game like men.*

His only surviving son, **John Stewart Lindsay-MacDougall DSO MC**, Major, Argyll and Sutherland Highlanders, died while a prisoner of war on 5th August 1943, aged 33. He is buried in grave IV.S.15 in Naples War Cemetery.

Brothers,

WILLIAM GEORGE EDWARD 'GEORGE' WRIGHT

and

JOHN HENRY 'JACK' WRIGHT

PRIVATES 3689 AND 3944, 1ST/3RD BATTALION, LONDON REGIMENT (ROYAL FUSILIERS).

Died on 1st July 1916, aged 20 and 18, during the fighting at Gommecourt.

They were two of the six children of Albert Edward (a provisions dealer) and Lucy Emily Wright (née Browning) of Kennington, London.

They enlisted at Harrow Road in February and March 1915 and went to France together on 17th April 1916.

Both wrote letters to their eldest brother, Albert. The last known letter from George was dated 17th June 1916: *I thought I would write today as we are expecting to go into the trenches again very soon… I have been out here nearly two months, how time goes… Mama asked what we should like sent us, will you tell her to use her own discretion we are glad to eat anything now. We are not so dainty as we used to be, we are only too glad to get anything at all… Don't be alarmed if you don't hear from me for a little time as I expect to be busy for a few days.*

Their major wrote: *…excuse my not having written to you before but I have had no opportunity. It is my painful duty to tell you that both your sons who were reported missing were killed. They were in a very tight corner where nearly everyone was either killed or wounded & it was difficult to get any information, but I have satisfied myself that our worst fears are true… It is especially hard for you to have lost two such brave boys.*

JOHN ROBERT SOMERS-SMITH MC

CAPTAIN, 1ST/5TH BATTALION, LONDON REGIMENT (LONDON RIFLE BRIGADE).

Died on 1st July 1916, aged 28, during the fighting at Gommecourt.

John was one of at least five children of Robert Vernon (a solicitor) and Mary Gertrude Wellington Somers-Smith (née Radcliffe) of Hersham, Surrey.

He married Marjorie Duncan on 25th July 1914 and they lived at Walton on the Hill, Surrey. They had one son, born in 1915.

Educated at Eton, he was a keen runner and rower. He soon became prominent on the river, was Captain of the Boats in 1906 and won the School Pulling.

He then went to Magdalen College, Oxford; he was considered unfortunate in not being in the University Eight, for which he was twice spare man. He was a member of the Magdalen

coxless fours, which won many events in 1907. Their success continued in 1908 and they were selected to represent Great Britain in the Olympics that year, winning the Gold Medal.

Gazetted a second lieutenant in the London Rifle Brigade in 1906, he was promoted to captain on 9th June 1914 and went to France on 3rd November. He was mentioned in despatches, and awarded the Military Cross on 13th May 1915, for services at the Second Battle of Ypres.

His Colonel wrote: *Alas! I have to break to you the very very sad news that your husband has met a true soldier's end in action in the enemy trenches. He took part yesterday in an assault, and I have news of him up to 4pm, and perhaps a little later. I am writing this at once, hoping you may get it before the official telegram. We all feel his loss most awful. He was a perfect officer, and always of the very greatest help to me especially in the trenches. He was quite fearless and was loved by his men who would have followed him anywhere.*

The commanding officer wrote: *I always liked Bob not only as a personal friend but as one of the best officers and he was I know equally popular with officers and men.*

FRANK DENISON CHANDLER

CORPORAL, 300251, 1ST/5TH BATTALION, LONDON REGIMENT (LONDON RIFLE BRIGADE).

Died on 1st July 1916, aged 23, during the fighting at Gommecourt.

Frank was one of at least seven children of Gibbs William (a manager of an insurance broker) and his first wife Lizzie Chandler (née Humes) of Blackheath, London. There were also at least four children from his second marriage to Alice Ann Catt.

He was educated at Wilson's School and then worked for Nelson, Donkin & Co. at Lloyds of London.

He enlisted in London on 7th August 1914 and went to France on 4th November.

LLOYDS OF LONDON WAR MEMORIAL

The company's war memorial lists 216 members and representatives who died in the war. Of those at least twenty one are commemorated on the Memorial.

The following five are all from the London Rifle Brigade and, like Frank Chandler, their names appear on Pier and Face 9D.

Eric H. Poland	Stanley A. Crook	Leicester A. Dixey	Reginald J. Moore	Bertram H. Norton
Lance Corporal	Rifleman	Rifleman	Rifleman	Rifleman
1st July 1916, 23	9th October 1916, 20	1st July 1916, 23	9th October 1916, 20	1st July 1916, 26

SAMUEL HART

RIFLEMAN, 300116 (9521), 1ST/5TH BATTALION, LONDON
REGIMENT (LONDON RIFLE BRIGADE).

Died on 1st July 1916, aged 22, although the War Office
did not declare his death official until 22nd February
1918.

Samuel was one of five children of Emanuel (a boot
manufacturer) and Matilda Ann Hart (née Moses) of
Cricklewood, London.

Educated at Hackney Downs School, he was later
employed as a precious stone cutter and engraver and enlisted in London.

In September 1916 a comrade wrote to the *Territorial Service Gazette* saying that, as he was
retiring along the German front line on the evening of 1st July, he met Samuel, who suggested
making a dash for it to the British lines. Having agreed that they should try, Samuel got up on
the parados and immediately a German machine gun opened fire and he was hit. The machine
gun continued to fire, so the comrade could not see whether Samuel was killed or only wounded.

BRITISH JEWRY

The Jewish community published a record of the part played by Anglo-Jewry in the war – the
British Jewry Book of Honour. The book lists around 60,000 Jews who served in the Forces,
including over 2,300 who died in the services.

At least 165 are known to be commemorated on the Memorial. The following four are all
from the London Regiment and, like Samuel Hart, their names appear on Pier and Face 9D.

Hyman Franklin	Colman Katz	Abraham Prins	Barnet Griew
Private	Private	Private	Rifleman
7th October 1916, 20	9th September 1916, 22	7th October 1916, 33	1st July 1916, 19

PIER 10

A

- Welsh Regiment - **Private R. Shakespeare to Private B. A. Young**
  (completed from Pier and Face 7A)
- Black Watch (Royal Highlanders)
- Ox & Bucks Light Infantry - **Captain W. R. Birch to Private E. Lowe**
  (continued on Pier and Face 10D)

B

- Northumberland Fusiliers - **Private J. Keenan 12867 to Private N. A. Yull**
  (completed from Pier and Face 11B)
- Royal Warwickshire Regiment - **Lieutenant Colonel E. A. Innes to Lance Sergeant A. Cross**
  (continued on Pier and Face 9B)

C

- Sherwood Foresters (Notts and Derby Regiment) - **Second Lieutenant J. P. Teahan to Private E. White**
  (continued from Pier and Face 10D)
  (continued on Pier and Face 11A)

D

- Ox & Bucks Light Infantry - **Private W. J. Lukies to Private J. Zusman**
  (completed from Pier and Face 10A)
- Essex Regiment
- Sherwood Foresters (Notts and Derby Regiment) - **Lieutenant Colonel L. A. Hind to Second Lieutenant F. H. Talbot**
  (continued on Pier and Face 10C)

PETER ROSS HUSBAND

SECOND LIEUTENANT, 1ST BATTALION, BLACK WATCH (ROYAL HIGHLANDERS).

Died on 25th September 1916, aged 30, during fighting near Flers.

Peter was one of at least three children of Peter Fair Husband and Jessie Husband (née Ross) of Dundee.

He was educated at the High School, Dundee and University New College (United Free Church), Edinburgh, where he took his MA, and was a Licentiate of the United Free Church of Scotland.

Initially enlisting in the Inns of Court OTC on 3rd January 1916, he received a commission on 14th July and went to France on 5th September. During the following three weeks he mentioned in his letters: *This is a good time to be going out, when all the signs are encouraging. But it is the men who went out a year ago, when everything was black, who deserve the honour;* and *I expect the life will become boring in the course of time, but at present I find it thrilling... One has to be out here to realise how tremendous the whole affair is.* A week before he was killed he wrote: *There is a possibility that we may be busy this week.*

A lieutenant wrote: *I knew him and loved him he was a fine, brave and unselfish gentleman and officer. When he was killed he was bravely leading an attack, a successful one, on a length of German trench. I was quite near him when he was killed and am able to tell you that he was killed instantaneously. He was not in any way disfigured, and just lay very peacefully with a smile on his face.*

His brother **James William Husband**, a captain in the 5th Battalion wrote: *I had been feeling very unhappy about him last week, and on Sunday I cycled over to his battalion…looking forward to a happy after-noon… Then the news was told me very abruptly… He had been smiling at the time he was hit, and to one who has a little idea of the hell he was in, it would seem that he had been 'seeing the glory of the eternal' - a phrase in his note-book… His has been a great ministry! … I know I shall miss Ross all the days of my life. I have been so accustomed to turn to him for inspiration and help. There was so little ostentation about him that only those who knew him well knew of his great powers of mind, and of his great qualities of heart. He has glorified all these things by his great sacrifice, and his influence on me at any rate will be everlasting.*

Shortly after his death the family published a memoir, *A Scottish Minister and Soldier*, to provide *a sketch of one aspect of his life – his relation to war.* In the preface Peter's uncle wrote that the book had been written, *as an illustration of the spirit that has been inspiring the young men of our country to do 'the utmost for the highest'.*

David Cargill
labourer
Arbroath
14th November 1916, 18

ARBROATH AND DISTRICT MEN

There are over forty men from the area commemorated on the Memorial.

The following ten are all from the 5th (Angus & Dundee) Battalion, Black Watch (Royal Highlanders). David Cargill was a lance corporal, the others were privates.

All their names appear on Pier and Face 10A.

Harry Alexander
apprentice engineer
Arbroath
3rd September 1916, 18

George Craig
grocer
Arbroath
3rd September 1916, 19

James Lundie
labourer
Arbroath
3rd September 1916, 19

George Meldrum
lapper
Brechin
3rd September 1916, 19

James Nairn
shepherd
Friockheim
14th October 1916, 20

Arthur C. Petrie
machineman
Arbroath
14th October 1916, 19

Hugh Robertson
farm labourer
Returned from New Zealand
13th November 1916, 37

Charles Weir
apprentice moulder
Arbroath
14th October 1916, 18

Robert S. Wilson
farm servant
Inverkeilor
3rd September 1916, 22

WILLIAM KEITH CARRUTHERS

SECOND LIEUTENANT, 1ST/1ST BUCKS BATTALION, OX &
BUCKS LIGHT INFANTRY.

Died on 3rd April 1917, aged 25, during the fighting at
Le Verquier, while attached to 2nd/4th Battalion
Lincolnshire Regiment.

William was one of at least four children of Sir William
(General Manager of Barclays Bank) and Lady Margaret
Carruthers (née Cameron) of Beckenham, Kent.

He graduated from the Stationers' Company School in
London and went to Canada in 1910, where he was a cashier in the Calgary office of the Bank
of Montreal. A keen sportsman, he had been the champion athlete of his year at school and,
while in Canada, played football and also won prizes for lawn tennis.

Although rejected a number of times, because of his defective eyesight, he was eventually
accepted and went to France in June 1916 as a private in the Canadian Expeditionary Force. He
rose to the rank of sergeant before receiving his commission on 18th December and returned
to France in February 1917.

His commanding officer wrote that he was, *killed last night when gallantly leading his men in
a night attack on a German position. He has only been with me a short time, but I realised at once
what a staunch fellow he was. He was killed instantaneously by a rifle bullet, actually at the German
wire… Your son's body was lying near the wire, and two men went back to bring it in, but it was found
to be impossible, one of them being killed and the other wounded… He has done everything he has
been called upon to do in a most gallant manner, and I have forwarded to my Brigade Headquarters
a report on a patrol he took out a few night ago. His patrol was spotted and in order that they might
return, he stood and fired his revolver at the Germans at a range of only ten yards until they had got
away. He was indeed a brave officer.*

His brother, **Cameron Roy Carruthers**, Captain, 4th Battalion,
Cameron Highlanders, died on 31st July 1917, aged 28. He is
commemorated on the Menin Gate Memorial.

PERCY GEORGE BIRCH

Lance Corporal, 1635, 1st/4th Battalion, Ox & Bucks Light Infantry.

Died on 24th August 1916, aged 24, during fighting near Ovillers.

Percy was one of nine children of Calvin (an accounts clerk) and his first wife Charlotte Alice Birch (née Brough) of Wolverhampton, Staffordshire.

Educated at Wolverhampton Grammar School, he then went to Culham Training College, Oxford, where he obtained the Board of Education Certificate, qualifying him as an elementary school teacher. He also gained first class results in the Archbishop's Divinity Certificate. At Culham he played the violin in the college orchestra, rowed for his college and was a member of the Territorials.

He had been appointed to a teaching position with Buckingham County Council but never took up the posting, deciding instead to enlist.

He was in France by May 1916 and on 25th July he wrote to his eldest sister, Gertie: *Just a line to let you know that we have at last been "over the Top"! It happened at about 1 A.M. on Sunday morn. last. Our Platoon and No 14 had the honour of leading the Oxfords who in turn had the honour of being the 1st Battn. over. I am pleased to say I am quite well, although losses were heavy. I believe 300 (about) came back out of 600 (about). All our company officers were either killed or wounded and we have only 2 N.C.O.s left in our platoon.*

A friend wrote: *He had been shifted…to take charge of a bombing position close to a barricade – a most difficult undertaking and one given as a rule only to very competent men. Needless to say he went cheerfully and was doing all that could be done to help and cheer his men. Whilst observing from his position he was struck by a piece of shell, being killed instantaneously… Percy is buried where he fell at a spot east of Ovillers close to Albert where the advance is being made… I have been able to collect various little articles that he prized and will send them to you as soon as it can be arranged.*

He had been promoted to lance corporal shortly before his death.

In May 1925 the Imperial War Graves Commission confirmed that no grave had been identified and that Percy would be commemorated on one of the memorials that were to be erected. An extract from the letter to Percy's father was given in Chapter One.

HARRY PRICE

Private, 23/888, 23rd (Tyneside Scottish) Battalion, Northumberland Fusiliers.

Died on 1st July 1916, aged 31, during the attack on La Boisselle.

Harry married Ethel Tingle in 1913. They lived in Choppington, Northumberland and had a daughter, born in 1914. He enlisted in Newcastle-upon-Tyne.

On 2nd February 1916 he wrote to Ethel: *We are now only 5 miles from the Firing Line, and we are supposed to go to the Trenches tomorrow… I cannot read your letters without having a terrible regret at been so far away from you xx and my delightful little treasure xx I do feel it Ethel xxxx my true and noble Love I will never forget the day that releases me from this terrible Crisis, to join you once more for Life, and if God*

wishes it so, I hope time will not be so cruel to prolong the realization of Home Life again. I bet everyone is making a gold mine at present in the pits.

In a card, dated 4th February 1916, he wrote to some friends: *Just a really slight acknowledgement for your nice gifts which you sent me, I am now receiving fairly good water and that lemonade compound which you sent makes nice drinks, I now fill my bottle with it. We are now only 1 mile from the Firing line & we expect to go the trenches in a day or two. I have seen a lot of ruin we are fairly among it all now, it is realy wonderful how our comrades have bray'd back the Germans from this place, they were 4 or 5 miles past us and almost every house is wired round, & loop holes made, we have lost a lot of men in doing it.*

In his last surviving letter, dated 23rd June 1916, he wrote: *Just a few lines True Love to let you know that the Final has come at last. We go to the trenches tonight and remain there during the Bombardment and finally take part in the Advance, so bear up my True and Faithful being xx. I realy do sincerely hope that nothing befalls me, for you and my little Treasure's sake It is far better to get it over than stand and be shot at for nothing and that's what we have gone through, he has hurled Death at us all every day now since the War began so we are going to try and end it all now and this will be the end, so don't expect any letters or correspondence whatsoever for probably a fortnight, as the Bombardment will last a week probably. We are just going to get biscuits and water. We will get the last hot tea tonight so with my most Beautiful thoughts of everlasting true love for you.*

DONALD WILLIAM ALERS HANKEY

SECOND LIEUTENANT, 1ST BATTALION, ROYAL WARWICKSHIRE REGIMENT.

Died on 12th October 1916, aged 31, in the fighting between Morval and Le Transloy.

Donald was the youngest of six children of Robert Alers Hankey and Helen A. Hankey (née Bakewell). The family lived in Australia before returning to England.

Educated at Brighton Day School and Rugby and then went to the Royal Military Academy at Woolwich. In 1903 he was gazetted to the Royal Garrison Artillery (RGA) and he served for five years, two of them in Mauritius.

In 1907, following a serious operation, he resigned his commission and went up to Corpus Christi College, Oxford, intending to take Holy Orders. He took his degree in 1910, with a Second Class in the Theological School. After a holiday in Africa and Mauritius he joined the Leeds Clergy School but then lived in Bermondsey and worked with the Oxford and Bermondsey Mission. In order to test the process of taking boys from London slums to a new life in Australia, he took a steerage passage in 1913 and worked there for some months on the land.

When the war broke out he enlisted in the 7th Battalion, Rifle Brigade, went to France in May 1915, and was wounded in July. In September he was granted a commission in the RGA but he wanted to return quickly to the Front, so he transferred to the Warwicks. He was then able to return to France in May 1916.

An author, his first book, *The Lord of all Good Life*, was published while he was a sergeant in the Rifle Brigade; and he contributed to the essays in *Faith or Fear?*, published early in the spring of 1916. He is best known for a series of articles that initially appeared anonymously in *The Spectator* in May 1916 and were published, after his death, under the title *A Student in Arms.*

On 23rd September 1916 he wrote to his sister: *It is difficult to believe that the war will heal the nations. I should not be surprised if, when we are old, we see a repetition of this war. I have little doubt that it will take most of our lifetime (if we survive the war) for the belligerent nations to recover their strength. But I have little doubt that if, as seems likely, we beat the Hun pretty badly, he will start the moment peace is signed to prepare for his revenge. A depressing thought, isn't it? Also, I doubt if we shall have such a horror of war as lots of people seem to think. The rising generation won't know what we know, and we shall forget much that is bad. When a soldier can write that the brotherhood of the trench will be "a wistful radiant memory" now, what shall we be writing twenty years hence!*

STEPHEN HENRY PHILIP HEWETT

SECOND LIEUTENANT, 19TH BATTALION ATTACHED TO 14TH
BATTALION, ROYAL WARWICKSHIRE REGIMENT.

Died on 22nd July 1916, aged 23, during an attack on
Wood Lane near High Wood.

Stephen was born in Bengal, India, one of five children of
John Stephen (Indian Telegraph Service) and Mary
Catherine Hewett. The family settled near Exeter after John's
retirement.

Educated at Downside School, he was a distinguished
student and sportsman as well as being a fine actor and singer. He was the Head of School for
nearly two years. Although only 16, he gained a place at Balliol College, Oxford, in 1909 but
decided to wait and took up the place in 1911. He continued to excel, gaining a First in
Moderations in 1913; whilst also participating in the sporting and artistic aspects of the
university.

In 1914 his poem *Patriae domus decorum,* set to music by Dom Alphege Shebbeare, was
adopted by Downside as their School Song. By the end of the year he had a commission in the
Warwicks. After a long period of training in England he went to France in February 1916.

An attack was planned for the evening of 22nd July 1916, and he volunteered with his
platoon to join the first lines. The attack started at 7 p.m. in the daylight, but it was a failure
owing to the intensity of the machine gun fire. Stephen never returned.

His commanding officer wrote that he had, *...most unwillingly arrived at the conclusion that
your poor boy is dead. It appears that his body was found by the unit relieving our own, and that it
was buried by them on the actual battle ground. Believe me that it is with the utmost regret that I have
to write you sad news, and for my own part also the blow is a bad one. Your son was one of my very
best officers and such a keen soldier, energetic and hard working; his loss will be a great one to the
battalion. Apart from his professional qualifications, I liked the boy so much for his fine, manly
qualities and general cheery bearing.*

A selection of his poems, entitled *Before the Mellowing Year,* was published privately at
Oxford in 1916. Some of his letters were also published in 1918 in a volume *A Scholar's letters
from the Front,* which included the following, written in June 1916, concerning the conclusion
of the war: *And when it is over, what terrible shame and remorse and indignation for the survivors,
and for posterity! What a poor show the war has been! And even granting that a life is well laid down
if it contributes to our victory, what a multitude of lives have been simply wasted.*

ERIC DOUGLAS SMART

SECOND LIEUTENANT, 10TH BATTALION, ROYAL
WARWICKSHIRE REGIMENT.

Died on 18th November 1916, aged 24, during the
fighting near Grandcourt.

Eric was the youngest of three children, all sons, of William
Henry (a commission agent) and Sarah Smart of Tanworth-
in-Arden, Warwickshire.

He was educated at Edgbaston Preparatory School and
King Edward's School, Birmingham. Afterwards he joined
the staff of Lloyds Bank and worked at the Moseley, Birmingham branch. He enlisted as Private
729, 14th Warwicks, was subsequently promoted to lance corporal and went to France on 21st
November 1915. He received his commission in the 10th Battalion on 22nd August 1916.

On the day Eric died his father had written to him analysing the 'deadlock' in the war.
Foreseeing a turn in fortunes for the Allies, he wrote: *My dear little Boy, As you say it does really
seem sometimes as tho the war had reached a deadlock, that it is quite impossible for either side to
gain any real advantage over the other, and that the state of war had become a permanent condition.
But this position of affairs is of course only seeming… Theoretically France, Russia, England, Italy,
should have been utterly crippled within the first 12 months… But our enemies have made a whole
budget of huge blunders. They have ignominiously failed at Paris, Calais, London. They have permitted
themselves to be hemmed in within a ring fence, and meantime they have actually permitted us to
organise, mobilise, arrange until we are all of us rapidly becoming a vast international War Machine,
coordinated and united far beyond what had hitherto been thought possible… By the coming spring
our superiority will be so manifest that the enemy if wise will be anxiously seeking home. If still blind
to their helpless position they may continue the struggle another few months, but the end is humanly
speaking, now inevitable… But meanwhile you are feeling like a helpless brick in the vast edifice, a
part of a cog in a huge machine. But don't forget dear boy that you are not a helpless atom, but a living
Soul, a subject and a soldier of the Great Captain, an immortal son of God, not a hair of whose head
can be injured without His consent. Tho you pass through the Valley of the Shadow of Death, He is
caring for you… I am delighted to note you are not taking to the Military life except as a duty. Keep
your mirror clean, clear, and bright. Try and get leave near as possible before Xmas. We are longing
more than I can say to see you. Your loving Dad."*

The letter was returned, marked 'Missing'.

WILLIAM ALLCOCK MM

SERGEANT, 8380, 2ND BATTALION, SHERWOOD FORESTERS (NOTTS AND DERBY REGIMENT).

Died on 16th September 1916, aged 35, whilst in action at The Quadrilateral, east of Ginchy.

William was one of sixteen children of Edmund (a printer's labourer) and Kezia Allcock (née Woolley).

He married Cecilia Cosgrove on 24th February 1912 and they lived in Sneinton Dale, Nottingham. They had two sons.

He enlisted in Nottingham on 21st January 1902 and served overseas in Hong Kong, Malaysia and India (1903 to 1910).

After leaving the Army he was employed as a picture framer for Boots & Co. He was mobilised from the Army Reserve on 5th August 1914, appointed lance corporal on 7th September and went to France on 10th October. He was promoted to corporal in the field on 3rd January 1915 and to sergeant on 7th June. On 8th August he was wounded in the face by shrapnel, having twice previously been wounded in the shoulder and leg.

In April 1915 one of his letters was published in the Boots staff magazine *Comrades in Khaki,* under the title *The Mud Hut,* in which he described trench life as being *…cold and muddy beyond description.* He also said that he presented a pretty picture dressed in long top boots and wearing several days of beard and dirt. From their position about 600 yards from the German line he had been in a group that had to inspect the barbed wire and also to dig an advanced post. They had succeeded in their task: *It was all right, we got back safe, for though the sniper had a shot or two at us he did no harm.*

On 14th March 1916 he was part of a six man patrol which had returned safely having bombed the German front line trenches. The next morning broke foggy and they saw a German advance post about 25 yards away from their position. An officer, William and three men surprised the group, killing three. They also brought one in as a prisoner, together with rifles, helmets and the German telephone apparatus. They were also able to cut the wires connecting a mine that the enemy had been preparing. For this action he received a written commendation from the Major General commanding the Division. The award of the Military Medal was gazetted on 3rd June 1916.

He was originally reported to have been buried south-east of Ginchy, but the grave was subsequently lost.

JOHN CONNAUGHTON

SERGEANT, 7039, 11TH BATTALION, SHERWOOD FORESTERS (NOTTS AND DERBY REGIMENT).

Died on 1st July 1916, aged 41, during an attack on Ovillers.

John was the eldest of at least four children of James (a moulder's labourer) and Bridget Connaughton of Chesterfield, Derbyshire.

He married Bridget Hester on 24th December 1896 and lived in Chesterfield, Derbyshire. They had nine children, born between 1898 and 1914.

Educated at St Mary's infant and junior schools, afterwards he was employed as a miner at the Bond's Main Colliery. He was a steward at the Working Men's Club and an amateur boxer. He also managed a gymnasium for local children.

He had seen service during the Boer War and, as a Reservist, he re-enlisted on 9th September 1914 in Derby, and was promoted to acting corporal one month later. Appointed as lance sergeant on 13th February 1915, he was promoted to acting sergeant on 29th May. He was confirmed in his rank on 26th August and went to France the following day.

A Chaplain wrote: *I am very sorry to tell you that no news has come to the battalion of your husband since the attack on July 1st. He was seen to be hit, and it was almost certain that he was killed, so that he is reported as missing believed killed. The Commanding Officer was wounded as well as many other officers and men otherwise you would have heard before. The fact that our Brigade after reaching the German lines had to retire to our own trenches has made it difficult to obtain exact particulars of all who have fallen. I know that if the Colonel were still with us he would have written to tell you how valuable Sergeant Connaughton's services had been to the battalion.*

A comrade wrote: *I saw the photo of Jack in The Derbyshire Times and your request for definite news. I am sorry to inform you that it is only too true. He was killed in action at [censored] on July 1st, about 8.30 a.m. We had a very bad time and lost a great many of our comrades before getting half way across No Mans Land. The officer of your husbands platoon was Mr. Brittain of Chesterfield and he was wounded as soon as ever we went over the top. Your dear husband immediately took command, and led his men up to the German barbed wire, where he was shot. He died a soldiers death, and I consider him one of the bravest men of the day. I have known Jack for a number of years, and the finish up of his life was a hero's death.*

HERBERT GRIFFITHS

CORPORAL 14096, 17TH BATTALION, SHERWOOD FORESTERS
(NOTTS AND DERBY REGIMENT).

Died on 5th October 1916, aged 20, near Thiepval, when
he accidentally kicked an unexploded bomb.

Herbert was one of ten children of Joseph (a coal miner) and
Mary Jane Griffiths (née Brown) of Hucknall,
Nottinghamshire.

Employed as a coal miner, he enlisted on 1st September
1914, went to France on 27th December and was wounded
in the left arm on 9th May 1915.

He went to the Dardanelles on 28th August 1915 and served at Mudros, Alexandria and on
the Suez Canal before returning to France. He served in various battalions, joining the 17th in
September 1916.

His platoon commander wrote: *Since I have been his platoon officer, I have always noticed that
your son has set a splendid example to his men. He did not know what fear was. Also, it might interest
you to know that I had recommended your son for his sergeant's stripes.*

A comrade wrote to Herbert's brother: *Well, I am sorry to say I've some very bad news to tell
you, and hope you will take it all right. Your dear brother Bert was killed on October 5th. We were just
going into action at the time, and I can assure you it was absolutely a pure accident. Very seldom
anything happens like it. He was walking over some capture ground from the Germans, and there were
a few shells here and there which had failed to explode… He was walking along, and he happened to
kick one by accident, with the result that it exploded and killed him instantly. He suffered no pain and
I saw him a few seconds after it was done, being only just behind him… I knew him so well by working
with him in the pit… He looked well, and was making a fine big fellow. It's hard lines, after being out
here all that time. He has seen some hard fighting, and it was a pity for him to be killed like that…
He died like a brave British soldier. If anyone has done his bit it was poor Bert.*

FREDERICK WILLIAM THURMAN

PRIVATE, 9109, 1ST BATTALION, SHERWOOD FORESTERS
(NOTTS AND DERBY REGIMENT).

Died on 8th July 1916, aged 26, during fighting at
Fricourt Wood.

Frederick was the younger of two children, both sons, of
Frederick (a brushmaker) and Florence Emily Thurman (née
Ballard). After her husband's death, Florence married Fred
Staveley and lived in Sneinton Dale, Nottinghamshire.

He was educated at the Wesleyan School and at London
Road Congregational Sunday School, Newark. Later he moved to Nottingham and was
employed in Boots' Stores Department.

He enlisted in the Sherwood Foresters as a boy soldier on 21st January 1904, aged 14 years
and four months. His overseas service included Singapore (1904 to 1906) and India (1906 to
1914), where he was acting Drum Major and stationed at Deololi. Once war was declared the
regiment returned to England and went to France on 5th November 1914. He had a short leave
in late 1915 but was back in France on 5th November. He was wounded twice and had also
suffered from fever and frostbite.

A comrade wrote to his stepfather: *I now take the opportunity of writing to you concerning poor
Fred, and I hope you will be able to explain to Mrs. Staveley better than I can. Well I must come
straight to the point. Poor Fred got killed on the 7th. It happened like this. We went into action at
[censored] on the morning of the 7th and when evening came and we had not had anything to eat,
the O.C. sent Fred and the Drum-Major down to the transport, so Fred and the Drum-Major made up
their minds to bring us some soup up, and they got within 20 yards of us, when a shell came and killed
them both. I ran out to Fred and got him under cover and did what was possible but it was too late as
there was no chance of him living. It might be some consolation to you that he said good-bye to all
before he passed away, and to know that he died a noble death. My heart is too sore to say any more
this time. I have got some photos belonging to him and I will send them to you. All the Drums send
their deepest sympathy to you, so good-bye for the present.*

HENRY ARTHUR WYATT PEAKE

CAPTAIN, 3RD BATTALION ATTACHED TO 9TH BATTALION,
ESSEX REGIMENT.

Died on 3rd July 1916, aged 25, during an attack on
Ovillers.

Henry was the eldest of six children, and one of three sons,
of Henry Arthur (a solicitor) and Alice Anne Peake (née
Wyatt) of Sleaford, Lincolnshire.

He was educated at Rottingdean, Charterhouse and
Oriel College, Oxford, where he took a degree in History and
rowed in the college boat.

After graduating he was articled to his father's firm of H. A. Peake, of Sleaford.

On 4th August 1914, he joined the Inns of Court OTC and on 16th August was granted a
commission in the 3rd Battalion, Essex Regiment. In December he went out to the Front and
was gazetted temporary captain in May 1915. On 9th June he was wounded and spent time
recuperating in England. His rank of captain was confirmed in April 1916 and he returned to
France on 29th May.

Henry was the last of the three brothers to be killed during the war.

Cecil Gerald Wyatt Peake, Captain, 2nd Battalion, Lincolnshire
Regiment, died on 10th March 1915, aged 23.

He is buried in grave III.A.4 in Rue-Petillon Military Cemetery.

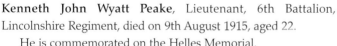

Kenneth John Wyatt Peake, Lieutenant, 6th Battalion,
Lincolnshire Regiment, died on 9th August 1915, aged 22.

He is commemorated on the Helles Memorial.

JOHN FRANCIS RAIKES

SECOND LIEUTENANT, 3RD BATTALION ATTACHED TO 9TH BATTALION, ESSEX REGIMENT.

Died on 10th October 1916, aged 20, during fighting at Gird Trench.

John was the only child of the Rev. Thomas Digby Raikes and Elizabeth Raikes (née Higgins) of Shipston-on-Stour, Worcestershire.

Educated at the Dragon School, where he won a number of prizes, he was remembered as *…a good-hearted, merry little fellow, with a keen sense of humour.* He then won a scholarship at Radley, where he became House Prefect. It was noted that although he *had not perhaps a wide circle of intimate friends, he was greatly liked by the members of his House and by all who knew him. He bore a spotless character, and he had a keen sense and appreciation of the humorous, and the recollection of the twinkle in his eye is abiding.*

He gained an exhibition in mathematics at Corpus Christi College, Oxford, but the war intervened and in October 1914 he enlisted as Private PS/1967, 18th Battalion (1st Public Schools), Royal Fusiliers and went to France on 14th November 1915.

In December he had time in hospital for a damaged knee. He wrote at the time to Dragon School: *I damaged it through tripping over something or other…we were put into some of the worst trenches of the line, and our section seemed to hit about the worst bit. We arrived in them with several of us having left our boots in the mud and some men having got so stuck that they had to be dug out. To move about was practically an impossibility.*

He returned to England in March 1916 for officer training, was granted a commission on 4th August and went back to France on 14th September.

His platoon sergeant wrote: *Although only with us for a short time he soon became very popular with all ranks. At all times he would study the men under him, looking after their comfort and doing all that an officer could do for them… The loss was deeply felt by the whole Company.*

His commanding officer wrote: *He has been a very short time with us, but he was a very good officer, and we miss him very much.*

John's servant, also aged 20, was killed by the same shell. This lad, writing home to his mother a few days before, had said: *You needn't worry about me. I am with a proper gentleman.*

Charles E. Chaplin
loader and checker at
Provender Depot
20th July 1916, 22

GREAT EASTERN RAILWAY

The company's war memorial on Liverpool Street Station in London commemorates over 1,000 of its staff who died. During the war the monthly staff magazine featured many letters from those serving as well as recording many of the deaths with pictures and obituaries. The pages of the magazine record at least eighty five men commemorated on the Memorial.

The names of these ten men (two NCOs and eight privates from the Essex Regiment) all appear on Pier and Face 10D.

William F. V. Wells
boilermaker at
Parkeston Quay
1st July 1916, 20

George T. J. Auker
clerk at Head Office
1st July 1916, 21

William G. Blyth
porter at Bishopsgate
1st July 1916, 32

Ernest W. O. Bruce
van guard at Bishopsgate
20th July 1916, 21

Joseph A. Frost
clerk at Romford
23rd October 1916, 26

John Hasler
stores at
Squirrel's Heath
1st July 1916, 22

Edward R. Markham
van guard, London
Cartage Committee
8th February 1917, 21

Samuel Ware
porter at
Bishopsgate
26th September 1916, 24

William A. West
porter at
Epping
20th July 1916, 19

ROBY MYDDLETON GOTCH

CAPTAIN AND ADJUTANT, 7TH BATTALION, SHERWOOD
FORESTERS (NOTTS AND DERBY REGIMENT).

Died on 1st July 1916, aged 26, during the fighting at
Gommecourt.

Roby was the younger of two children, and only son, of John
Alfred (an architect) and Annie Gotch (née Perry) of
Kettering, Northamptonshire.

Educated at Cottesmore School, Hove and Rugby, he
then went to New College, Oxford, taking his degree in Law
with Second Class Honours in 1911, and passing in 1912 for the Bachelor of Civil Law with
Third Class Honours. On leaving Oxford, he was articled to firms in Nottingham and then
London. He passed the Final Law Examination in 1914 with Second Class Honours. Whilst
working in Nottingham, he was a member of the 7th Sherwoods and was a lieutenant when
he went to France in February 1915. He was mentioned in despatches on 30th November,
gazetted temporary captain and adjutant in July 1916. The rank of captain was confirmed on
5th July, four days after his death.

The regimental history notes: *The Battalion were most unfortunate in the early stages of the
attack to have the Commanding Officer, Lieut.-Col. L. A. Hind*, and the Adjutant, Capt. R. M. Gotch,
killed. As far as can be ascertained these two Officers proceeded with the first wave and passed over
No Man's Land to within about 50 yards of the German trenches.*

The brigade commander wrote: *He was such a splendid fellow - standing out as quite one of the
best Officers in the whole of my Brigade. His work as Adjutant was most excellent, and he set all the
young Officers a wonderful example in devotion to duty. As a Company Officer he showed great
gallantry and determination on more than one occasion. I have always regretted that my
recommendations for a distinction were not accepted, and I was looking forward to pressing his claims
at the earliest opportunity. I had the greatest admiration for him, and feel that not only the Battalion
but the whole Brigade has suffered a great loss.*

His old Headmaster at Rugby wrote: *It is indeed a fresh and sad blow to me, for I do feel very
keenly the loss of so many of my old School House boys, about 50 of
whom have now fallen.*

*Lawrence Arthur Hind MC was aged 38. A solicitor, married
with three children and he was promoted to lieutenant colonel in
May 1916. He is also commemorated on Pier and Face 10D.

PIER 11

A

- Sherwood Foresters (Notts and Derby Regiment) - **Private G. H. White to Private J. Young**
  (completed from Pier and Face 10C)
- The Loyal North Lancashire Regiment
- Northamptonshire Regiment - **Major G. M. Clark to Private F. Hart**
  (continued on Pier and Face 11D)

B

- Northumberland Fusiliers - **Lance Corporal D. Clark to Private J. Keenan 324**
  (continued from Pier and Face 12B)
  (continued on Pier and Face 10B)

C

- Queen's Own (Royal West Kent Regiment)
- King's Own Yorkshire Light Infantry - **Major W. N. Tempest to Private E. Bowers**
  (continued on Pier and Face 12A)

D

- Northamptonshire Regiment - **Private H. J. Hayes to Private C. Wrighton**
  (completed from Pier and Face 11A)
- Royal Berkshire Regiment

THOMAS ORDE LAWDER WILKINSON VC

Lieutenant, 7th Battalion, The Loyal North Lancashire Regiment.

Died on 5th July 1916, aged 22, during the fighting near La Boisselle.

Thomas was one of at least six children of Charles Ernest Orde Wilkinson (a land agent) and Edith Mary Wilkinson (née Lawder) of Foynes, Co. Limerick.

Initially educated at a preparatory school in Ewell, Surrey, he then went to Wellington College, where he was one of the two senior prefects, head of the gymnasium and a member of the OTC; and for three successive years represented his school in the Public Schools Boxing Competition.

He then worked as a surveyor, having emigrated to Canada in 1912, where he worked in Comax and North Burnaby in British Columbia. In 1913 he passed the preliminary surveyors' examination at Victoria, British Columbia.

He enlisted as Private 28804, 16th Canadian Scottish, in Valcartier, British Columbia, on 23rd September 1914 and left Canada on 7th October. He was commissioned in The Loyal North Lancashire Regiment in January 1915 and went to France in July. He was promoted to lieutenant on 1st February 1916, later becoming machine gun officer.

The citation for the award of his Victoria Cross reads: *For most conspicuous bravery. During an attack, when a party of another unit was retiring without their machine-gun, Lieut. Wilkinson rushed forward, and, with two of his men, got the gun into action, and held up the enemy till they were relieved. Later, when the advance was checked during a bombing attack, he forced his way forward and found four or five men of different units stopped by a solid block of earth, over which the enemy was throwing bombs. With great pluck and promptness he mounted a machine-gun on the top of the parapet and dispersed the enemy bombers. Subsequently he made two most gallant attempts to bring in a wounded man, but at the second attempt he was shot through the heart just before reaching the man. Throughout the day he set a magnificent example of courage and self-sacrifice.*

His VC was presented to his father on 29th November 1916 by HM King George V at Buckingham Palace.

THOMAS STANLEY WORRALL

LANCE SERGEANT, 15228, 8TH BATTALION, THE LOYAL
NORTH LANCASHIRE REGIMENT.

Died on 7th July 1916, aged 20, shot while leaving the
trenches near the Leipzig Salient.

Stanley was one of five children of Thomas (advertising
manager of the *Bolton Evening News*) and Nancy Worrall (née
Ormerod) of Bolton, Lancashire.

Educated at St Augustine's School, Bolton, he was later
employed as a clerk for a local firm of brass founders and
played for Bradshaw Cricket Club.

He enlisted in Bolton on 1st September 1914 and went to France on 25th September 1915.
Stanley was a regular letter writer, these are some excerpts:

28th December 1914: *Many thanks for your letter of the 26th I have received the Chicken etc
and thanks very much to all of you. The Landlady cooked him up and we all chewed him up.*

4th June 1915: *We have to rise at 5 am it nearly breaks my heart, and go to bed at 9.30. The grub
is rotten, some of our chaps say they have had better grub in gaol. I should be glad if you would send
me some grub, I am going like a shadow.*

29th June 1915: *I have received a parcel this a.m. from Annie M., some fags in, Toffee and
Shortcakes and a nice large Fruit Cake A1 I'll give it wallop.*

23rd July 1915: *You say something about another stripe they can keep 'em, I don't want to dine
with these Sgts. I have seen some of them "grubbing" at meal times, they eat like pigs I think some of
'em were Rag Merchants before they joined this lot.*

28th September 1915: *Further to my P.C. of Sunday. When I sent it we had just arrived in
France. We stopped at the Coast Town for 2 nights and now we have moved further in. I can't tell you
where, as a matter of fact I don't know.*

9th October 1915: *I have been up to the trenches to-day and our Artillery has been firing all day,
but the German Artillery has not returned one shot. One of our chaps says there are no Germans in
this part of the line only a Caretaker and his wife. It may be true according to the shots they fire only
a Sniper or two reply to our fire.*

17th October 1915: *We have only had 2 casualties in our Bn up to to-night both wounded, and
one very slight. We are going to have some luck I can see. By the way Ma, I will be careful alright,
don't fret with a bit of caution a chap is safe as the Bank of England…I have got a champion dug out,
nice and warm and well sand-bagged on top. Shell proof and bullet proof.*

THOMAS MYERSCOUGH

LANCE CORPORAL, 13346, 1ST BATTALION, THE LOYAL
NORTH LANCASHIRE REGIMENT.

Died on 26th September 1916, aged 24, whilst in the
front line at Eaucourt l'Abbaye.

Thomas was the youngest of three children, all sons, of
Thomas Edward (a cotton packer) and Sarah Ellen
Myerscough (née Collinson) of Chorley, Lancashire.

He was employed as an overlooker at Lawrence's Mill
and enlisted in Chorley on 4th September 1914 in the 10th
Battalion.

Promoted to lance corporal on 22nd July 1915, he went to France nine days later.

Wounded during the fighting on 1st July 1916, he was evacuated to England and spent a
week in Netley Hospital. He was posted to the 11th Battalion on 20th July and returned to
France on 19th August, joining the 1st Battalion in the field two weeks later.

A comrade wrote: *He was a good lad, and so kindhearted. He lost his life trying to save another.
We have lost eight out of our platoon.*

A comrade, who was killed ten months later, wrote: *He died a good death. He had seen a
wounded lad keep rising up in 'No Man's Land,' about 500 yards away, and Tom set off to go and bring
him in. The lad had been there from the charge the night before. They succeeded in getting the lad part
way back, when he died in their arms, and they had to leave him… He had just got back to the parapet
when a sniper shot him through the stomach, and he died in about ten minutes' time.*

Another comrade, who was killed some three months later, added that Thomas had been
wounded in the thigh during the rescue attempt but had continued until he was shot by the
sniper. He also said that Thomas was well thought of by both the officers and men, was sadly
missed and had met his death like a British hero.

Another comrade who had worked with Thomas, said that he proved himself a good
soldier, who was always ready to help and comfort others. He felt his loss as he would that of
a brother.

JOHN GOODLEY

PRIVATE, 3/10225, 7TH BATTALION, NORTHAMPTONSHIRE
REGIMENT.

Died on 17th August 1916, aged 39, during an attack on
Guillemont.

John was one of at least seven children of John (a
brickmaker) and Alice Goodley of Whittlesey,
Cambridgeshire.

He married Nora Elizabeth Chambers in 1899 and lived
in Nottingham. They had three children, born between 1901
and 1908.

He enlisted in Northampton and went to France on 6th July 1915. Originally reported
missing on 20th October 1916, he was officially reported as presumed killed in August 1917.

In a letter to his wife he wrote: *I am well & in the best of spirits we have just come out of the
trenches for a few days... I can assure you we are goeing strong & a finer lot of fellows I don't wish to
be with they all have had a good Baptism from our most hated enemy & they have proved themselves
capable of the task which lays before us. which I hope will not last long… I received papers & parcel
with cake & cigars which I thank you very much for what I should like you to do is send me a stick of
shaving soap & some new socks which the game plays havock with foot wear you can send me a scarf
also has the nights begin to be very cold the pass word his keep your head down & I find if you want
to keep it on that is the only thing you can do when we are in the trenches… Now keep smiling & keep
a stout heart & look on the best side I am looking forward to come home & have a good time with you
all.*

His platoon commander wrote: *I very much regret to have to inform you, in answer to your
letter, that there seems to be very little hope of your husband being alive. I have made full and extensive
enquiries and interviewed several men who were with him at the time. It appears that he went over
the top with his regiment and was hit almost immediately and I very much fear badly. He was helped
back into our trench by a machine gun corporal, who was himself badly wounded immediately
afterwards. He was afterwards seen walking towards the dressing station but he never returned there.
The dressing station and trenches leading to the same, were at this time being heavily shelled. There
is of course, a very small chance that he may be still alive but I do not wish to give you any false hopes.
I will not try and sympathize with you in your great loss but would like to remind you that if he proves
to be dead, he died like a brave man fighting for his Country.*

ADOLPHUS VICTOR TRUTTMAN

LANCE CORPORAL, 12303, 9TH BATTALION,
NORTHUMBERLAND FUSILIERS.

Died on 7th July 1916, aged 25, during an attack on
Mametz Wood.

Adolphus was one of eight children, the only surviving son,
of Philip and Isabella Truttman (née Ferguson) of
Newcastle-upon-Tyne

Educated at Barnard Castle School, he was a keen athlete
and footballer. He joined the choir, against his wishes, as the
best singers were *forced to join*. In 1907 he joined the family firm of P. Truttmann & Co. Ltd. and

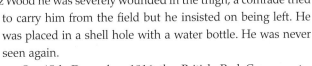

had become a director by the time that war
broke out. He enlisted on 4th August 1914,
being only the third man to join the 'Quayside'
Company of the 9th Battalion.

On 18th June 1916 he wrote: *If you want an
amusing book get "The First Hundred Thousand"
by Ian Hay*. It is absolutely true to life and quite
accurate.*

On 25th June 1916 he wrote: *I am still in
billet, far from the maddening crowd, so our easy
time continues. Different times are ahead. I cannot promise regular news, but will do my best.*

During the attack on Mametz Wood he was severely wounded in the thigh; a comrade tried
to carry him from the field but he insisted on being left. He
was placed in a shell hole with a water bottle. He was never
seen again.

On 15th December 1916 the British Red Cross wrote:
*…we are sorry to have received a report from Private T. Mason,
12154, now in hospital in France, who says he knew Corpl.
Truttman and was told by Private W. C. Robson B. Coy: that when
last seen Truttman was lying wounded on the ground and shouting
to the lads to "Carry on"…we feel constrained to agree with you
that there is no real hope left to you that your son is alive, but that
he died gallantly, encouraging others in the attack.*

After his death the family drawing room included a
collection of items in his memory.

*The book, published in 1915 as a good humoured account of Army life, was a best seller.

RYTON MEN

The village war memorial in Ryton, Co. Durham lists 272 men from the area. Twenty five of those men are commemorated on the Memorial, eighteen from battalions of the Northumberland Fusiliers and seven from other regiments.

The six remembered below were members of the Tyneside Scottish or Tyneside Irish battalions of the Northumberland Fusiliers.

They all died on 1st July 1916 during an attack on La Boisselle and are commemorated on Pier and Face 11B.

Edward Johnson
Lance Corporal
24th Battalion, 38

Mason Carr
Private
25th Battalion, 31

William Cook
Private
22nd Battalion, 33

Robert Forster
Private
22nd Battalion, 23

Joseph Graham
Private
23rd Battalion, 34

Richard Hogg
Private
20th Battalion, 38

PIPERS OF THE TYNESIDE SCOTTISH BATTALIONS

In the fighting at La Boisselle on 1st July 1916, the Tyneside Scottish battalions of the Northumberland Fusiliers were played into action by their pipers.

The pipers' behaviour on that day was an inspiration to the men who followed them. They were exposed to very heavy fire and to every sort of obstacle on the ground. Many, having played their companies up to the German trenches, then took an active part in the fighting as bombers.

During the action ten pipers were killed and at least five wounded. The two below are commemorated on Pier and Face 11B.

JOHN WILLIAM ERWIN FELLOWS

PIPER, 20/1585, 20TH BATTALION, 21

John was the elder child and only son of William and Martha Fellows of Walker, Newcastle-upon-Tyne.

ALEXANDER FINDLEY

PRIVATE, 22/1079, 22ND BATTALION, 38

Alexander married Catherine Lee in 1900 and lived at High Mickley, Northumberland. They had six children, born between 1901 and 1915.

EDGAR HINDLE

PRIVATE 15039, 14TH BATTALION, NORTHUMBERLAND FUSILIERS.

Died on 14th July 1916, aged 21, during fighting near Bazentin-le-Petit.

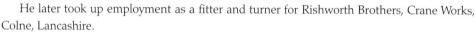

Edgar was the only son, the younger of two children, of William Spencer Hindle (a sailor) and Amelia Hindle (née Ashton) of Skipton, Yorkshire.

He was educated at Skipton Grammar School, where he was noted as having great promise.

He later took up employment as a fitter and turner for Rishworth Brothers, Crane Works, Colne, Lancashire.

Enlisting in Bradford on 31st August 1914, he had been at the Front about eleven months and was a member of the machine gun section.

His lieutenant (who was killed in August 1918) wrote: *Unfortunately I wasn't present when the incident happened, and can't give you any first hand news. Upon enquiries I find that Pte. Hindle was killed by a shell at Bazentine-le-Petit Wood on 14th July. The shell hit him on the side and lower part of the body. He did not suffer any pain but was killed outright. He would probably be buried where he was killed by one of the burying parties… Lance-Corporal Walsham…tells me that he was present at the time, and he or myself will be only too pleased to give you any information that you may desire. Please accept my deepest sympathy for I was very fond of your son, and was grieved at his death, but am proud that he died in such a noble way. My Captain also wishes his sympathy and heartfelt sorrow to be conveyed to you.*

A friend wrote: *It is with a heavy heart that I write these few lines to you. I saw in the paper about poor Edgar having been killed… When I saw it I could not believe it was true, for I have lost one of my very best friends. I hope you will bear it with a good heart, but I know it will be a great blow to you. He has died with great honour and he will live in my memory for ever.*

HENRY GEORGE THOMAS MM

CORPORAL, G/567, 6TH BATTALION, QUEEN'S OWN (ROYAL WEST KENT REGIMENT).

Died on 5th August 1916, aged 25, whilst in the line at Ration Trench near Pozières.

Henry was the eldest son, one of five children, of Walter (a gardener) and Jane Thomas (née Young) of Chislehurst, Kent.

Employed as a gardener, he enlisted in Bromley, Kent, on 31st August 1914, was appointed lance corporal on 5th February 1915, promoted to acting corporal on 16th April and corporal on 11th May.

He went to France on 1st June 1915 and was wounded on 3rd August and on 7th March 1916. He was promoted to acting sergeant on 3rd July 1916.

The award of the Military Medal was gazetted on 22nd August 1916 in respect of an action on 3rd July at Ovillers.

A second lieutenant wrote that he was: *seriously wounded on the afternoon of the 5th inst., and died as we were getting him down to the station. During the morning of the 3rd and 4th inst. we had captured a line of trenches, and it was during the enemy's heavy bombardment of our newly acquired position that Sergeant Thomas was hit by shrapnel. It is a source of great regret to every officer, non-commissioned officer, and man in this fighting battalion that he should no longer be with us. I realise only too well how difficult it will be to replace a non-commissioned officer having the soldierly qualities and pluck that Sergeant Thomas undoubtedly possessed.*

Another officer wrote: *…he was badly wounded by a shell, which blew in our dugout… He was our most promising non-commissioned officer and the battalion's best bomber. He did most gallant work on July 3rd in our attack, and well earned the King's Military Medal recently awarded him…he was extremely popular, and I am truly sorry to have lost such a gallant comrade and a man I could rely on to do a job thoroughly.*

ORAZIO ABBOTT CORTE

PRIVATE, G/11593, 7TH BATTALION, QUEEN'S OWN (ROYAL WEST KENT REGIMENT).

Died on 18th November 1916, aged 24, during the fighting at Grandcourt.

Born in Turin, Italy, Orazio was the son of Ferdinando and Maria Corte.

His father died in 1905 and his mother was an invalid; so in 1908 he was adopted by George and Edith Abbott of Tunbridge Wells, Kent.

He was educated at Skinners' School and the Technical Institute in Tunbridge Wells and then went to University College London. In June 1912 he won the prize for Applied Maths at the end of his second year. He read for Maths Honours, and took a first in his BSc in 1913. He decided to research and teach Mathematics and arranged to stay a further two years at the College, with a view to earning his MA. A paper by him, *Note on the product for sin x*, was published in the *Messenger of Mathematics* in November 1914. He took a large part in the activities of the Christian Union and other College Societies. A fellow student wrote: *I knew him as a member of the Philosophical Society, which he joined in 1915, but I remember his reading a paper on the Trisection of an Angle, some years before, at a meeting of the Mathematical Society, of which he was Treasurer.*

When Italy declared war in the spring of 1915, he tried, without success, to join the Italian Army. He twice attempted to join the OTC, but was rejected on account of bad eyesight. In December 1915 he enlisted at Kingsway, London as a private in the Royal West Kents. He became a first class machine gunner and went to France in July 1916.

A fellow student wrote: *At College he was a steady worker, and much given to undertaking advanced and difficult pieces of work on his own account. Most of all he cared for the philosophical side of his subject.*

WILSON BELL

CAPTAIN, 2ND/4TH BATTALION, KING'S OWN YORKSHIRE
LIGHT INFANTRY.

Died on 15th March 1917, aged 36, while in trenches
between Miraumont and Puisieux-au-Mont.

Wilson was the only child of Thomas Pearson Bell and
Elizabeth Bell (née Wilson) of West Kirby, Cheshire.

He married Dora Ellen Hughes on 7th July 1911. They
subsequently lived in Wakefield, Yorkshire and had two
daughters, born in 1912 and 1916.

He was educated at Calday Grange Grammar School, The Institute, Liverpool, and
Liverpool University, where he took his LLB degree with Honours in 1902. In his final
examination in Law in 1902 he came out fourth in all England in Honours, being awarded two
gold medals. He served his articles with the Liverpool firm of Mason, Grierson & Martin and
was admitted as a solicitor in July 1904.

He took up the post of Assistant Solicitor to the West Riding County Council. On the
passing of the National Insurance Act, he was entrusted with the organisation of that
department at the County Hall.

He had previously been a member of the Volunteers and as a result he was commissioned
on 28th November 1914; promotions followed to lieutenant in March 1915 and captain in May.

A lieutenant colonel wrote: *your husband was shot through the back and died instantly. I cannot
say how terribly grieved we all are. For over two years we have been training together, and looking
forward to coming out and doing our bit, and then returning home with a firmly established
friendship; but it was not to be, and we are feeling his loss most deeply. His men were devoted to him,
and since we had been out here their devotion had increased, and they had got to love him. His conduct
was always most thoughtful, and he was a most clever and capable officer and his loss to the battalion
and to the country is very great. Such a man is not dead, and that whilst his influence and example
remains, he lives with us all.*

He was reported buried on the battlefield in a grave that had a cross at the top and a board
at the bottom. The cross carried the inscription: *In loving memory of Captain Wilson Bell, 2/4
King's Own Yorkshire Light Infantry. Killed in action 15.3.17.* Shell cases were placed around the
grave; two crosses were laid on it - one of white chalk stones, and the other formed of ten
bullets or cartridges placed upright. The grave was subsequently lost.

ARTHUR FREDERICK RYDER

SERGEANT, 12178, 6TH BATTALION, KING'S OWN YORKSHIRE LIGHT INFANTRY.

Died on 15th September 1916, aged 24, during an attack to the east of Delville Wood.

Arthur was the only son, younger of two children, of Thomas Bainbridge Ryder (a printer compositor) and Clara Ann Ryder (née Moores) of Skipton, Yorkshire.

Educated at Ermysted Grammar School, Skipton, he was later employed as an assistant architect with the West Riding County Council at Wakefield, Yorkshire.

He enlisted in Wakefield in August 1914 and went to France on 21st May 1915.

In a letter published in the local newspaper he wrote of a local village: *It was deserted except for a few soldiers billeted there, quiet except for the bursting of an occasional shell well beyond us, and the noise of artillery firing at too-venturesome aeroplanes. Half-way down the street is covered with debris - the remains of a house, furniture, etc. A little further on the side of a house was blown away, exposing to the view beds, chairs, and pictures hanging at rakish angles on the remaining wall. So you go on meeting with scenes of destruction and ruin. Whole streets are demolished and one building was irreparably damaged. This is the inevitable mark of modern warfare. Think of the people who were there and are now wanderers: then you know what we are fighting here for in order that the scenes I have attempted to describe shall not be seen in Britain.*

He was wounded in July 1915 whilst in the reserve trenches. He wrote that he: *had the unfortunate luck to get in the way of a piece of shrapnel which went through the right calf;* and later he commented, *That's the worst of being in the reserve trenches, you cannot see the enemy, though every now and then they give you a warm time.* He was eventually invalided home, not rejoining his unit until the end of the year.

It was reported that he had been wounded in the hand and was making his way back to the British lines for treatment but he was never seen again.

A private wrote: *Such a thing as being taken a prisoner seems nearly impossible as our lads went forward a long way in advance of where Arthur got hit. The Germans did not put up much of a fight after their machine guns were put out. They were only too glad to be made prisoners themselves… We were the only two in this Battalion from Skipton so I shall miss him very much.*

His commanding officer wrote: *He is a great loss to me for he was quite one of my best platoon sergeants. I seldom met a man with a higher sense of duty and he always set a splendid example to those under him.*

WILLIAM ANSELL

Lance Corporal, 12824, 6th Battalion, Royal Berkshire Regiment.

Died on 5th October 1916, aged 19, during fighting in the Thiepval area.

William was the eldest of ten children of Edgar Hedley Ansell and Bertha Ansell (née Edwards) of Sonning, Berkshire.

Enlisting in Reading, he went to France on 25th July 1915 and became a member of a Lewis gun team.

His officer wrote: *I am the officer in charge of the Lewis guns and was with him and a friend of his when he was killed. He was a splendid fellow and a soldier and everyone spoke highly of him. The circumstances were unfortunate the Huns had broken into a part of the line on our left, which was held by another regiment, they had passed along for a Lewis gun and I sent for one. Your son was the first chap to come, although he had further to come than several others and his gun was not working well. His bravery and keenness gave me the greatest assistance in a crucial position where fellows had lost their heads. He placed his gun on the parapet and incautiously looked over hardly had his head appeared over the top than a German sniper shot him. He did not suffer as he was killed straight out. I may say incidentally that he practically saved my life as I was about to look over myself. The German sniper at close range rarely misses. His friend Maskell* collected his belongings and they will be sent to you. We laid him on the side of the trench and as soon as the Huns had been thoroughly driven out he will be decently buried. His loss is greatly felt by all and the battalion to which he was a credit has lost a brave and good soldier. However he has died for a great cause which so many other brave men died for and his life was not uselessly thrown away. Let me offer you again my deepest condolences and regret.*

*Believed to be **George Maskell**, Lance Corporal 12874; he died of wounds on 2nd August 1917 and is buried in grave III.E.6 in Mendinghem Military Cemetery.

ERNEST JESSE SAUNDERS

LANCE CORPORAL, 200621 (2752), 1ST/4TH BATTALION, ROYAL BERKSHIRE REGIMENT.

Died on 23rd July 1916, aged 20, during an attack on Pozières.

Ernest was the eldest of three children of Jesse (a machine fitter with the Great Western Railway GWR) and Flora Saunders (née Brown) of Caversham, Berkshire.

He was educated at Swansea Road Council School and in 1910 he joined GWR as a machinist in the Reading Works. In 1913 he transferred to be a tracer in the GWR Signal Engineer's office at Reading.

A member of Reading Swimming Club, he enlisted in Reading and went to France on 30th March 1915, becoming a member of a Lewis gun team.

His captain wrote: *I am most dreadfully sorry to have to tell you that your son who was in charge of a Lewis Gun team, was sent to a flank trench to be ready to assist the advance with covering fire while there he was subjected to a very heavy bombardment, and one shell pitched clean on the gun, blowing in the trench. Soon after the trench had to be given up, and it was then found that your son and another* of his party were missing. A search was made but no trace could be found and the two men must have been killed and buried by the explosion. Our company had to move elsewhere, or we would have waited till night and dug the trench out again, but in the shell fire that could not be done. Your son was a most promising NCO, keen willing and capable, invariably cheerful; his loss will be severely felt in the company. He was noted for further promotion had he been spared. It may be some consolation to you to know that our attack was entirely successful but nevertheless your loss is a heavy one. I know what a devoted son he was, and you probably knew how popular he was with all ranks of the company, the officers and men alike.*

*The other member of the gun team was **Reginald Cyril Arthur Mulford**, Private 200361 (2293), 1st/4th Battalion, Royal Berkshire Regiment, aged 18. He is also commemorated on Pier and Face 11D.

ARTHUR THOMAS KNOTT

Private, 2616, 1st/4th Battalion, Royal Berkshire Regiment.

Died on 14th August 1916, aged 21, during an attack on Skyline Trench near Mouquet Farm.

Arthur was one of eight children of Frederick Edward and Ellen Knott (née Collier) of Reading, Berkshire.

The family made brushes and ran a hardware shop. Educated at the Central Schools, Reading, he was a staff sergeant in the St Mary's, 7th Reading, Boys' Brigade. Later he worked in the family business and enlisted in Reading.

On the eve of the 'Big Push' he wrote to his mother: *We have just been told to write if we wish to has no more letter's will be taken after six tonight which is another hour from now so I suppose we shall soon be busy. I am quite well so pleased to hear all at the dear Home are… We must all look on the bright side and be cheerful through these anxious times, and I will write a field card has often has possible. Give my fond love to All, I shall do my best in whatever lies before me. God grant that I shall return safely to you all. Goodbye mother be brave and cheerful. With love and Hope. Your loving son Arthur.* Added at the end was: *God bless you all I shall never forget a loving Mother, Father Brother's and Sister's*

kindness to me through all these weary anxious months. Ever yours Arthur.

He came through that fighting but was wounded on 24th July 1916, returning to the front line only three days before he was killed.

A comrade wrote: *Arthur's company sergeant major told me that Arthur was killed by a bullet wound in the stomach, and it was probably certain that death was instantaneous. He also said that a better fellow than Arthur it was impossible to find, for he was always in the best of spirits and was never lacking when there was duty to be done. I have found him a very good chum all through my Army career.*

WALTER ERNEST WEBB

Private, 2017, 1st/4th Battalion, Royal Berkshire Regiment.

Died on 24th July 1916, aged 19, near Pozières.

Walter was one of nine children of Samuel C. (a carpenter) and Frances Elizabeth Webb (née Nicholl) of Reading, Berkshire.

Educated at Battle School, he then worked for the Reading Tobacco Supply Company before working for Mr. A. C. Drew, wholesale tobacconist, in Reading.

He played football for the South Reading Wednesday FC and was a member of the Territorials. He enlisted in Reading and went to France on 30th March 1915.

His employer, Mr. Drew, wrote: *All on the firm feel that I should write you something to show our very great sympathy with you all in your sad loss. Everyone who knew Walter, and worked with him here (since he joined us on September 1st 1913) held him in the very highest esteem. We did not hear a cross or unkind remark from him from the first day we knew him. Your loss is shared somewhat by us, as we all looked forward to him returning to the firm at some distant date.* Quoted in the local newspaper he also said that Walter was: *One of the best. One cannot speak too highly of a lad like that. He was so gentle and kind and so willing in every respect. We feel his loss very keenly.*

His captain wrote: *It is with the deepest regret that I have to tell you that your son, Private W. E. Webb was killed in action in the early morning of the 25th July, while he was most pluckily assisting to repel a bombing attack which the Germans were making on a trench we had taken the day before. His body was lying on the parapet where the fighting had been thickest, and those near told me he was the first man to begin throwing bombs back, and he stuck at it most bravely till he was killed. His name has been sent in for distinction, but, of course, one cannot guarantee that he will receive any, though he well earned it. I knew your son well, for he had served in my company for three years, and he had always shown himself a keen and willing soldier. A good footballer, he was universally popular with all ranks. Latterly he had been employed as a 'runner' to carry messages, a task calling for strength and coolness, both of which qualities he displayed to the full. I had learnt to rely greatly on his quickness and ability. He died fighting, setting a fine example to others.*

PIER 12

A

- King's Own Yorkshire Light Infantry - **Private H. Boyes to Private E. C. Young**
  (completed from Pier and Face 11C)
- King's Shropshire Light Infantry - **Captain P. J. Bellasis to Private A. Grady**
  (continued on Pier and Face 12D)

B

- King's Own (Royal Lancaster Regiment) - **Private W. Cottam to Private C. Young**
  (completed from Pier and Face 5D)
- Northumberland Fusiliers - **Lieutenant Colonel A. P. A. Elphinstone to Lance Corporal J. Chrisp**
  (continued on Pier and Face 11B)

C

- 22nd Bn. London Regiment (The Queen's) - **Private R. D. Cope to Private F. G. Wilson**
  (completed from Pier and Face 13C)
- 23rd Bn. London Regiment
- 24th Bn. London Regiment (The Queen's)
- 25th Bn. London Regiment (Cyclist Battalion)
- 28th Bn. London Regiment (Artists' Rifles)
- Herefordshire Regiment
- Hertfordshire Regiment
- Army Cyclist Corps
- Northern Cyclist Battalion
- Huntingdon Cyclist Battalion
- Machine Gun Corps (Infantry & Heavy Branch) - **Captain W. Baddon to Private F. Aldred**
  (continued on Pier and Face 5C)

D

- King's Shropshire Light Infantry - **Private G. F. Grant to Private J. Yates**
  (completed from Pier and Face 12A)
- Middlesex Regiment - **Major M. C. Scarbrough to Private T. Emmett**
  (continued on Pier and Face 13B)

LAWRENCE COOPER

and

SAMUEL COOPER

PRIVATE, 19878, 9TH BATTALION, KING'S OWN YORKSHIRE LIGHT INFANTRY, AGED 20.

LANCE CORPORAL, 19877, 9TH BATTALION, KING'S OWN YORKSHIRE LIGHT INFANTRY, AGED 23.

Both killed by the same shell on 1st July 1916, during the fighting at Fricourt.

They were two of at least eight children of Mark (a coal miner) and Emma Cooper of Wales, near Rotherham, Yorkshire.

Employed at the Kiveton Park Collieries, they enlisted together in Sheffield on 11th November 1914 and both went to France on 13th October 1915.

A comrade wrote: *They were well respected by their comrades and platoon officers…both of them were killed instantaneously by the same shell. I have his little pocket book…so I will bring it with me when I come home to Sheffield, and I can tell you full details. I and a few more comrades buried them side by side, between our lines and the Germans. You must excuse bad writing, as I feel the blow as much as anyone.*

On 12th July 1916 their eldest brother, **James**, wrote to another brother, **Enoch**, who was serving with the Military Police in Egypt: *I really don't know how to break the sad news to you, but I must tell you of Sam & Lawrie getting killed in action near Albert, both the dear lads got knocked out with one shell, & are buried side by side…mother is terribly upset.*

Although the brothers enlisted and died together, the difference in their ranks means that Samuel is commemorated on Pier and Face 11C.

ARTHUR GRUNDY

Private, 37549, 10th Battalion, King's Own Yorkshire Light Infantry.

Died on 25th September 1916, aged 21, during an attack on Gird Trench.

Arthur was the youngest of five children of Thomas (a brick company employee) and Annie Grundy of Bradford, Yorkshire.

Employed at a firm of woollen merchants and shippers in Bradford, he enlisted in the 5th Battalion, Duke of Wellington's (West Riding Regiment) on 1st January 1916. He went to France on 29th June and on 11th July was transferred to the 10th Battalion, King's Own Yorkshire Light Infantry.

While in training and in France he wrote many letters to family members. The following extracts are from letters to his married sister, Ethel, that were published in 1991 in *Arthur Grundy* by John A. Richardson.

3rd July 1916: *As you will most likely know we are under canvas, it is much different to sleeping in huts, but it is a change. We have had half day off today, to wash, and that was a change too…well, it is official this time, we are undoubtedly on the last lap. I can't say more, but it is a toss up whether I shall ever see any fighting or not - I hope I do now that I am in France.*

27th July 1916: *I got three letters from home - one registered with 10/- enclosed, and have just changed it for 14 francs (11/8). I received 10 francs (8/4) on Tuesday, pay, so am fairly well off. The country here is splendid and the weather lovely, the food very good and the work very little.*

1st August 1916: *France is much more beautifull than England as far as views and scenery goes, but it is too warm in the day time for my liking. As I told Tom and Beaty the other day, I never used to perspire in England, but here I have no need to wash handkerchieves… In five days I have had fifteen letters, three parcels and one newspaper - not bad eh.*

21st August 1916: *Am pleased to say that we are going out of the trenches tomorrow, for a six days rest, to the village we were last in. We shall be shure of eight hours sleep every night and ten if we choose - we shall also get a bath and a change of clothing, so when those six days are up, I should just about be ready for another eighteen days in here, then with a bit of luck, the war will probably be nearly at an end. I hope so anyway, for I don't fancy doing a winter in here. If it has to be though, you can rely on my doing it smiling.*

9th September 1916: *Very many thanks for Syrup enclosed in last parcel. If I remember correctly, I asked Ma to let me have it fairly often, if I didn't, will you please ask Mother to sent it every fortnight until I say "when".*

COLIN JOHNSTONE MACLAVERTY

Captain, 1st Battalion, King's Shropshire Light Infantry.

Died on 18th September 1916, aged 37, during fighting near Leuze Wood.

Colin was one of seven children of the Rev. Alexander and Mary Eugenia MacLaverty (née Tombs) of Llangattock, Monmouthshire.

He was educated at Rossall School, Fleetwood, Lancashire.

He married Geraldine Antoinette Hewat at Hereford on 14th October 1915. They had one son, who was born just two days before Colin was killed.

He served in the Boer War and was awarded the Queen's Medal with four clasps. He subsequently joined the 4th Battalion, King's Shropshire Light Infantry in 1908 and on the disbanding of the battalion transferred as a captain to the 3rd Battalion, The Scottish Rifles, from which he resigned in May 1914.

He then went prospecting in Northern Nigeria; when the war broke out he immediately volunteered for service with Nigerian troops. He landed at Duala, Cameroon, with the original Expeditionary Force, attached to the 1st Battalion, The Nigeria Regiment and took part in the main actions until wounded at Roga in June 1915, from where he was invalided to England.

When he recovered he rejoined the King's Shropshire Light Infantry and was gazetted a captain in the 1st Battalion on 30th June 1916.

He was buried on the railway bank near to where he fell. An officer wrote: *His company was the leading company, and it was thanks to his fine and gallant leading the whole attack was such a magnificent success. After having captured the first trench he was killed, collecting his men to go and attack the second.*

His wife dedicated a stained glass window to him in St Cadoc's Church, Llangattock.

CHARLES VINCENT HOLDER

SECOND LIEUTENANT, 5TH BATTALION, KING'S SHROPSHIRE LIGHT INFANTRY.

Died on 24th August 1916, aged 31, during the fighting at Delville Wood.

Charles was one of eleven children of Edward Henry (a landscape artist) and Annie Fowler Holder (née Seals) of Harlesden, London.

As a child he was known as 'Sunshine' and the name stuck amongst family and friends.

Educated at Reigate Grammar School, he went on to the Schools of the Royal Academy of Arts, where he was twice awarded the silver medal for *Heads from Life* and won several other minor distinctions. In 1915 and 1916 he had paintings exhibited 'on the line' at the Royal Academy Exhibition, the latter being a portrait of his sister Edith.

He enlisted on 8th August 1914 as Private 1895, 2nd Battalion, London Regiment (Royal Fusiliers) and went to France on 6th January 1915.

He saw action at Armentières, Ypres and Arras before obtaining his commission on 30th October.

His body was recovered after a few days and interred near Combles; however, the grave was subsequently lost.

A brother officer wrote: *He was a dear fellow, loved and respected by all who knew him. As a soldier he was quite fearless, and behaved magnificently up to the last. He was one of the coolest men when in action that I have ever met.*

A friend from civilian life wrote: *Most of us knew and admired him, first at the Academy school, where he won our esteem as much for his stalwart character as for his talent in art. His ready wit and genial manner made everyone his friend, and as such we always knew he could be depended upon an estimation he has amply proved we were justified in holding. In joining the Army at the very outbreak of the war we knew he made very considerable personal sacrifices, of which we are all proud, and he relinquished a career which promised to achieve distinction… His was a noble sacrifice, and from our knowledge of his character we are sure that he never flinched at facing the enemy as he led his men to the charge... He was a very model of fastidiousness of conduct, not easily ruffled, magnanimous. He was manly, and though he now lies silent in France, the fine and splendid quality of his character will always remain with us in our memories to stimulate us.*

GEORGE YATES

PRIVATE, 2178, 1ST/5TH BATTALION, KING'S OWN (ROYAL LANCASTER REGIMENT).

Died on 15th August 1916, aged 24, while carrying a wounded officer.

George was one of eight children of Abraham (a labourer) and Ann Jane Yates of Lancaster, Lancashire.

He was educated at St Thomas's School and later worked as a labourer in the production of oil cloth at the Lune Mills Works. He was an enthusiastic amateur footballer.

Enlisting in Lancaster on 3rd September 1914, he went to France on 14th February 1915. He was wounded by shrapnel in April and again in May. Whilst on leave, he married Ellen. E. Hargreaves on 3rd July. He returned to France in November.

The first news of his death came from his brother in law, **Private Jack Hargreaves**, who reported that he had been shot through the head, the bullet entering near his left eye.

George was a stretcher bearer. His captain wrote: *He was shot through the neck whilst carrying a wounded officer down, and death was instantaneous…he had proved himself thoroughly reliable, however trying the circumstances, and he died doing his duty in that quiet and efficient way so characteristic of him.*

Another captain wrote: *…his work has at all times been invaluable…and had been doing excellent work during a difficult period…a good stretcher bearer is always worth his weight in gold.*

A corporal expressed the thoughts of the stretcher bearer section when he wrote: *He had gained the respect and esteem of all by his quite cheerfulness, and the knowledge that he gave his life nobly in the execution of his arduous duties should be a great comfort to you. The circumstances of his death were such as to make us proud to call him comrade. He was laid to rest close to where he so gallantly fell, and a cross will mark his grave.*

JOHN MACFARLAN CHARLTON

Captain, 21st (Tyneside Scottish) Battalion,
Northumberland Fusiliers.

Died on 1st July 1916, his twenty fifth birthday, during a charge on a German strongpoint near La Boisselle.

John was the younger of two children, both sons, of John (a well known artist) and Kate MacFarlan Charlton (née Vaughan) of Cullercoats, Northumberland.

He was educated at The Mount, Hindhead, and at Uppingham, where he served in the Cadet Corps.

He was an enthusiastic naturalist, amateur taxidermist and gifted artist. He had written and illustrated several short works on ornithology, among them *The Birds of South East Northumberland*; his drawings of birds were often featured in the magazine *British Birds*.

In October 1914 he joined the Northumberland Yeomanry, receiving his commission to the 21st Battalion, Northumberland Fusiliers in the following month. He was promoted to lieutenant in January 1915, and captain on 21st September.

He went to France with his regiment in January 1916, was appointed to the command of C Company in February and later served temporarily with the divisional headquarters staff as transport officer. He was mentioned in despatches. His commanding officer wrote: *I recommended him for the Military Cross. It happened one night, midnight, a Saturday, when the Germans made a raid on his section; he collected three or four men and went along this trench and drove the Germans out. He personally shot dead the Officers who led the raiders.*

An officer wrote: *He was laid to rest in front of the captured trench he had helped to take; I put up a small wooden cross to mark the spot. He was greatly loved and respected by his men. They saw he was a leader and would have followed him anywhere. He did not know what fear was.*

His brother, **Hugh Vaughan Charlton**, Second Lieutenant, 7th Battalion, Northumberland Fusiliers, died on 24th June 1916, aged 32. He is buried in grave VI.A.7 in La Laiterie Military Cemetery.

A memorial service for the two brothers was held in Lanercost Abbey on 27th July 1916.

JOHN WILFRED ROBINSON

CAPTAIN, 4TH BATTALION, NORTHUMBERLAND FUSILIERS.

Died on 15th November 1916, aged 22, during fighting at the Butte de Warlencourt.

John was one of five children of John William (a draper) and Elizabeth Anne Robinson (née Stobbs) of Hexham, Northumberland.

He was educated at Battle Hill School, Hexham and then at St Bees School; later he joined a firm of solicitors in Hexham, and was studying for his final examination at the outbreak of the war.

In 1914 he joined the 4th Battalion, Northumberland Fusiliers and was gazetted second lieutenant in September. He went to France in April 1915 and a few days later was wounded during the fighting at St Julien. After recovering he was on home duty and returned to France in November. He was promoted to lieutenant on 12th August 1916 and captain the following month. After a successful attack had been made on the German trenches, he went out to reconnoitre the enemy position, and in doing so was shot and died instantaneously.

His eldest brother **Francis** (then a Major and second in command of the same regiment), wrote: *Wilf was killed to-day. I would rather it had been myself. He died in the way most of our lads have died, leading his men on to what we hear has been a victorious attack on the German trenches… The Colonel has told me on many occasions how pleased he was with him. The last time we were in the trenches he was out on patrol with an N.C.O. and man. The N.C.O. was hit and evidently did not know what he was doing, for he started to walk towards the enemy trench. Wilf went after him…and brought him back, but unfortunately the N.C.O. was hit again.*

His commanding officer wrote: *Wilfie was a very gallant boy, and was doing splendid work when he fell. He was shot through the head and died at once. This was close to the enemy's trench. We have not as yet been able to get his body, but will make every effort to do so.*

His brother, **George Sydney Robinson**, Private G/25152, 1st Battalion, The Buffs (East Kent Regiment), died on 26th April 1918, aged 19. He is buried in grave V.A.32 in Haringhe (Bandaghem) Military Cemetery.

The **Tynedale Rugby Football Club's Roll of Honour** commemorates forty nine members who fell during the war. John and three others are commemorated on the Memorial. The stories of two of those, **William Richard Thew** [1A] and **William Braidford** [14A], appear elsewhere.

HAYDON BRIDGE MEN

The village war memorial in Haydon Bridge, Northumberland lists fifty six men and one woman from the area. Of these, five are commemorated on the Memorial. One is from the Yorkshire Regiment but the other four were Territorials from the 1st/4th Battalion, Northumberland Fusiliers. The four died on 15th September 1916 during an attack towards High Wood.

The two NCOs are commemorated on Pier and Face 12B.

BENJAMIN CUFFE MM

SERGEANT, 27

NORMAN CHARLTON

LANCE SERGEANT, 23

The eldest of four children of Edward and Jane Cuffe of Stublick Hill, Northumberland. He went to France on 20th April 1915 and was wounded in June.

The award of the Military Medal was gazetted on 11th October 1916.

One of eleven children of George and Mary Ann Charlton. He married Evelyn Taylor in 1916 and they had a daughter the same year. He went to France on 20th April 1915.

His brother, **Walter**, was killed in action in 1918.

The other two men killed on the same day were privates; they are commemorated on Pier and Face 11B and 10B respectively.

John Pearson Hutchinson
Private, 20

James Edward Robinson
Private, 20

JOHN ALLEN RUTHERFORD

CAPTAIN, 7TH COMPANY, MACHINE GUN CORPS (INFANTRY).

Died on 24th August 1916, aged 27, during fighting near Thiepval.

John was the only son, the eldest of at least two children, of John Adam (a colliery agent) and Agnes Jane Rutherford (née Allen) of Holcombe Brook, near Manchester.

Educated at the Secondary School for Boys, Bootle, he entered Liverpool University in September 1905, with a Tate Scholarship, and took a four year course in electrical engineering. He obtained a Bachelors degree in 1907, gained honours in 1908 and his Masters degree in 1914.

After working in Manchester for a short time he went, in 1910, to work in Rangoon as assistant engineer for the Rangoon Electric Tramway & Supply Company. He served in the Rangoon Volunteer Rifles, rising to the rank of sergeant in December 1913. He came to England with the First Burma Contingent in January 1915. The following month he was commissioned in the 10th Battalion, Cheshire Regiment. Promoted to lieutenant on 2nd April, he went to France on 25th September.

On 12th January 1916 he transferred to the Machine Gun Corps and was sent to Bailleul, where he organised, commanded and trained the 7th Company for a couple of months until it was ready to take the field.

A brother officer wrote: *I want to let you know…what splendid work he did and what admiration we had for him… My impression is of a relentlessly hard worker, exacting at times to those under him but all through with a determination to maintain the utmost efficiency and attention to duty… Four of our guns were to go across following an attack and occupy the captured trench. He arranged everything thoroughly beforehand, but, not content, went by himself to see that all should go well. He had not the satisfaction of seeing the highly successful result, for a bullet struck him in the head about 4 o'clock in the afternoon, a few minutes before the attack went over. He lies buried, as near as I can say, in the old German trench system, called the 'Leipzig Salient,' about half a mile south of Thiepval. Close to him lie Colonel Brown* of the 1st Wiltshire's, who made the attack, and Bird^, one of our officers who was killed the same night, and he could not lie in finer company.*

***Lieutenant Colonel Walter Sidney Brown's** body was recovered later and he now lies in Blighty Valley Cemetery.

^Like John, **Lieutenant Reginald William Bird's** body was not recovered, and he is now commemorated on Pier and Face 13A; his story is told later.

ALEC FRANK EVELYN PRESCOTT

LIEUTENANT, 124TH COMPANY, MACHINE GUN CORPS
(INFANTRY).

Died on 8th October 1916, aged 22, during fighting at
Gueudecourt.

Alec was one of five children of James (a printing works
manager) and Annie Prescott (née Hill) of Newton-le-
Willows, Lancashire.

He was educated at Leigh Grammar School and then
became a mechanical engineer with the Linotype and
Machinery Co. and later was in the electrical department of the Liverpool Corporation.

He initially enlisted as a private in the 19th Liverpools and gained a commission after six
months. Later he transferred to the Machine Gun Corps and went to France on 17th June 1916.

His officer commanding wrote: *Speaking the simple truth, I can say he was the most beloved
officer in my company. His cheerful, open and loyal nature made an irresistible appeal. He was my
second in command. He was very young to have such a responsibility, but he was the most suitable
officer for the position, and that is why he was appointed… We cannot replace the boy himself. I had
come to have a great affection for him, and I am happy to think that this was reciprocated on his part
in a great measure… On Saturday last he accompanied me into action with the reserve guns about 6
p.m. We arrived at the front of the line, and were finding suitable positions for the guns when he was
hit by a rifle or machine-gun bullet. I was a few yards away, and he shouted to me that he was hit. I
rushed to him, and with the help of one of the men of his old section, bandaged up the wound, which
was in his side. He said, 'I shall not get over this sir.' He became unconscious in about two minutes,
and only lingered about ten minutes altogether. Everything was done for him that could possibly be
done, and I think he suffered very little.*

One of his men commented that *his manifest integrity of character made it a pleasure to serve
him.*

ALBERT CHARLES CRANE

CORPORAL, 20877, 13TH COMPANY, MACHINE GUN CORPS
(INFANTRY).

Died on 22nd July 1916, aged 22, during the fighting at
Delville Wood.

Albert was the eldest of seven children of Albert Charles (a
government clerk) and Flory Eleanor Crane (née Eldred), of
Southend, Essex.

He was educated at Acton Commercial College and
Southend Technical School; and later studied law at
University College, London. He was a member of the Union Committee and Secretary of the
Inter-Collegiate Law Students' Society. He was a keen sportsman, playing cricket for the First
XI, was an excellent swimmer and had won numerous athletic prizes.

On leaving college he was articled to a firm of solicitors in Lime Street, London.

A friend wrote: *He was a regular attendant at the debates of the Law Students' Society, and was
a fluent speaker. Always full of good humour and high spirits, he succeeded in imparting liveliness into
the driest of subjects. He made an excellent chairman; he had a short, sharp way with interrupters,
and on points of order was never at a loss for swift decision. Crane was always keen on the position
of the Laws Faculty in the University. With him it occupied the premier place, and he never missed an
opportunity of putting forward its claims… It was owing to his persistence that the Society drew up
some resolutions dealing with that part of the Commission's report on London University teaching
which dealt with the position of the Laws Faculty, and forwarded them to the University.*

As soon as war broke out, he enlisted in Southend in the 9th Battalion, London Regiment
(Queen Victoria's Rifles) and rose to the rank of corporal. He went to France on 4th November
1914 and transferred to the Machine Gun Corps on 4th April 1916.

A comrade wrote that *He was caught by a shell whilst stopping to bandage another's wounds.*

His three younger brothers also served; the youngest, **Edgar Leslie**, enlisted a couple of
months before his fifteenth birthday. He served in France and was wounded before being
discharged due to his age.

NORMAN ARMITAGE LISTER MM

CORPORAL, 22579, 165TH COMPANY, MACHINE GUN CORPS (INFANTRY).

Died on 7th August 1916, aged 25, during fighting near Trônes Wood.

Norman was the only child of Thomas (a brass founder) and Emma Lister (née Armitage) of Brighouse, Yorkshire.

He was educated at Rastrick Grammar School and then worked in Liverpool and later in Manchester.

A pre war Territorial, he enlisted in Liverpool as Private 1837, The King's (Liverpool Regiment) and went to France on 12th March 1915.

He was wounded in the leg by shrapnel during the fighting at La Bassée in May 1915. After an operation and further treatment in England, he was able to return to France in October and subsequently transferred to the Machine Gun Corps.

The award of the Military Medal was gazetted on 11th November 1916.

RASTRICK GRAMMAR SCHOOL

In 1921 a Roll of Honour book was published containing pictures and short obituaries relating to the one master and thirty one pupils from the school who died in the war.

As well as Norman, there are four other former pupils commemorated on the Memorial.

JAMES O'CONNOR KESSACK

CAPTAIN, 25TH BATTALION ATTACHED TO 17TH BATTALION, MIDDLESEX REGIMENT.

Died on 13th November 1916, aged 36, during an attack on Redan Ridge.

James was the eldest son, one of at least seven children, of James O'Connor Kessack (a baker's journeyman) and Isabella Kessack (née Davidson).

He married Margaret Weir Cunningham on 6th June 1902. They lived in Glasgow and had three children, born between 1903 and 1911. After his death the family moved to Australia.

He was reported to have had an adventurous career as a seaman, a cowboy, a miner, a navvy, and then as a dock labourer. Afterwards he became a prominent labour activist and campaigner, writing many pamphlets. Eventually he was appointed as the chief organiser for the Dockers' Union. He was a notable Scottish Labour leader, and unsuccessfully contested the Camlachie Parliamentary Division of Glasgow on two occasions as the Labour Party candidate.

In 1914, during a visit to Liverpool to speak to striking miners, he dived into a local canal to rescue a boy who was drowning. James had to miss another speaking engagement later that day while his clothes were dried.

He enlisted in the Scottish Horse as a private, rising to the rank of sergeant. Afterwards he was given a commission in the Navvy Battalion and transferred to the Middlesex Regiment on 13th July 1915; subsequently he was promoted to captain.

Both of James's sons died in the Second World War.

James Henry Hyndman Kessack GM, Lieutenant, Royal Australian Naval Volunteer Reserve, died on 28th April 1941, aged 38. The posthumous award of the George Medal, in June 1941, was in respect of his actions in the disposal of unexploded mines. After previously successfully dealing with a total of ten mines, he was killed while attempting to make safe an eleventh. He is commemorated at Glasgow Crematorium.

The younger son, **David Stevenson Kessack,** a private in the Australian Infantry, died on 31st August 1941, aged 36. He is buried in grave 2.A.10 in Beirut War Cemetery.

LIONEL ROBERT 'LEO' LAST

SERGEANT, PS/462, 16TH BATTALION, MIDDLESEX REGIMENT.

Died on 1st July 1916, his twentieth birthday, during an attack on Beaumont Hamel.

Lionel was one of ten children of William Henry (a master mariner and later a provisions merchant) and Elizabeth Emma Last (née Haile) of Clacton-on-Sea, Essex. In this family group, taken in 1909, Leo is standing at the left of the back row.

Educated at Cranleigh School, he was then employed as a journalist, working as a cartoonist on the *Daily Sketch*. He enlisted in London on 11th September 1914 and went to France on 17th November 1915. A qualified grenadier, he was promoted lance corporal (unpaid) on 15th March 1916 and to acting sergeant on 1st May.

In his last letter (dated 28th June 1916) to his sister he wrote: *I cannot write any more, Old Girl. I am very sorry but I seem a bit jumbled up in myself, but I want you to pray for me especially in the days that are coming, that I may do my duty as I ought.*

In a letter dated 28th July 1916 (subsequently returned marked Missing) his older sister Dorothy wrote: *These last weeks I have thought a great deal about you, Dear Boy, I pray that God will give you strength to go through all that you have to face and I trust that He will keep you all safe and bring you back to us all at home again – You are always in our prayers and remembering this may give you help.*

The father of Leo's captain told the family that the bombing party had gone into *a sunken road and started throwing in the midst of very heavy fire.* His son was then hit and did not rise again but then Leo *led the men as if nothing had happened and nothing more was seen of them.*

His brother, **Harold Haile Last**, Private 1012, 1st Battalion, Honourable Artillery Company, died of wounds on 26th April 1915, aged 22. He is buried in grave E.101 in Clacton Cemetery.

ROY HERRICK TOPLIS

CORPORAL, PS/2597, 23RD BATTALION, MIDDLESEX
REGIMENT.

Died on 13th September 1916, aged 22, during the
fighting at Delville Wood.

Roy was born in Little Sark, Channel Islands, one of at least
eight children of William Arthur (an artist) and Eleanor
Toplis (née Dickinson).

Educated privately, he was both artistic and musical. In
March 1911 he went to Western Canada to learn agriculture.
Four days into the voyage a violent gale broke the vessel's wireless gear and he helped the
operator to repair the damage and then, whilst a terrible sea was running, fearlessly climbed
the mast to place the wire in position. He was cheered by all on board for his pluck and daring.
After being invited to visit the engineroom, he astonished the chief engineer by asserting that
he could make improvements on the cylinders, and proceeded to illustrate his idea by means
of a sketch, with the result that both the engineer and captain were convinced that his
suggestions were really an improvement and easily workable.

Whilst in Canada he designed a number of time and labour saving appliances for farming
operations, including a combined plough and harrow, a potato planter, and a horse powered
drill for boring holes for fenceposts.

When war broke out he was on the point of entering a Theological College at
Saskatchewan, to study for the Church. He returned to England, and enlisted in the 14th
Battalion, Manchester Regiment on 30th November 1914. Promoted to lance corporal on 17th
February 1915, he then undertook a number of courses, and became an expert marksman and
signaller. He transferred to the Middlesex Regiment on 23rd July 1915. Promoted to corporal
four weeks later, he formed a signalling section for the battalion and was subsequently
transferred to the 23rd Battalion. He went to France on 16th March 1916.

His company quartermaster sergeant wrote: *Your son met his death like the gallant soldier he
was, working under a terrific heavy fire, and by his heroism and devotion to duty he encouraged his
men, and by his example prevented what might have been a serious state of affairs. He was most
popular with all ranks here, and his tactfulness, generosity, and, above all, unfailing cheerfulness and
comforting words will be remembered by all.*

He is commemorated on a stained glass window in St Peter's Church, Sark.

WALTER NORMAN BALDERSON

Private, F/130, 17th Battalion, Middlesex Regiment.

Died on 28th July 1916, aged 18, during the fighting at Delville Wood.

Walter was one of nine children of Alfred and Eleanor Elizabeth Balderson (née Clarke).

Employed at F. H. Benson Advertising, Kingsway, London, he enlisted in London and went to France in December 1915.

On 5th June 1915 while in camp in Dorking he wrote to an older sister: *We are in trouble down here. Spotted & Enteric Fever have broken out down here; the chap who had Spotted Fever died last night. Every morning from now onwards we have to be on parade at 5.15 in the morning & gargle our throats with Candys Fluid "vot a go" you should have heard the row this morning; it sounded like a ship sinking or water going down a sink.*

In a letter to a sister and her husband, dated 1st January 1916, he wrote: *As it's New Year day we have been given a day off and I've taken the opportunity of writing a letter to you. In the way of grub we are O.K. except we could do with a change from bacon. The place where we are stationed now when we first came here was under water and the streets resembled rivers of waterfalls. Up in the trenches the water comes past the knees but it's soon got out by pumps. When you are in them it reminds you of London; the names, if it wasn't for these you would never get out. The worst part of life in the trenches is the feet, through standing about and not keeping your feet warm you get frostbite and it's more terrible than shells, bombs or bullets.*

In a letter to his mother dated 24th June 1916, he wrote: *Just a few lines as I haven't much time to spare as the Boche needs a lot of attention… France is looking grand now all the trees and flowers are out, even the trenches don't look so grim… Our platoon officer went under, you remember me speaking about Mr Skerry don't you? He was an officer and a gentleman, our platoon caught it and many faces I shan't see again I'm sorry to say. Anyway, I came through without a scratch one thing to be grateful for…our general said "What was done was done grand" and we carried the raid out to a T. We captured the largest mine blown up on the British Front. Well dear, I must close now. Sorry to say can't tell you when I shall come home, still, keep smiling.*

In a letter to a sister dated 25th July 1916, he wrote: *Just a few lines to thank you for your letter… Things are going smoothly at present but there's plenty of noise. I'm glad Bobs is getting on alright, so he wants to hear about the Gerluns. We are hearing about them all the time. Tell Charlie to stick it, if they could only see what their shells are doing it would make them work harder… Please excuse this scribble as it's very uncomfortable and nothing to ly the paper on in a German dugout. Well dear I must close now nothing more to say so Goodbye.*

PIER 13

A

- King's Royal Rifle Corps - **Lance Corporal J. Farrington to Rifleman G. C. Young**
  (completed from Pier and Face 13B)
- Wiltshire Regiment
- Manchester Regiment - **Captain H. K. Birley to Second Lieutenant A. D. Walker**
  (continued on Pier and Face 14C)

B

- Middlesex Regiment - **Private P. A. England to Private P. H. Young**
  (completed from Pier and Face 12D)
- King's Royal Rifle Corps - **Lieutenant Colonel E. W. Benson to Lance Corporal J. A. Exall**
  (continued on Pier and Face 13A)

C

- 14th Bn. London Regiment (London Scottish) - **Private A. A. McKichan to Private A. Young**
  (completed from Pier and Face 9C)
- 15th Bn. London Regiment (Prince of Wales's Own Civil Service Rifles)
- 16th Bn. London Regiment (Queen's Westminster Rifles)
- 17th Bn. London Regiment (Poplar and Stepney Rifles)
- 18th Bn. London Regiment (London Irish Rifles)
- 19th Bn. London Regiment (St Pancras)
- 20th Bn. London Regiment (Blackheath and Woolwich)
- 21st Bn. London Regiment (First Surrey Rifles)
- 22nd Bn. London Regiment (The Queen's) - **Second Lieutenant W. G. Beaumont-Edmonds to Private A. A. Connell**
  (continued on Pier and Face 12C)

D

(Blank)

JOHN WILLIAM MARINER VC

Also known as WILLIAM WIGNALL

RIFLEMAN, A/2052, 2ND BATTALION, KING'S ROYAL RIFLE CORPS.

Died on 1st July 1916, aged 34, in the area south of Loos.

William was one of two children of Alice Ann Mariner, a cotton weaver. Alice later married John Wignall and lived in Lower Broughton, Manchester.

He was educated at the Parochial School, Chorley, Lancashire.

He enlisted in 1900 and served for seven years in South Africa and India. At one time he was the regimental lightweight wrestling champion. He was court martialled on two occasions - for striking an officer and threatening behaviour - resulting in long jail terms with hard labour.

Employed as a collier from 1909 to 1914, during which time he was on the Reserve; he also spent time in prison. On 26th August 1914, he re-enlisted and went to France on 29th November.

The award of the Victoria Cross was gazetted on 23rd June 1915: *During a violent thunderstorm on the night of 22nd May, 1915, he left his trench near Cambrin, and crept out through the German wire entanglements till he reached the emplacement of a German machine gun which had been damaging our parapets and hindering our working parties. After climbing on the top of the German parapet he threw a bomb in under the roof of the gun emplacement and heard some groaning and the enemy running away. After about a quarter of an hour he heard some of them coming back again, and climbed up on the other side of the emplacement and threw another bomb among them left-handed. He then lay still while the Germans opened a heavy fire on the wire entanglement behind him, and it was only after about an hour that he was able to crawl back to his own trench. Before starting out he had requested a sergeant to open fire on the enemy's trenches as soon as he had thrown his bombs. Rifleman Mariner was out alone for one and half hours carrying out this gallant work*

He was presented with the VC by HM King George V at Buckingham Palace on 12th August 1915. He was also presented with an illuminated address and a gold watch and chain by the people of Salford. Whilst on leave he was asked to assist with recruitment but then overstayed his leave by two days. He escaped with a caution when he wore his VC at the court appearance, the Magistrate concluded by saying, *Well, take care not to bring that Cross into court again in such circumstances.*

He returned to France on 12th October 1915.

SYDNEY FRANK MARLOW

Rifleman, R/30888, 1st Battalion, King's Royal Rifle Corps.

Died on 17th February 1917, aged 25.

Sydney was the youngest son, one of four children, of George Henry (a grocer) and Williamena Marlow (née Buston) of Mansfield, Nottinghamshire.

He was educated at Queen Elizabeth's Boys Grammar School, Mansfield; and was also a keen member of the Mansfield 1st Scout Troop.

Employed as a railway clerk, he served two years in the Mansfield Rifle Corps and four years in the 8th Battalion, Sherwood Foresters (Notts and Derby Regiment).

On 5th June 1914 Sydney followed his elder brother, Alfred, to Fiji and became a civil servant in Suva.

He was responsible for starting the Scouting Movement in Fiji in 1914. He also served in the Fiji Rifle Association and was a member of the 1st Fiji Reinforcement, Fiji Defence Forces.

In April 1916 he left Fiji as part of a group of European Volunteers bound for England. Following their arrival, he enlisted in the King's Royal Rifle Corps in London on 18th July and became a member of the regiment's Fijian Lewis gun team.

A member of the team wrote: *Marlow was hit on the head by shrapnel immediately before he went forward. He was opposite me when this occurred. We did what was possible, but had to leave him unconscious.* Later the same comrade wrote that Sydney *is now known to have been killed. His body has been found and buried. He must have died shortly after we left him and without recovering consciousness… We feel his loss as though we had lost a brother, for he was liked by one and all who knew him.*

In 1929 scouts from Fiji attended the World Jamboree which was held in Birkenhead. During their time in England they visited Mansfield and presented a Fijian flag to the Mansfield troop in Sydney's honour.

GERALD HOLT ROTHWELL

Rifleman, R/9693, 8th Battalion, King's Royal Rifle Corps.

Died on 15th September 1916, aged 24, during an attack towards Flers.

Gerald was one of ten children of Nathan (a confectioner and shopkeeper) and Betty Rothwell (née Holt) of Hebden Bridge, Yorkshire.

Educated at the Central School, Hebden Bridge, he then won a county minor scholarship to Heath Grammar School, Halifax. Deciding on a teaching career, he worked at Burnley Road, Mytholmroyd, as an uncertified assistant. He completed his education at University College, Reading, gaining the schoolmaster's certificate of proficiency. While there he was a member of the OTC. He was admitted as an Associate of University College Reading in 1913.

He then held a post at a school at Worsborough Dale, near Barnsley, but eventually he returned to the Central School about two or three years before the war. Latterly he had been responsible for an evening school as well as taking a part-time horticulture course at Leeds University.

He enlisted in Halifax in early 1915 and went to France on 29th December. He was an excellent shot and became a sniper.

His lieutenant wrote: *I was most awfully grieved and sorry to lose him, as he was one of my "snipers." If there was ever anything to be done, no matter what, he could always be relied upon to do it well. He was very brave, and liked by all his officers and comrades alike. Only a month ago he volunteered to stay up in the trenches for an extra time when I wanted to relieve him. He died quite painlessly, being hit by a small piece of shell during the battle of the 15th of this month. He was in the act of carrying up rations to his comrades. He fell and was buried just to the north of Delville wood. All the surrounding country is in our hands.*

His brother, **Clifford Holt Rothwell**, Gunner 149016, C Battery, 83rd Brigade, Royal Field Artillery, died on 10th August 1917, aged 23.

He is commemorated on the Menin Gate Memorial.

REGINALD 'REX' WILLIAM BIRD

LIEUTENANT, 1ST BATTALION, WILTSHIRE REGIMENT, ATTACHED
TO 7TH COMPANY, MACHINE GUN CORPS (INFANTRY).

Died on 24th August 1916, aged 23, during fighting near
Thiepval.

Reginald was one of six children of William Frederick (an
architect and surveyor) and Florence Emily Bird (née
Stratup) of Midsomer Norton, Somerset.

Educated at Wycliffe School, he excelled both
academically and as a sportsman. He was Head of School in
his last year and also passed the Junior and Senior Cambridge examinations with honours and
many distinctions. He was first in England in each examination in different subjects. Leaving
school, he entered his father's office and showed promise of becoming an architect of
exceptional ability. In his leisure time he helped to start a scout troop for local boys.

Just after the start of the war he enlisted as a private in the 12th Gloucesters and, in the
autumn, he was commissioned in the 1st Wiltshires. He went to France in May 1915. He wrote
the following after returning from five days' leave: *The country itself had altered since I saw it last.
The village was absolutely razed to the ground, except for the remains of two walls in the chateau. A
few piles of bricks were the only evidence that it had existed. It was with difficulty that I traced our
old trenches. The long grass which had grown up between our trenches in old time had been completely
swept away, and in the Hun line the ground had been everywhere disturbed by shells, in many parts
literally pulverised for a depth of several feet, and remained a place of strange confusion.* He was
slightly wounded during fighting around Ypres in September, but was back in the firing line
after a few weeks.

A comrade wrote that: *just after he had his lunch he was so very quiet. I asked him if he was
not well... He said, 'I am quite well, Chalk, but there is something. I do not know what it is.' How he
worked that terrible day! If any man ever earned the V.C., he did! At ten minutes past midnight he
had just wished me good-night and told me to get some sleep, when a shrapnel shell came over and a
piece struck him in the right temple. He was buried in the old German trench, formerly known as the
Leipzig Salient, half a mile south of Thiepval village. His former C.O.* in the 1st Wilts. and many
others^ lie close beside him...none can ask for finer company in death.*

*Lieutenant Colonel Walter Sidney Brown's body was recovered later and he now lies in
Blighty Valley Cemetery. It was reported that the Colonel had, in his pocket, a written
recommendation for Rex for the DSO.

^One of those was **John Allen Rutherford**, Captain, Machine Gun Corps, who is
commemorated on Pier and Face 12C. His story appeared earlier.

17TH MIDDLESEX REGIMENT (THE FOOTBALLERS' BATTALION)

There are a number of professional and amateur footballers commemorated on the Memorial. These two were members of the 17th Middlesex and are commemorated on Pier and Face 13B.

WILLIAM WEBBER WALTER 'BILLY' GERRISH

PRIVATE, F/936.

Died on 8th August 1916, aged 27, during the fighting at Guillemont.

William was one of twelve children of Wesley Charles (a timber salesman) and Annie Florence Gerrish (née Webber) of Bristol.

During his career he played football for Bristol Rovers, Aston Villa (where he was signed for £200), Preston North End and Chesterfield. In the three seasons 1909 to 1912 he made a total of fifty eight League and Cup appearances, scoring a total of eighteen goals.

He enlisted in Bristol on 25th February 1915 and went to France on 17th November. Whilst in hospital in 1915, recovering from an operation, he gave some of his blood to save the life of another patient.

WILLIAM JONAS

PRIVATE, F/32.

Died on 27th July 1916, aged 26, during the fighting at Delville Wood.

William was one of at least seven children of William James and Elizabeth Jonas. He married Mary Jane Anderson in 1911 and worked in coal mining before becoming a professional footballer.

He played for Jarrow Croft, Havannah Rovers and then Clapton Orient. Whilst at the latter he was particularly popular with the female supporters and received regular fan mail. In one of the match programmes he said he was flattered by the attention but could they please stop as he was happily married to his sweetheart!

Just before he was killed he had spoken to another Orient player (who was killed three months later) saying, *Best of luck, special love to my sweetheart Mary Jane and best regards to the lads at Orient.*

ALFRED RIEU

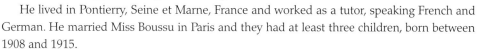

PRIVATE, PS/2260, 16TH BATTALION, MIDDLESEX REGIMENT.

Died on 1st July 1916, aged 37, during the fighting at
Beaumont Hamel.

Alfred was the youngest of at least five children of Dr
Charles Pierre Henri Rieu and his first wife. Dr Rieu was
keeper of Oriental Manuscripts at the British Museum and
Professor of Arabic and Persian at Cambridge University.

He was educated at Mill Hill, University College School
and Christ's College, Cambridge where he graduated BA.

He lived in Pontierry, Seine et Marne, France and worked as a tutor, speaking French and
German. He married Miss Boussu in Paris and they had at least three children, born between
1908 and 1915.

In August 1914 he was too old to enlist in the British Army, so he and his brother Charles
joined the French Foreign Legion. They came to England with other members of the Legion in
1915. Given their lack of military experience, they declined commissions.

Enlisting in Southampton on 3rd February 1915 into the Army Service Corps, they
transferred to the 16th Battalion, Middlesex Regiment, in which their brother Henry was
already serving, on 19th May. All three went to France on 17th November.

Henry Rieu, Private 512, died on 30th January 1916, aged 39.
He is buried in grave L20 in Cambrin Churchyard Extension.

Charles Rieu, Private PS/2261, died on 13th September 1917,
aged 42.
He is buried in grave III.F.20 in Hazebrouck Communal
Cemetery.

ERIC WILLIAM BENSON MC

LIEUTENANT COLONEL, 9TH BATTALION, KING'S ROYAL RIFLE CORPS.

Died on 15th September 1916, aged 29, during the fighting at Gueudecourt.

Eric was the eldest of two children, the only son, of Sir Frank and Lady Constance Gertrude Benson (née Featherstonhaugh) who together ran a touring company and acting school specialising in Shakespearian productions. He was educated at Lee's School, Forest Row, Sussex and then Winchester. After school he served for a time in the Jersey Militia before transferring, with a commission, to the Cheshire Regiment. He spent four years in India, during which time he captained the regimental hockey team that won the Calcutta Cup at Bombay.

He retired from the Army just before the war broke out; in August 1914 he was transferred to the King's Royal Rifle Corps in the rank of captain. On 30th July 1915 he was severely wounded in the head during the fighting at Hooge. He was promoted to major in January 1916 and a few months later, at the then early age of 29, he was promoted to lieutenant colonel. He was mentioned in despatches by Sir Douglas Haig and awarded the Military Cross for *distinguished and gallant service in the Field.*

Whilst home on a short leave he married Muriel Taylor on 17th June 1916, returning to his regiment the following day.

On the day he died he had defied his doctors and left hospital during treatment for an injured ankle and then insisted on hobbling along before his advancing regiment. The exact circumstances surrounding his death are slightly confused, but appear to be the result of bullet wounds to his legs, which severed the arteries. His reported last words were: *I don't mind. I'm only sorry for my people. Give them my love.*

The Medical Officer wrote: *How much I owe personally to his charm, his kindness, his leadership his thoroughness, and his high standard in everything - a standard he set to none more rigorously than himself ! His grave lies in the path of the advance, about three-quarters of a mile in front of Delville Wood. That little corner will be 'for ever England'.*

After Eric's death his father, who was too old to enlist, drove ambulances for the French Red Cross, whilst his mother opened a canteen for French troops coming out of battle. In 1918 his father was awarded the French Croix de Guerre in recognition of his bravery in driving his ambulance through heavy enemy shelling.

A window in the Royal Shakespeare Theatre, Stratford-upon-Avon, commemorates ten members of the Benson Dramatic Company who died in the war.

STEPHEN RALPH PERRY

LIEUTENANT, 12TH BATTALION, KING'S ROYAL RIFLE CORPS.

Died on 18th September 1916, aged 23, during the fighting at Ginchy.

Stephen was the youngest of three children, all sons, of the Rev. Samuel Edgar and Ellen Sarah Perry (née Banks) of Lowestoft, Suffolk.

After preparatory school, he went to Tonbridge School where he was a lance corporal in the OTC in his last term. He was apprenticed to an engineering company, although his plan was to become a tea planter in India. He had just completed his apprenticeship when war broke out.

He immediately enlisted in the Honourable Artillery Company and went to France with the 1st Battalion on 23rd January 1915. After six months he volunteered for the stretcher bearer section. When he left them to take up his commission he received a letter from the Medical Officer of the battalion: *To my knowledge no one in the Section has done a larger or more willing share of difficult work than yourself. Personally I have placed absolute confidence in your excellent judgment and long experience of the conditions of trench warfare. For these and for personal reasons I much regret your loss in the Section.*

He was gazetted on 16th January 1916 and promoted to lieutenant on 1st December. In one of his last letters he wrote about the capture of Guillemont: *It is what our war correspondents are pleased to describe as Inferno of 'Hell let loose.' I must say I thought I had seen the worst of the War, but I didn't conceive anything could be so awful as this. To make it worse it rained solid the whole time, and we couldn't get food or water up for two days... I have hardly had a wink of sleep for eight days.*

An officer wrote: *They were being counter-attacked, and the enemy got a footing in a small portion of the trench. Stephen immediately took his men over the parapet, and turned them out. He was killed while on top of the parapet, directing operations.*

The adjutant wrote: *He was perfectly splendid and absolutely regardless of his own personal safety, running about in the open and organising his Company.*

His servant wrote: *I bandaged Mr. Perry; brought him a stretcher, but I could see he would not last long - he had a wound in the back and one in the abdomen. His last words were, 'Do the boys love me?' The boys thought very well of him. A better officer we couldn't have had; his heart and soul were in the Company.*

He was buried by the chaplain at a spot about a half mile south-west of Morval. A cross inscribed with his name was erected; but the grave was subsequently lost.

CHARLES BERTRAM STALLEY

Private, 2812, 1st/15th Battalion, London Regiment
(Prince of Wales's Own Civil Service Rifles).

Died on 15th September 1916, aged 32, during an attack
on High Wood.

Charles was one of at least six children of Alfred (a builder's
foreman) and Sarah Stalley (née Hardy) of Romford, Essex.

He was employed by the Great Eastern Railway for
eighteen years and was a clerk in the Chief Traffic Manager's
Ledger Accounts Office when he enlisted at Somerset
House, London in September 1914. He went to France on 17th March 1915.

Whilst on active service his letters and sketches were published in the staff magazine. This
particular sketch of the interior of a dugout was used as the cover for the December 1915 issue.

The August 1916 issue included one of his anecdotes:
*I've seen a few ruined towns but none to equal this - its
desolation struck me more forcibly than ever. Picture those
marches to the trenches… We do not look like the smart
soldiers you see at home. We move off in fours, and as we
approach the fighting zone drop to two deep, later to single
file. No smoking, no talking. By the time we approach the
trenches we are fatigued. About the only word one hears is
'hole' as a man warns the one following of a shell hole, or
perhaps a swear from the latter because he has received the
warning too late… The roads were full of planks, bricks,
puddles and shell holes… I plodded along in deep thought
when I noticed a strong smell of pickles - the pickle bottle in
my sack was leaking… Whilst we halted I fished out the
offending article; the cork had become loose. There was still*

INTERIOR OF A DUG-OUT IN FRANCE.
(Drawn by Pte. C. B. Stalley, Chief Traffic Manager's Office, Great Eastern Railway.)

*a half-bottle left. The man next to me offered to carry it. A pity to waste it – very nice with cold meat.
He carried it until we jumped into the trench when it slipped out of his hand. No pickles.*

The staff magazine in November 1916 included the following: *His loss will be regretted by all
who knew him, owing to his genial personality. He took an active part in sports, particularly
distinguishing himself in cricket and football matches which have taken place from time to time
between the staff of the Chief Offices at Liverpool Street. He was also an artist of some
accomplishment.*

CHARLES DAVID WALLER

RIFLEMAN, 550444 (2327), 1ST/16TH BATTALION, LONDON REGIMENT (QUEEN'S WESTMINSTER RIFLES).

Died on 1st July 1916, aged 22, during the fighting at Gommecourt.

Charles was the only son, one of seven children, of David (a builder and decorator) and Anna Alice Waller (née Stovell) of Croydon, Surrey.

He was educated at Whitgift School, where he earned Senior House colours at football and was a private in the OTC.

Having worked as a master builder for his father's firm, he enlisted in the 16th Battalion on 28th August 1914 and went to France on 19th February 1915.

Hospitalised in April 1915, he returned to England the following month. A keen motorcyclist, he felt the weight of the law during his convalescence when he was fined £1 for exceeding the 20mph speed limit. He returned to France on 24th May 1916 and rejoined the battalion two weeks later.

He was recommended for a commission.

His adjutant wrote: *I regret that I cannot give you any definite information of your son. He was seen to be hit, but if wounded or killed I cannot find out. I can only hope that he is a prisoner in the hands of the enemy and that you have good news of him before this. If such is the case I should be very glad of a line, as there are many friends here who will be glad to hear that all is well with him. Sorry I cannot give you anything further in spite of the exhaustive inquiries that were made from the few that did return to the Battn.*

In August 1917, the British Red Cross wrote: *Now that over a year has passed without news, notwithstanding our diligent enquiries at home and abroad we fear that the soldiers of the 16th Londons who were missing in the attack of July 1st 1916 cannot have survived. This was as you know the first day of the great offensive on the Somme front and the battle was everywhere very violent... In the stress of the incessant fighting, men had little opportunity of noticing the movements of their comrades. After questioning every reliable witness whom we could find, we have reluctantly had to give up all hope of hearing anything of your son's fate, though we never cease to watch the Prisoners Lists from Germany for the names of all the missing.*

PHILIP CHARLES HOSMER

Private, 5870, 1st/19th Battalion, London Regiment (St Pancras).

Died on 15th September 1916, aged 19, during the fighting at High Wood.

Philip was the youngest of four children of Philip (a railway platelayer) and Ellen Hosmer (née Mobbs) of Aylesford, Kent.

Educated at the Council School, Aylesford; afterwards he became a postman.

He was awarded a Certificate of Honour from the Royal Humane Society for rescuing three people from drowning on 21st August 1914. The local newspaper reported: *Dr Palm, who was present, told an interesting story. He said on that day he was urgently called to Millhall to render aid to several persons who had been nearly drowned. A little girl, aged 9 had accidentally got into deep water in a stream adjoining the Medway. A young woman, aged 20, immediately endeavoured to rescue the child, but was soon in difficulties herself. The mother of the little girl then assisted, and she was soon dragged under. Hosmer, without a moment's hesitation, dived in and first got the child out, and next the young woman. Then, after two dives, he found the mother under the water, and was successful in bringing her ashore. He immediately set to work and applied artificial respiration, which proved successful… The Vicar, the Rev T. K. Sopwith, then presented the certificate to Hosmer, and congratulated him on his gallant act…The recipient acknowledged the gift, and in very appropriate words thanked the Vicar and Dr Palm for the kind words spoken, and the ladies and gentlemen present, together with the teachers and scholars of the school, for the hearty feeling shown. – The boys gave three hearty cheers in honour of their old school-mate.*

Later Philip worked for a wholesale clothier and draper in London. He enlisted at St Paul's Churchyard on 1st February 1916. He went to France on 15th June, where he was a member of the Lewis gun section.

His officer wrote: *I am very sorry to have to inform you that your son was killed in action on September 15th… He was killed instantaneously, by the same shell which killed the Lewis Gun Sergeant and several others of the team. We all much regret his loss, as during the time he had been with us he had done good work and made himself liked by all. He is buried with many of his comrades near High Wood. I am afraid it is poor consolation to you to say that he died a true soldier's death, fighting for his King and country, and for all that we hold best.*

GILBERT HALFORD SHEAF

LANCE CORPORAL, 3045, 1ST/21ST BATTALION, LONDON
REGIMENT (FIRST SURREY RIFLES).

Died on 15th September 1916, aged 32, during the
fighting at High Wood.

Gilbert was one of eleven children of Halford and his first
wife Elizabeth Rebecca Sheaf (née Asman) of Shipston-on-
Stour, Worcestershire.

Employed as a mechanical draughtsman, he enlisted in
Camberwell, Surrey.

In November 1915 he wrote to his brother in law (Bert Starbuck): *Many thanks for your letter
and also for the cigarettes which came just at the right moment to keep me from running dry. We had
a very rough time in the trenches during our last stay… I am very pleased to be out of this muck again
as I got very sick of all the red tape etc. We are in a very decent billet now which we reached by
travelling a part of the way by train as they thought most of the fellows too tired to march all the way.
This is the first train ride I have had since our original journey of 20 miles when we first landed… A
lot of our fellows go for leave each week now, but I am afraid it will be a long time before I get my 5
or 6 days. They sent me to attend some lectures and demonstrations at the Engineers out here for
making modern trenches and repairing existing ones so expect I shall have to lecture to the rest of the
company upon what I have seen and heard… Please excuse the bad writing as I am doing it on my
knee on the floor with cold hands.*

The chaplain of the 1st/22nd Battalion (who was killed in July 1917) wrote: *It fell to my lot
to bury your son Lance Corporal G. H. Sheaf after the action which took place near High Wood. He
was buried with many others of his Battalion who fell at the same time among the trenches in front
of High Wood and the place is marked with his name, rank and date of death. We did all we could for
our fallen brothers who died so gloriously but you will understand that the difficulties are great, when
the ground is being fought over and has only just come into our hands. His Company Commander
Captain Heppell was killed at the same time leading his men in to the attack. It was we are proud to
think owing to the valour of our London Regiments and your son's sacrifice among others, that the
High Wood was taken and held, for us a position of extreme importance and value in the Somme
region.*

PIER 14

A
• York and Lancaster Regiment - **Private E. Keddy to Private C. York**   *(completed from Pier and Face 14B)*   • Durham Light Infantry - **Captain A. H. P. Austin to Private S. Wilson**   *(continued on Pier and Face 15C)*

B
• North Staffordshire Regiment - **Second Lieutenant W. G. Fletcher to Private A. H. Youngs**   *(completed from Pier and Face 14C)*   • York and Lancaster Regiment - **Lieutenant Colonel R. P. Wood to Private C. J. Judd**   *(continued on Pier and Face 14A)*

C
• Manchester Regiment - **Second Lieutenant H. Wilks to Private R. Young 25634**   *(completed from Pier and Face 13A)*   • North Staffordshire Regiment - **Major J. Carnegy to Second Lieutenant C. T. Eaddy**   *(continued on Pier and Face 14B)*

D
(Blank)

WILLIAM BRAIDFORD

SECOND LIEUTENANT, 19TH BATTALION, DURHAM LIGHT
INFANTRY.

Died on 24th July 1916, aged 22, near Longueval.

William was one of nine children of William (a mining engineer) and Laura Emma Braidford (née Garbett) of Rowlands Gill, Co. Durham.

He was educated at St Bees School and was a prominent member of its rugby team for three seasons.

Afterwards he continued to play rugby for the Tynedale Club, Durham University and Durham County. He continued his studies at Newcastle-upon-Tyne, with a view to becoming a mining engineer and had nearly completed his course when the war broke out.

He married Beatrice Myra Lax in 1913 and they had one son, born in 1914.

Initially he enlisted in a Public Schools Battalion and afterwards was granted a commission in the Durham Light Infantry. He went to France on 29th May 1916.

On 10th June 1916 he had written to his sister: *At present I am at a farm not far behind the firing line and have been up once at night. There was a lot of shooting going on but we had no casualties. Our artillery was peppering away at the Huns and gave them a hot time. Its very funny that I am in the same place as Frank and Percy* were. It is quite a nice little place and has not suffered much from shellfire. You would be surprised at the thousands of birds here which whistle all day long in spite of the guns roaring nearly all day.*

On the day he was killed his company were ordered to dig themselves in and whilst superintending this he was buried by a shell. When his body was recovered it was found that his head had been entirely shattered by the explosion.

The **Tynedale Rugby Football Club's Roll of Honour** commemorates forty nine members who fell during the war. William and three others are commemorated on the Memorial. The stories of two of those, **William Richard Thew** [1A] and **John Wilfred Robinson** [12B], appeared earlier.

*These two brothers also served in the DLI. The eldest, **Frank Garbett Braidford**, survived the war. The younger, **Percy Braidford MC**, Second Lieutenant, 3rd Battalion, died on 21st September 1917, aged 22, and is commemorated on the Tyne Cot Memorial.

ARTHUR SELWYN MORLEY MC

SECOND LIEUTENANT, 15TH BATTALION, DURHAM LIGHT INFANTRY.

Died on 16th September 1916, aged 26, in the fighting near Gueudecourt.

Arthur was one of nine children of William (a sanitary inspector) and Hannah Morley (née Moore) of Houghton-le-Spring, Co. Durham.

Educated at Royal Kepier Grammar School, he was involved in long distance running and rugby. He then worked in a solicitors' office in Houghton-le-Spring before taking up a position at the National Insurance Commission in Glasgow.

He married Mary Crake Wilson on 13th January 1916.

He initially enlisted as a private in the Durham Light Infantry, was quickly promoted to sergeant and on 4th April 1915 was commissioned in the Manchester Regiment. Later he transferred back to the DLI and went to France on 10th February 1916.

On one occasion whilst bathing in the river Somme, he got entangled amongst some weeds and was rescued by a soldier, a strong swimmer, who dived into eight feet of water and brought him to the surface. Very much to Arthur's regret this same soldier (a Bishop Auckland man) who saved his life was killed in action the following week.

After the attack on 1st July he wrote to his parents: *The charge over 1,200 yards of ground was the most magnificent sight I have seen, and I shall never forget nor cease to marvel that human beings are capable of such calm resolution... I am thankful I was able to keep a clear head to lead my brave men, who were simply splendid, and never turned a hair during the three days of action. The North Countrymen were too good for even the famous Prussians, who whined for mercy after shooting us down with hellish machine-gun fire to the moment we reached them. Shelter Wood and Crucifix trench were hard, but we (and no one else) took them. I was slightly wounded in the knee by a blow from an almost spent shrapnel, and several bullets ripped my tunic, but am A1. My friend Lieut. Martin, was treacherously shot through the neck by a wounded German, whom he passed but then turned and slew. The Huns deserved no mercy for treachery like that... We marched from the battlefield singing "Keep the home fires burning," and every man had a German Spiked helmet or other trophy.*

The award of the Military Cross was gazetted on 25th August 1916: *For conspicuous gallantry in action. He took command of his company when the senior officers became casualties, led several attacks on enemy position, and behaved with great coolness and courage until the battalion was relieved.*

JOHN CARR

LANCE SERGEANT, 18/246, 18TH BATTALION, DURHAM LIGHT INFANTRY.

Died on 1st July 1916, aged 23, during an attack on Serre.

John was one of five children of John Thomas (a tailor and postmaster) and Mary Jane Carr (née Rumney) of Cowshill, Co. Durham.

Educated at Wearhead School and Wolsingham Grammar School, he then served his time at Wolsingham Steelworks before taking up a position with a company in Nenthead, Cumberland. He enlisted in Spennymoor, Co. Durham in September 1914. He was serving in Hartlepool, Co. Durham, when German warships bombarded the town on 16th December 1914 leaving 102 people dead (including nine soldiers, seven sailors and fifteen children) and 467 wounded.

He went to Egypt on 22nd December 1915 and France in mid March 1916. During his time on active service, his experiences were a regular feature in the local newspaper, featuring as the *Diary of a Weardale Soldier*. In April 1916 he wrote: *…before we arrived at the communication trench the rain had begun to fall, and continued to fall until the third day of our stay… Our work consisted chiefly in carrying provisions from the rear up to the front line, and journeys had to be made down an extremely long communication trench… Now in fine weather this would have been all right, for it is quite pleasant walking along a nice evenly-boarded trench. But when the average height of the water is well over the ankles, and there are innumerable sump-holes into which one goes up to the waist (the covers having become loose and floated away), then you can imagine that things are decidedly unpleasant, to say the least. We were provided with high waders which effectively kept out the water so long as one did not drop into a sump-hole. But on getting into one of these holes the waders became full of water, and you can more easily imagine the situation than I can describe it when the waders became full of water… I cannot withhold my sympathy and admiration for the courageous men who passed the winter months under conditions which must have been ten times worse than the few unpleasant days that we have just had.*

Two local comrades wrote: *Jack was killed when leading his section to the charge. He was liked by all. He was so cheerful, and none mourn his loss more than we do, who knew him so well.*

The quartermaster wrote: *Jack was noted for daring and coolness, and his men had the utmost confidence in him. He was afraid of nothing, and died advancing with his face to the foe. He was one of my best men, and had just acquired his third stripe. He was admired by officers and men, and was always conscientious in his work. He never grumbled and was ever ready to volunteer for the most dangerous jobs. If Jack were in charge volunteers were always ready.*

EDWARD HOPE DCM

Private, 21266, 15th Battalion, Durham Light Infantry.

Died on 1st July 1916, aged 17 years and four months, shot by a sniper during fighting in the Fricourt area.

Edward was born on 28th February 1899, one of ten children of Thomas (a coal miner) and Mary Jane Hope (née Harris) of Pelton Fell, Co. Durham.

He was educated at the Council School, Pelton Fell and enlisted in Chester-le-Street, Co. Durham on 2nd November 1914 when only 15. He went to France on 9th October 1915 and worked as a signaller.

He was a member of the Sunday School of the Primitive Methodist Church in Pelton Fell. The school sent him a copy of the Bible and he wrote: *I thank you from the bottom of my heart. I am a regular goer to the Chapel here. I was showing one of the teachers here and they say it is splendid and very thoughtful of you. I shan't forget the good advice you have put in your letter, and will try my best to do it. I have so far succeeded from being tempted to drink and gamble and I hope I shall do so all the rest of my life.*

The award of the Distinguished Conduct Medal was gazetted on 15th March 1916 in respect of an action in January 1916: *For conspicuous gallantry. During an intense and prolonged bombardment by the enemy, Privates Coates and Hope remained in their Signal Station maintaining communication. They repaired wires under heavy fire, and finally, when their Station was demolished by shells and aerial torpedoes, they took turns in carrying message over 150 yards of open ground to the Company Commander.*

To celebrate the award, over £30 was subscribed in his neighbourhood, and a gold watch valued at £25 was purchased for presentation to him. His old school bought a wrist watch to give him and hung his portrait in one of the schoolrooms. He was unable to obtain leave to receive the presents.

In a letter home on the eve of the attack he wrote: *I received your ever-welcome parcel this morning and was ever so pleased to receive it this morning, because if it had been a day late - well I might never have got it, as we are in for it now… A chap has only to die once.*

A comrade wrote: *Not a day goes by but we are talking of him… For he was the youngest in the Battalion.*

Unaware of his son's death, his father wrote to the Infantry Records Office on 4th July 1916, enclosing a copy of Edward's birth certificate, as *an application for his relegation to the Army Reserve as he is under age for foreign service.*

HORACE BIRCHALL JONES

SECOND LIEUTENANT, 1ST/6TH BATTALION, NORTH
STAFFORDSHIRE REGIMENT.

Died on 1st July 1916, aged 24, leading his men in action
near Gommecourt.

Horace was one of three children of William Thomas (a
draper) and Clara Elizabeth Jones (née Chambers) of Arden
Vale, Olton, Warwickshire.

He was educated at Wellesbourne School and Wycliffe
College. After leaving school he went to gain business
experience in Liverpool and London, and a few years later he became a junior member in his
father's firm of Messrs. W. T. Jones & Co. in Birmingham.

He was a good boxer and swimmer, an enthusiastic motorcyclist (he raced as an amateur
at Brooklands) and a breeder of prize poultry on a large scale.

About one month after war was declared he was offered, from the Birmingham University
OTC, a commission in the South Wales Borderers. He refused and, with several of his friends,
enlisted in the 1st Birmingham City Battalion as Private 14/175, 14th Battalion, Royal
Warwickshire Regiment. His commission in the North Staffordshire Regiment was gazetted on
22nd September 1914.

In his last letter he wrote: *I am not writing to you individually because it is too hard. I am
leaving this behind to be posted in the event of my not being here to write or see you again. A big attack
is coming off - in fact we are on the eve of it - and they have honoured me by selecting me and my
platoon to lead the attack so far as my Company is concerned. I have a grand lot of boys and am
certain we shall succeed - nothing will stop us - but of course we must pay the price of victory, and
many of us will not answer the roll. I do not want you to think that I am going in with a faint heart
- on the other hand, I go in with every confidence, but realising that I may fall, and cannot do so
without expressing my gratitude to you all, I write this. I thank you all from the bottom of my heart
for the wonderful kindness and love you have always shown towards me. I hope I may come back to
you all again, but if God wills that I shall not, my last prayer is with you all.*

His major wrote: *From statements of men who saw him I fear that there can be little doubt that
he died fighting hard on July 1st. He is missing, so that there is a chance that he is wounded and a
prisoner, but I can hold out little hope… Your son was a wonderfully good soldier, who did not know
what fear was, and his loss is a heavy blow to the regiment. He was so popular with everybody, always
cheery and in good spirits. Many of his comrades have, alas, gone with him.*

AUGUSTUS ANDREW DENYER MC

SECOND LIEUTENANT, 9TH BATTALION, YORK AND LANCASTER REGIMENT.

Died on 7th June 1917, aged 38.

Augustus was one of at least three children of Andrew (a grocer) and Fanny Helena Denyer (née Smith) of Southsea, Hampshire.

He married Edith Florence Feest in 1906 and they lived in Worthing, Sussex. They had a son (born 1907) and a daughter (born 1910).

He was also a grocer and enlisted as Private 2935, Royal Sussex Regiment in 1914, subsequently being commissioned and joining the York and Lancs.

On 21st March 1917 he had written this letter to his wife with the instruction, *Please forward if I am killed.*

> *My Darling Edie,*
>
> *I am writing these few lines to you as I go to my regiment in the line.*
>
> *Not knowing what may be before me, though I have prayed that I may be restored again to you I feel I should like to write a few lines to let you know my thoughts are of you and the little ones.*
>
> *Should the worst happen dearest, be brave and try to see it was for the best, kiss the little ones for me and tell them that my last wish was that they should always look after you.*
>
> *As for you dearest, you have been a better wife to me than I could have ever hoped or deserved, your love so true has been my greatest comfort during these trying times and I know it has been a comfort to you to know that my love for you has been no less, no two have spent a happier 10 years than we.*
>
> *Let these thoughts dearest strengthen and comfort you in the future.*
>
> *May God protect you and the little ones.*
>
> *With fondest love*
> *From Your ever loving*
> *Gus*

The award of the Military Cross was gazetted on 26th May 1917: *For conspicuous gallantry and devotion to duty. In spite of being subjected to the most intense hostile bombardment, he maintained his position, and throughout set a splendid example to his men.*

PHILIP KENNETH PERKIN

SECOND LIEUTENANT, 12TH BATTALION, YORK AND
LANCASTER REGIMENT.

Died on 1st July 1916, aged 22, during the fighting at
Serre.

Philip was one of three children of Emil Scales Perkin (a
headmaster of a technical science and art college) and Isabell
Lillian Perkin (née Bebb) of Oxford.

Educated at Blundell's School as a day boy, he afterwards
studied in France.

Although about to take up an important post in the firm of Huttons of Sheffield, he
enlisted as Private 213, 12th Battalion, York and Lancaster Regiment. He gained his
commission on 14th September 1915.

On the day he died he was in command of the first wave of his battalion. Although
wounded twice, he continued to advance until he was unable to carry on.

A private wrote: *…he was well out in front of his men and was using his revolver and shouting
encouragement to them and at the same time trying to work his way through the wire when a hand
bomb burst close to him. He reeled and half fell but most pluckily pulled himself together for another
effort but another bomb burst which brought him down. Immediately afterwards another bomb
exploded which took two pieces out of my leg and peppered me generally and I know nothing beyond
this.*

The commanding officer wrote: *The report that your son was wounded was from one of our own
wounded who crawled back later, the only hope is that he was taken prisoner but I pray that you do
not put too much reliance on this. A few of our men got to the enemy's third line but as the enemy, to
his eternal disgrace, shot our wounded as they lay in the open. I fear the worst for all our missing.*

The chaplain wrote: *I think that there is little doubt that your brave young son was killed… So
much is said of our brave soldiers that some of the force may be lost when applied to individuals. His
calmness and coolness were unique… His confidence and courage were infectious and you cannot
realise what a blessing this is to others in this difficult time out here. He was last seen sitting on the
German line calling his men on. Many of our wounded told me with admiration what he was doing
and that he was shot in the head by a machine gun. We are all very sad about it. I cannot tell you
officially that he was killed, we do not know, but that is the general opinion, his men saw him fall and
spoke of him with pride.*

ALEXANDER ROBERTSON

CORPORAL, 12/220, 12TH BATTALION, YORK AND LANCASTER REGIMENT.

Died on 1st July 1916, aged 34, during the fighting at Serre.

Alexander was one of at least three children of Robert (a headmaster) and his first wife Maggie Russell Robertson (née Niven) of Edinburgh.

Educated at George Watson's College from 1890 and later at Edinburgh University where he gained an MA in History and won medals in Latin, Education and Political Economy.

For three years he was senior master in History at George Watson's College and then in Caen, France, where he also attended the university. From there he spent three years at New College, Oxford gaining a BLitt in 1913.

The following year he became a lecturer in History at Sheffield University and he enlisted in Sheffield on 11th September 1914. He was promoted to lance corporal (unpaid) on 10th November 1915, (paid) on 28th May 1916 and to acting corporal on 29th June.

Serving in Egypt from 1st June 1915 to 10th March 1916, he was hospitalised with fever in Marseille on 16th March 1916, only rejoining his battalion on 31st May.

He was the author of *Life of Sir Robert Moray*, a book of his own poems, *Comrades*, published in May 1916 and *Last Poems*, published posthumously in 1918.

Alexander is at the left of this picture, which was taken during training.

The others are (left to right) **H. E. Bailey**, **William Wyatt Bagshawe** and **Edward Stanley Curwen**.

William and Edward were also

posted missing on 1st July 1916 (aged 24 and 37 respectively) and are commemorated with Alexander on Pier and Face 14B. H. E. Bailey is understood to have survived the war.

THOMAS BROADBENT

Sergeant, 6960, 16th Battalion, Manchester Regiment.

Died on 9th July 1916, aged 23, during the fighting at Trônes Wood.

Thomas was the eldest of four children of John (a building surveyor) and Annie Broadbent (née Dunnicliff) of Altrincham, Cheshire.

Educated at the British Schools, Altrincham and Lymm Grammar School, he later went to the Manchester School of Technology.

Employed as an engineer at Crossley's Ltd, Openshaw, Manchester, he enlisted in Manchester on 3rd September 1914 and went to France on 8th November 1915. During his time in the Army he was a regular letter writer as well as keeping a diary that he started on 30th October 1915. He also collected many photographs of his army life.

In his last letter written to his sister on 4th July 1916, Thomas highlighted the success of their attack on the village of Montauban on 1st July: *All this time we were under heavy machine gun fire from the left which caused our fellows to drop like flies. On nearing the village the Germans seemed to lose heart and retire. We rushed right through the village and got to the other side cutting off a large number of Germans including the General staff of the brigade… The divisional and brigade Generals can't praise us enough as we are the first division which has done what we set out to do, that is to take the line. It seems a miracle that any of us returned as it was absolutely an inferno… Of course everyone now is in the best of spirits knowing that the way is open to Berlin? And fresh troops are carrying on. The Allemandes have had enough in my opinion now and the end is in sight… I have got a lovely German helmet with a huge bright silver plated badge about 6 inches wide with an eagle with outspread wings and a spike on top. While there we ran very short of water but found a large amount of German Perrier water and jolly good it was. Also most of us got a clean change of underclothing German this time…Captain Johnson* our company captain from Altrincham was shot through the head and killed during the counter-attack.*

William Morton Johnson, Captain, died on 2nd July 1916, aged 34. He is commemorated on Pier and Face 13A.

ADELPHI LADS' CLUB ROLL OF HONOUR

The Club, based in Salford, Lancashire, recorded 1,080 members who served during the war. Of those 203 were killed, at least twenty four of whom are commemorated on the Memorial.

These thirteen served in the Manchester Regiment and died during the fighting in July 1916. They are commemorated on Pier and Face 14C.

John W. Anderton	**Alfred Hunt**	**Arthur Williams**	**Thomas Barnett**
Corporal	Corporal	Corporal	Lance Corporal
7th July, 30	30th July, 29	23rd July, 21	10th July, 29

George W. Smith	**Harold Baume**	**John Dickens**	**Leonard V. Hind**
Lance Corporal	Private	Private	Private
1st July, 23	1st July, 23	14th July, 31	1st July, 23

William Litherland	**William T. Naylor**	**Arthur Prince**	**Ernest Royle**	**Reuben Schofield**
Private	Private	Private	Private	Private
9th July, 26	30th July, 27	1st July, 32	9th July, 21	1st July, 22

UTTLEY STANSFIELD

PRIVATE, 20953, 22ND BATTALION, MANCHESTER REGIMENT.

Died on 1st July 1916, aged 21, during an attack on Mametz.

Uttley was the youngest of four children of Joseph (a weaver) and Susannah Stansfield (née Sutcliffe) of Todmorden, Yorkshire.

He was employed at the Strand Drapery Department, Todmorden Co-op and also the Failsworth Co-op Society. A member of the Cross Stone Church choir, he was also connected with the Sunday School. He enlisted in Manchester in November 1914 and went to France on 12th November 1915, serving as a signaller.

Initially a private in the same regiment reported: *Uttley has been wounded in action, but it is not serious, and, as arranged, we opened his parcel and divided it among the boys that were left... I don't know to which hospital Uttley has been taken, but you will probably hear from him soon.*

With no more news the family made further enquiries and a chaplain wrote: *I have made inquiries as to your son, and all the information I have is, I am afraid, not very hopeful. Your boy was last seen with a bad wound near his heart, lying on the parapet of a trench... I expect your lad, with others, has been buried by a chaplain of another division.*

His mother remained optimistic, she reasoned that if he had been buried he would have been identified by the authorities and they would have informed her appropriately.

The subsequent official notification was supplemented by a letter from a fellow signaller who wrote: *We were all to have gone over with the second line at 7-30 a.m. on July 1st, but Smith was wounded before the attack started, thus leaving Uttley and myself to do the whole of the company's communications by our two selves. We two went over at 7-30, and both of us got as far as the second German trenches, and then I missed Uttley. I turned back a few yards, and found Uttley had been hit, and was laid down behind the parapet with another chap who was wounded, and they were helping each other, so I, being the only signaller with the company, had to go on and leave them both for the stretcher bearers, who I knew would very soon be up. That was the last I heard or saw of him, although I tried to find him when I was coming back two hours later, being wounded myself. I also asked at the signal headquarters and advanced dressing station, but neither place had seen or heard anything of him, and as the Germans never again came over that same ground, and all our stretcher bearers were out on the job, he could not have been taken prisoner, so I can only think that the worst has happened, and I offer you my deepest sympathy. He was a good friend and workmate of mine through the winter months of such trying times in the trenches. I don't think I can say any more than he met his death as a soldier would wish.*

ALBURY EVERSHED

LIEUTENANT, 1ST/6TH BATTALION, NORTH STAFFORDSHIRE REGIMENT.

Died on 1st July 1916, aged 24, during an attack on Gommecourt.

Albury was the youngest of at least four children of Sir Sydney Herbert (a brewer and MP) and Alice Constance Evershed (née Meakin) of Burton-on-Trent, Staffordshire.

Until 1910 he was educated at Burton-on-Trent Grammar School and Clifton College. He was then employed with John German & Sons, estate agents, Ashby de la Zouch. He was commissioned on 26th November 1914, promoted to temporary lieutenant on 1st July 1915 and went to France on 30th October.

As he was preparing to go to France he sent this card to his parents, indicating that it was going to be used in the battalion magazine *The China Dragon*. The picture is unusual in that the Lewis gun is on a modified Vickers machine gun mount, which might be why Albury thought it would appear in the magazine. Unfortunately, the magazine ceased production before the picture could be used and only restarted publishing in 1921.

PIER 15

A

- Royal Irish Rifles - **Lance Corporal T. Murphy to Rifleman W. Young**
  (*completed from Pier and Face 15B*)
- Royal Irish Fusiliers
- Connaught Rangers
- Argyll and Sutherland Highlanders - **Captain T. Russell to Private T. Powrie**
  (*continued on Pier and Face 16C*)

B

- Gordon Highlanders - **Private A. Duthie to Private A. Yule**
  (*completed from Pier and Face 15C*)
- Cameron Highlanders
- Royal Irish Rifles - **Captain H. P. Beggs to Lance Corporal S. Mercer**
  (*continued on Pier and Face 15A*)

C

- Durham Light Infantry - **Private T. Wilson 283 to Private W. Young**
  (*completed from Pier and Face 14A*)
- Highland Light Infantry
- Seaforth Highlanders
- Gordon Highlanders - **Major R. D. Oxley to Private R. Duncanson**
  (*continued on Pier and Face 15B*)

D

(Blank)

WILLIAM FREDERICK MCFADZEAN VC

RIFLEMAN, 18278, 14TH BATTALION, ROYAL IRISH RIFLES.

Died on 1st July 1916, aged 20, in trenches in Thiepval Wood while preparing for the attack.

William was the eldest son of William (a linen yarn salesman) and Annie Pedlow McFadzean, of Cregagh, Belfast.

He was educated at Mountpottinger Boys' School and the Trade Preparatory School of the Municipal Technical Institute, Belfast. He was an enthusiastic rugby player. Later he was apprenticed to Spence Bryson & Co. Ltd, engaged in the linen trade.

Prior to the war he was a member of the Ulster Volunteer Force, No. 1 Battalion, Ballynafeigh and Newtonbreda, East Belfast Regiment. On 22nd September 1914 he enlisted in the 14th Battalion, Royal Irish Rifles. He went to France on 5th October 1915.

A general wrote: *I know that his battalion, the 14th Royal Irish Rifles (the Y.C.V.'s), are immensely proud of his memory, and I am sure you must find consolation in the fact that he died so magnificently in saving the lives of his comrades and friends. Indeed I shall always be proud to remember that such a brave and heroic man was a soldier of the Brigade.*

The award of the Victoria Cross was gazetted on 9th September 1916: *For most conspicuous bravery. While in a concentration trench and opening a box of bombs for distribution prior to an attack, the box slipped down into the trench, which was crowded with men, and two of the safety pins fell out. Private McFadzean, instantly realising the danger to his comrades, with heroic courage threw himself on the top of the bombs. The bombs exploded blowing him to pieces, but only one other man was injured. He well knew his danger, being himself a bomber, but without a moment's hesitation he gave his life for his comrades.*

His VC was presented to his father on 28th February 1917 by HM King George V at Buckingham Palace. The King said: *I have very great pleasure in presenting to you the Victoria Cross for your son, the late Private McFadzean. I deeply regret that he did not live to receive it personally, but I am sure you are proud of your son; nothing finer has been done in this war for which I have yet given the Victoria Cross, than the act performed by your son in giving his life so heroically to save the lives of his comrades.*

GEOFFREY ST GEORGE SHILLINGTON CATHER VC

LIEUTENANT AND ADJUTANT, 9TH BATTALION, ROYAL IRISH FUSILIERS.

Died on 2nd July 1916, aged 25, while searching for wounded men near Hamel.

Geoffrey was the eldest of three children of Robert Gabriel Cather (a partner in Joseph Tetley & Son) and Margaret Matilda Cather (née Shillington) of Limpsfield, Surrey.

He was educated at Hazelwood, Limpsfield and Rugby. On leaving school he was employed by the Tetley Company, which sent him to America and Canada in 1912. Whilst in New York he appeared in the chorus of the opera *Aida,* for which he received a half-dollar in payment. He shared the stage that night with the famous tenor Enrico Caruso.

He returned home in May 1914 and in September enlisted in the 19th Battalion, Royal Fusiliers. In May 1915 he was appointed to the 9th Battalion, Royal Irish Fusiliers, went to France in October and was in action at Thiepval on 1st July 1916.

His colonel wrote: *On the night after the attack he went out and brought in numerous wounded; again, about 7 a.m. the next morning, he was out again at the same work. He heard a man calling and went over the parapet in broad daylight, gave him water, called out to see if there was anyone else within hail, saw a hand waving feebly, went on and was shot through the head by a machine-gun and killed instantaneously. So brave and fearless: such a fine character. As an Adjutant he was perfectly wonderful, and the Battalion has sustained a severe loss by his death… I cannot tell you what a help he has been to me, and I only now realise how much I leant on him.*

The award of the Victoria Cross was gazetted on 8th September 1916: *For most conspicuous bravery near Hamel, France, on 1st July 1916. From 7 p.m. till midnight he searched 'No Man's Land', and brought in three wounded men. Next morning at 8 a.m. he continued his search, brought in another wounded man, and gave water to others, arranging for their rescue later. Finally, at 10.30 a.m., he took out water to another man, and was proceeding further on when he was himself killed. All this was carried out in full view of the enemy, and under direct machine gun fire and intermittent artillery fire. He set a splendid example of courage and self-sacrifice.*

He was buried where he fell, south of Beaumont Hamel; the grave was subsequently lost.

His VC was presented to his mother by HM King George V at Buckingham Palace on 31st March 1917.

ARTHUR CARSON HOLLYWOOD

LIEUTENANT, 9TH BATTALION, ROYAL IRISH FUSILIERS.

Died on 1st July 1916, aged 24, during the attack on the north bank of the River Ancre near Beaucourt.

Arthur was one of at least four children of James (manager of the local Workshops for the Blind) and Elizabeth Hollywood of Helen's Bay, Co. Down.

He was educated at the Royal Belfast Academical Institution and the Friend's School, Lisburn. He joined the Royal University of Ireland in 1909 and served as a company commander in the Ulster Volunteer Force in 1913 and 1914. Employed in his father's business as a rent agent, he enlisted in the 108th Field Ambulance on 12th September 1914, as a staff sergeant. He was commissioned in the Royal Irish Fusiliers on 19th April 1915, and joined the 9th Battalion in January 1916. He was wounded in the left arm by a bomb while on patrol near Hamel on 22nd February A week later he was promoted to lieutenant.

A sergeant wrote: *The first wave of men left the British trenches followed by the second wave to which Lt Hollywood belonged. I followed them with the 3rd wave of men. I saw Lt Hollywood jump into the German trench. I was then wounded and saw no more*

Two privates stated that they saw Arthur being killed at Hamel, just after leaving the 1st line German trench about 13.00; a third said he saw Arthur *hit by a machine gun bullet during the advance*; whilst a fourth reported that he had been wounded in the attack and lay beside Arthur's body for a night. Another sergeant reported that he saw Arthur's body being brought in, and that it was buried in Hamel village graveyard.

His younger brother, **James Hollywood**, Second Lieutenant, 18th Battalion attached to 12th Battalion, Royal Irish Rifles, also died on 1st July 1916, aged 23, during the same attack.

He is also commemorated on Pier and Face 15A.

The telegrams announcing the deaths of the two brothers arrived one day apart.

JOHN MCGLADE

COMPANY SERGEANT MAJOR, S/3630, 11TH BATTALION,
ARGYLL AND SUTHERLAND HIGHLANDERS.

Died on 15th September 1916, aged 36, during the
fighting around Martinpuich.

John was the eldest of at least six children of John and
Catherine McGlade (née O'Farrell) of Denny, Stirlingshire.

He married Clara Dore at Birkenhead on 5th September
1910 and lived in Wigtown, Wigtownshire.

Enlisting in the Argyll and Sutherland Highlanders in
Stirling on 8th September 1914, he went to France on 7th July 1915.

His officer commanding wrote: *It was largely due to Sergt.-Major McGlade that C was accounted the best disciplined company in the battalion, and did so well at Martinpuich on 15 Sept. Shells were bursting all round us and amongst us. I heard Sergt.-Major McGlade's voice behind me encouraging on the men, and then we had a bad five minutes with shrapnel and machine-gun bullets. I was knocked down twice, and I think it was then that the Sergeant-Major fell. I not only regarded him as an highly efficient officer and a splendid soldier, but also as a friend.*

Another officer wrote: *He was instantaneously killed on the 15th, while advancing over the open with his Captain. He was buried at the same spot. Your husband was a very fine soldier - in fact, the best in the battalion. He worked from morning to night in the cause of his company. We miss him greatly many of his old friends are missing; but their cause was gained. I express to you deepest sympathy from both officers and men of the 11th Battn. in your great loss. Remember, he died for his country.*

His chaplain wrote: *I knew him well, as he was a great friend of mine, and regularly assisted at Sunday Mass when this was possible. Indeed, he used to lead the singing of our hymns from the very first. I saw him last near midnight, the day before he was killed, as he called a cheery, 'Good-night, Father,' from the trench. Next morning, 15 Sept., he was killed at the head of his company, an hour after he went over. I was out on the field immediately myself, but he was already dead. He was hit straight in front, fell on to his knees, then forward, and never moved after. I was too busy with the wounded to bury him then, or even to find him, but that night he was buried with his chums on the field in front of Martinpuich, which we took that day. He was an excellent soldier, brilliant, resourceful and brave as a lion. I can assure you that his Colonel has often bewailed his loss in my hearing.*

JAMES WILLIAM SINCLAIR

PRIVATE, 6391, 7TH BATTALION, GORDON HIGHLANDERS.

Died on 13th November 1916, aged 19, during an attack on Beaumont Hamel.

James was the eldest and only son, one of at least two children, of Robert (a seaman) and Barbara C. Sinclair of Lerwick, Shetland.

After completing his education he was employed in the County Clerk's Office.

A keen musician, he had been a drummer in the Lerwick Brass Band.

A member of the local Territorials from 1914, he enlisted in Lerwick; not long before his death he had applied for a commission.

SHETLAND

Three other privates of the Gordon Highlanders with Shetland connections are also commemorated on Pier and Face 15B.

George Groat	**Alexander M. Henry**	**William Kay**
(Lerwick)	(Gutcher)	(Lerwick)
13th November 1916, 20	18th July 1916, 20	13th November 1916, 24

GEORGE CAMERON MACLEAY

SECOND LIEUTENANT, 8TH BATTALION ATTACHED TO 7TH
BATTALION, CAMERON HIGHLANDERS.

Died on 17th August 1916, aged 32, in fighting near
Contalmaison.

George was the eldest son of John and Mary Ann Isabella
MacLeay (née Cameron) of Bonar Bridge, Sutherland.

Educated at Bonar Bridge, he enlisted in the Seaforth
Highlanders, but transferred to the Lovat Scouts on their
formation. He served with them, as a despatch rider, in the
Boer War and was awarded the Queen's Medal with three clasps. He then represented the
scouts at the Great American War Show, which travelled across the USA. Afterwards he
participated in track athletics, winning numerous cups and other trophies, both in North and
South America, and won the Championship of the Southern States for running in 1910.

He finally settled down as a hotel manager in New Orleans.

At the outbreak of war he returned to England, rejoining the Lovat Scouts on 7th August
1914, serving in Egypt and the Dardanelles in September and October 1915.

He was then gazetted as a second lieutenant in the Cameron Highlanders and went to
France.

A brother officer wrote: *Quite apart from my high estimation of Lieut. Macleay, his men adored
him, and he was a great favourite with all the battalion officers.*

One of his men wrote: *Lieut. Macleay was absolutely one of the best, and a kinder officer one
could not have. While on a forced march for three days in the heat of the summer, he carried the heavy
packs of many poor lads who were nearly dropping out by the way. He acted like a father to us all,
and his loss is great.*

ERNEST GEORGE BOAS

SECOND LIEUTENANT, 5TH BATTALION ATTACHED TO 13TH
BATTALION, ROYAL IRISH RIFLES.

Died on 1st July 1916, aged 19, during fighting at
Thiepval Wood.

Ernest was the eldest son, one of at least four children, of
Ernest Alexander (a linen manufacturer) and Maud Lloyd
Boas (née Burnett) of Belfast, Co. Antrim.

He was educated at Campbell College, Belfast, Clifton
College, Bristol and the Royal Belfast Academical Institution.
He was a member of the school and later the Queen's University, Belfast OTC.

He was working in his father's linen business, the Loopbridge Weaving Factory, Belfast,
when he enlisted.

He received his commission in June 1915 and went to France in May 1916. He was attached
to the 13th Battalion just three weeks before his death.

A sergeant wrote: *At 7.30 am, on the 1st July 1916, at Thiepval Wood, I advanced with No 3
Platoon 13th Royal Irish Rifles, of which 2nd Lt Boas was in command. Between the 2nd and 3rd
trenches, I found 2nd Lt Boas lying in a communication trench, as he was my platoon officer I
recognized him at once. He must have been hit by hand grenades as they were landing very thick and
we lost a lot of men at that place. I believed him to be dead as he never moved or spoke, but I put him
on the fire step and then advanced on; when we retired back 2nd Lt Boas was not lying where we left
him, and the trench had been blown in, in two or three places; he could not have been taken prisoner
as no Germans except prisoners under escort got through and I firmly believe he was blown to pieces
by a shell. I should like to state that 2nd Lt Boas led us most splendidly and did some excellent bayonet
work.*

A comrade wrote: *I'm sorry I cannot inform you as you would like, I saw the young Lt. before we
mounted the parapet but never since. I heard some of the men in his platoon, those who returned safe,
saying Lt Boas knocked a German to the ground with his fist and after that he was killed. They surely
must have saw it happen or they would not say that I know his platoon got badly cut up. Sir it may
be wrong but I believe he is dead.*

A lance corporal wrote: *I saw him in the 2nd line German trench at about 11am on July 1st. the
platoons were all mixed up and we were attacking the enemy who were bombing us. We were using
the bayonet. Lt Boas had a rifle and bayonet. I got wounded just as we reached the communication
trench and did not see Lt Boas afterwards.*

JAMES ALFRED WILLIAMS

Second Lieutenant, 3rd Battalion attached to 7th Battalion, Royal Irish Rifles.

Died on 6th September 1916, aged 18, during a night patrol between Guillemont and Ginchy.

James was the youngest of four children, all sons, of James Alfred and Emily Kate Williams of Londonderry.

Educated at Foyle College, Londonderry, he then became a medical student at Edinburgh University.

He enlisted as Private 25036, 16th Battalion, Royal Scots on 12th May 1915. He was commissioned in the Royal Irish Rifles on 23rd August and served in Ireland during the rebellion. He then joined the 7th Battalion in France on 18th June 1916.

All four brothers served, but only one, **Harold Patton Williams MC**, survived.

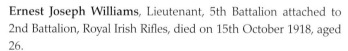

Charles Beasley Williams, Captain, 2nd Battalion Royal Irish Rifles, died on 28th August 1915, aged 20.

He is commemorated on the Menin Gate Memorial.

Ernest Joseph Williams, Lieutenant, 5th Battalion attached to 2nd Battalion, Royal Irish Rifles, died on 15th October 1918, aged 26.

He is buried in grave II.B.1 in Dadizeele New British Cemetery.

HUGH MARR WOODSIDE

SECOND LIEUTENANT, 9TH (GLASGOW HIGHLANDERS)
BATTALION, HIGHLAND LIGHT INFANTRY.

Died on 15th July 1916, aged 24, during an attack at
High Wood.

Hugh was one of five children, all sons, of the Rev. David and
Elizabeth Marr Calderwood Woodside of Bearsden,
Dunbartonshire.

Educated at Glasgow High School, he afterwards worked
in an office. After a few years he took up farming and then
went to Canada, where he was employed as a manufacturer's agent. He and his brother Thomas
enlisted in the Canadian Forces on 25th October 1914 in Winnipeg, Manitoba. He came to
England with the 2nd Canadian Division in May 1915 and went to France on 17th September.
After serving for three months at the Front he received a commission in the Glasgow
Highlanders on 6th December. He then returned to France at the beginning of June 1916.

A private declared: *I had got wounded and was finding my way to the Dressing Station. While
doing so, I saw Lieutenant Woodside fall evidently wounded. He then rose and I saw him fall again. I
passed close to him when he was lying on the ground and saw that he had been struck by a piece of
shrapnel on the chest and that he was dead.*

Hugh and his three surviving brothers all enlisted; only one, **Thomas Leadbeater Woodside**,
survived.

His older brother **David Cunninghame Woodside**, Second
Lieutenant, Royal Scots Fusiliers was wounded at the Dardanelles
on 31st December 1915. He died of his wounds in a Glasgow
hospital on 26th February 1916, aged 26, and is buried in grave
N.663 in Glasgow Western Necropolis.

A younger brother, **Archibald Mitchell Woodside**, Second
Lieutenant, 9th Battalion, Highland Light Infantry, died on 23rd
April 1918, aged 20.

He is buried in grave I.C.22 in Bagneux British Cemetery.

ROBERT ARCHIBALD SCARLYN WILSON

SECOND LIEUTENANT, 3RD BATTALION ATTACHED TO 7TH BATTALION, SEAFORTH HIGHLANDERS.

Died on 12th October 1916, aged 19, during an attack on Snag Trench near Eaucourt l'Abbaye.

Robert was one of three children of Dr Archibald Scarlyn Wilson and Sybil Mary Wilson (née Sanderson) of St Leonards-on-Sea, Sussex.

He was educated at Hill House, St Leonards, and Lancing College, where he was a member of the OTC.

Initially gazetted on 14th August 1915 in a temporary capacity, his commission was confirmed on 13th March 1916. He went to France on 8th July and was attached to the 7th Battalion.

A school friend, and fellow officer, wrote: *The Battalion, including Wilson, went up to the front line, just south of [censored] on Sunday night. I saw him there on Wednesday about 10pm he was very cheerful and smoking as usual, his favourite Savory's No.5. On Thursday afternoon the battalion went over the parapet to attack an important trench in front. Apparently the artillery had not strafed the machine guns sufficiently, for as soon as they got into the open the bullets came from both flanks, literally like hail… About 180 returned…of Wilson and his Company Commander nobody seems to know the fate. Probably all the men near them were also wiped out. At any rate, he was seen to fall, but, in spite of the nightly search-parties, no sign has been found of them. He had done very well since he came out here, and his men loved him… He used to spend all his money too on cigarettes and bread etc when they needed it. The Company had a great opinion of him. He promised great things apart from the army. During this last year he acquired a great power of conversation and could talk - and talk sense – whether he was discussing poetry or lecturing his platoon. I have never met anyone with such a flow of ideas. At first he might have been called inconsistent, but as he grew older the good ideas increased at the expense of the indifferent ones; and I had a great admiration for my friend, both as to his character and powers. He was only 19 when he was killed; but we have lost a man and a good one.*

A private wrote: *Your son was a great favourite with the men of No. 9 Platoon. He was always cheery and smiling and the whole time I was under him I never heard him speak a cross word with any of us; the regiment has lost a good officer and the country a gentleman. I shall always remember his face when he gave No. 9 the command to go over the top, cool and smiling as usual, and we had every confidence in him, and where he went we gladly followed.*

Another private wrote: *I don't think we shall ever get such a good officer (from the men's point of view) as he was. He was always pleasant and cheerful and never too proud to speak to a soldier and this is what a Tommy most likes in an officer.*

PERCY CHARTERS

PRIVATE, S/11551, 7TH BATTALION, SEAFORTH HIGHLANDERS.

Died on 14th July 1916, aged 25, killed by a sniper during an attack on Waterlot Farm.

Percy was one of at least eight children of James (a herb beer maker) and Emily Roberts Charters (née Caley) of Manchester.

The following are extracts from letters written to his eldest sister, Nellie.

13th March 1916: *…you say in your first letter I wont have seen much of France yet, but I think I have seen enough and had enough up to now. We are just going back to the trenches but anything you send will be alright I would have liked you to have been there when the parcel arrived they all crowded round as if they had not seen one before. I might say we had a right feast tell Ivy I got the dummy tit and I hope to fetch it home with me if I ever see home again you know it might save my life.*

15th April 1916: *I was put on sentry for the week and I had some narrow shaves while I was on one of my mates came to me and said I wish I could get a nice blighty one…just then the Huns started shelling us and this fellow walked away just as he moved away a piece of shell came down caught my coat sleeve and went through the bag he was sat on it was about five pounds weight if it had caught him it would have killed him dead so you can tell I was glad to get out of it as there has been five killed by snipers at the same spot.*

11th June 1916: *Well that march I was telling you about nearly killed me we covered 48 Miles in 3 days with full pack on and when we arrived it was 7 o'clock and I was put on Guard till 7 o'clock the following night without any rest at all that was 24 hours on my feet after the March they gave me. I am fairly fed up with it and I wish it was over what with the work and the food its enough to drive a man mad.*

A friend wrote: *I cannot help thinking about him as he was in my Section and with me all along till the morning of the 14th of July when we were to go and take what is called Waterlot Farm and there your dearest Brother got sniped. He was such a good chap to all of us and very obliging too and fullness to give you any thing of course no doubt that you will wonder how I came to have his address but it was when we came out of the Trenches when a letter came for him dated 15th July 1916 and of course I thought that I would get his address and write you a few lines concerning his death poor chap so I do hope that you wont be offended with me in any way by writing you a few lines.*

His sergeant wrote: *He was killed in Action and I assure you he was a great favourite amongst his Comrades, also he died as a soldier and man. As I'm not used to breaking news to anyone I think you already got information about Your Sad Loss.*

JOHN HENDERSON-BEGG

Captain, 4th Battalion, Gordon Highlanders.

Died on 23rd July 1916, aged 25, during fighting at High Wood.

John was the elder of at least two children of John Henderson-Begg (an Advocate, late Sheriff-Substitute of Aberdeen, Kincardine and Banff) and his second wife, Rosetta Cathrine Henderson-Begg (née Scott).

He was educated at Greenock Academy, Aberdeen Grammar School, Robert Gordon's Technical College, Aberdeen and Glasgow Technical College.

He married Dorothy Eleanor Spinks at Callander, Perthshire on 7th September 1915. They lived in London and had a daughter, born in 1916.

On completion of his training he was employed as a mechanical engineer with the Luther Engineering Company (Limited), London. In April 1914 he went to Russia as assistant superintendent at the company's works in Reval. On the outbreak of war he returned to Scotland via an indirect route through Finland, Sweden and Norway, which took a total of twelve days.

He was gazetted lieutenant on 12th September 1914, promoted to captain on 9th February 1915 and went to France ten days later.

When he was killed he was endeavouring to return to Headquarters to report, after being twice wounded during the attack. He was buried in the wood but the grave was subsequently lost.

An officer wrote: *Your husband was cool and stuck to his job until he absolutely couldn't do so any more, and his loss is greatly regretted by all the battalion, and especially by the officers, non-commissioned officers and men of his company.*

His half-brother, **Robert Henderson-Begg**, Captain, attached to 6th Div HQ, Royal Garrison Artillery, died on 24th December 1915, aged 37.

He is buried in grave P.22 in Kut War Cemetery.

PIER 16

A
• Royal Fusiliers - **Sergeant W. C. Gordon to Private S. F. Hutton**   *(continued from Pier and Face 9A)*   *(continued on Pier and Face 8C)*

B
• Rifle Brigade - **Rifleman S. E. Hughes to Rifleman C. F. Zwisele**   *(completed from Pier and Face 16C)*   • Monmouthshire Regiment   • Cambridgeshire Regiment   • 1st Bn. London Regiment (Royal Fusiliers)   • 2nd Bn. London Regiment (Royal Fusiliers)

C
• Argyll and Sutherland Highlanders - **Private A. Pratt to Private J. Young**   *(completed from Pier and Face 15A)*   • Leinster Regiment   • Royal Munster Fusiliers   • Royal Dublin Fusiliers   • Rifle Brigade - **Lieutenant Colonel D. Wood to Rifleman F. Hughes**   *(continued on Pier and Face 16B)*

D
(Blank)

EDWARD CHARLES CASS

LANCE SERGEANT, 4610, 20TH BATTALION, ROYAL FUSILIERS.

Died on 20th July 1916, aged 21, during the fighting at High Wood.

Edward was the only son, one of three children of William Hepworth Cass (a headmaster) and Sarah Cass (née Bulcock) of Colne, Lancashire.

He was educated at Colne Secondary School and Manchester School of Technology, where he was a member of the University OTC. Afterwards he was employed by Messrs Levenstein, dyers, of Harpurhey, Manchester.

He enlisted in Manchester in September 1914 and went to France on 14th November 1915. He had been accepted for a commission in the Duke of Wellington's (West Riding Regiment), but at the time of his death he was awaiting being gazetted.

A comrade wrote: *We cleared the wood of the Bosches, and got right through. Then, owing to heavy shelling, and there were so many in the line that some were ordered to retire a bit. Our company went back under machine gun fire, and I was glad to see Eddie when we assembled. Then we were ordered up again, but the fire was so strong that we couldn't get in, and made our way back again… I was told by the man who was next to him that as he was showing them the way he was hit by this machine gun. They did their best for him, but I am sorry to say he passed away almost immediately. He had no pain at all, and he died…doing his best to hold what was in reality an absolute hell. I went forward from the support trench to try and find him, but owing to the damage done to trees and the ground itself by shells, I simply couldn't find him, and I had to give up in despair. I meant to have another try, but we were relieved and that put it out of the question. He was shot straight through the head. You can imagine for yourself how I feel about it. When we lined up for roll call after the attack there were four only of the Colne and Nelson boys left. I felt like breaking down absolutely. Ernest* is posted 'missing, believed killed,' although someone said he was wounded in the head early on… We were congratulated by the General afterwards, but there are many sad homes in our district after this, I miss Eddie already. We were always together out here, just the same as at home. Everyone was sorry. I feel so sorry that I can't put it into words.*

*__Ernest Swire__, Sergeant, 5726, 20th Battalion, Royal Fusiliers, also died on 20th July 1916, aged 26. He is also commemorated on Pier and Face 16A.

JEREMIAH 'JERRY' DELANEY MM

Corporal, SPTS/1431, 23rd Battalion, Royal Fusiliers.

Died on 27th July 1916, aged 22, in the fighting at Delville Wood.

Jerry was one of at least seventeen children of William (a woolcomber) and Catherine Delaney (née Durkin) of Bradford, Yorkshire.

Educated at St Anne's School, Bradford he was afterwards employed as a newspaper seller.

One of five brothers who were boxers, he fought at lightweight. In July 1912 the *Boxing* magazine reported on his success in a bout at Newcastle-upon-Tyne and concluded: *Delaney, on the other hand, is a hard, rugged fighter who wins contests, no matter how severe may be the journey. With a little experience and the tuition of his brother Fred, Jerry will no doubt make a good boxer, but he will certainly have to use his head in the cultivation of the profession which he has adopted.*

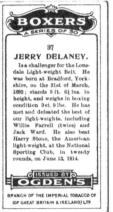

He enlisted in Bradford and went to France on 16th November 1915, where he was a bomber.

In December he wrote to a friend in Birmingham: *My time is fairly well occupied in occasional bouts with Huns... You can tell my Birmingham friends that I have no intention of relinquishing any claim to a championship contest, as I hope, providing that I come home safe and sound, to have a crack for the world's title... Anyway, I have just got some boxing gloves, and hope, in the intervals of Hun fighting to keep in touch with the 'game,' and not allow myself to forget any of it.*

In another letter, written early in 1916, he wrote: *I had a narrow squeak a few hours before we came out of the trenches...a German sniper sent a bullet which found its way through my cap and just grazed the top of my head. It was nothing. It just drew blood and that was all.*

His brother, **Edward Delaney**, Lance Corporal 201216, 1st/5th Battalion, Royal Warwickshire Regiment, died on 28th June 1916, aged 34.

He is buried in grave III.L.10 in Euston Road Cemetery.

LOUIS LAWRENT D'ABADIE

PRIVATE, 2276, 24TH BATTALION, ROYAL FUSILIERS.

Died on 31st July 1916, aged 38, in the fighting at Delville Wood.

Louis was born in Trinidad, the third son of St Luce d'Abadie (a landowner) and Ida d'Abadie (née Girod), of Port of Spain, Trinidad.

For a short time in 1887 he was a student at Stonyhurst College, before completing his education at St Augustine's College, Ramsgate. A diligent student and a keen sportsman, he was well read in the literatures of France and England, a brilliant debater, and had intended to study law.

He left Trinidad with Edward Ellis*, Thornton Warner^, **John Wilson** (all three members of the local constabulary) and **Bertie Russell** on 14th November 1914, arriving in England on 8th December. He enlisted in London and went to France on 15th November 1915.

A friend from Trinidad wrote: *He had great facility of speech, and a wonderful persuasive and winning manner. He took great interest in sport, was a thorough sportsman, and sometimes wrote in the local papers. He was a great favourite with everyone, a faithful friend, and, as you may imagine from what I have said, the pleasantest of companions. Louis was one of the first Trinidadians to leave Trinidad, after the declaration of war, to join the Army. Himself and a few others left together without fuss or show, and almost unnoticed. I must confess I never seriously thought he meant to join the Army. First of all he must have been very near the age limit, if not over it, and fighting did not seem me to be in his line. However, he proved that he was in earnest, and his colleges, Trinidad, and his family and friends have every reason to be proud of him.*

A comrade wrote: *Louis was killed in action while taking part in the advance…he was instantaneously killed by a shell on July 31st, 1916, while advancing through Delville Wood. The morning before we went into action he attended an open-air Mass, and, with the rest of us Catholics, received Holy Communion on the field, so that we were all prepared for any sacrifice.*

Another comrade wrote:*'Darby' (as we always called him) was beloved by all, and everyone of us will, deep in our hearts, treasure his memory as one of the finest men and truest comrades we have ever had the good fortune to meet.*

*__Edward Charles Ellis__, Lieutenant, Gloucestershire Regiment, died on 7th August 1915, aged 26. He is commemorated in Twelve Tree Copse Cemetery.

^**Thornton Sparr Warner**, Captain, Gloucestershire Regiment, died on 23rd July 1916, aged 33. He is commemorated on Pier and Face 5B.

SYDNEY FREDERICK HUTTON

PRIVATE, PS/10224, 8TH BATTALION, ROYAL FUSILIERS.

Died on 7th October 1916, aged 32, killed by shrapnel while assisting a wounded comrade during the fighting at Flers.

Sydney was the only son, eldest of at least three children, of the Rev. Frederick Robert Chapman Hutton and Maria Louisa Hutton (née Mort) of Ashton-under-Lyne, Lancashire.

After leaving Sedbergh School he was educated in France and Germany. Afterwards he joined the business of his uncle, James F. Hutton & Co. in Manchester, but after six years went up to New College, Oxford, taking a Second Class in Theology. He was ordained in September 1913 to the curacy of Swinton Parish Church, Manchester.

On the outbreak of war, having applied unsuccessfully for a chaplaincy at the Front, he enlisted as a private in the Royal Fusiliers on 27th January 1916. He went to France in August. On several occasions he acted as a voluntary chaplain, the last occasion being on the Sunday before his death, when his service was attended by several hundred men.

Just prior to his death he had written that one of the chief problems in the trenches was the rats: *One ran over me last night and the night before they ate one man's rations, and half another's haversack.* On 3rd October he wrote: *I am in a German dug-out, drinking German coffee out of a German bottle.*

Sydney and another man were acting as orderlies, and were waiting in the first British trench. The second man received a wound that Sydney dressed for him. He had just said *Good-bye* and sent him to the dressing station, when a shell burst, killing Sydney instantaneously and wounding the other man for the second time.

He was buried by a man from the Middlesex Regiment who wrote: *On the 8th of the month we went to relieve them, and I found him in the trench probably killed the day before with a lot more. I buried him as respectfully as possible… I am sending one of two photos I retained to you… It is my work to bury the dead, but it is not a very pleasant job, especially our own boys. I would sooner bury Germans, and we have had plenty of them just lately.*

His commanding officer wrote: *I greatly admired your son he was remarkably brave and always cheerful. He is a great loss to the company, and his death is felt very keenly by his comrades, to whom he was of great assistance.*

A plaque dedicated to him in St Peter's Church, Swinton describes him as *A very gallant gentleman.*

SIR HENRY GUY TRENTHAM BUTLIN BART

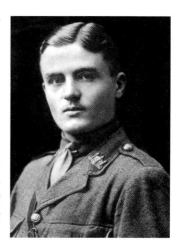

CAPTAIN AND ADJUTANT, 1ST/1ST BATTALION,
CAMBRIDGESHIRE REGIMENT.

Died on 16th September 1916, aged 23, at Beaumont
Hamel during a bombing attack.

Henry was the only son, one of three children, of Sir Henry
Trentham Butlin (1st Bart., President of the Royal College of
Surgeons) and Annie Tipping Butlin (née Balderson) of
London.

He succeeded to the baronetcy on the death of his father in 1912. The title became extinct
on Henry's death in 1916. Educated at Harrow and Trinity College, Cambridge, gaining a BA in
1914, he then became a student at the Inner Temple. He joined the Cambridgeshire Regiment
on 1st August 1914 and went to France in February 1915, as a second lieutenant, before
promotion to lieutenant, then captain and adjutant by June. He was mentioned in despatches.

Henry tried to rescue two officers reported as wounded. All three men died; the graves of
the two others* were found in German cemeteries but Henry's grave was never identified.

His commanding officer wrote: *Poor Guy was wounded in the act of binding up the wound of
a brother-officer while under very heavy fire at point-blank range… All we know is that he told one
of the stretcher bearers to go back for help and bring more ammunition. Every effort was made that
night - and very gallant efforts they were - to bring in your son, but without success. One of his
brother-officers crawled out in the daylight to find him, but was driven back. The following night
another effort was made. This time we found out for certain that he was in the hands of the Germans.
We are all very depressed at losing poor Guy. If he had a fault, it was that he always thought of others
and never gave a thought for himself - that was how he received his wound. We have lost a brave man
and a great friend.*

His major wrote: *Lieutenant Bradford^ made several determined efforts himself through-out the
night to reach your son, and was the last to come in after wading through a marsh, sometimes up to
his shoulders in water, in order to try and find a way round by a flank. He showed the greatest
gallantry… He will be greatly missed by all. I don't think there is an Officer in the Battalion who had
the welfare and comfort of the men more at heart than he had.*

*Arthur Innes Adam, Captain, also died on 16th September 1916, aged 22. He is buried in
grave IV.Q.12 in Achiet-le-Grand Communal Cemetery Extension. **William Shaw,** Lieutenant,
died of his wounds in Cambrai on 27th September 1916, aged 23. He is buried in grave II.A.33
in Porte-de-Paris Cemetery.

^Alfred Royal Bradford, Lieutenant, died on 14th October 1916, aged 22. He is buried in
grave IX.A.5 in Lonsdale Cemetery.

WALTER STANLEY CAMPBELL MC

SECOND LIEUTENANT, 1ST BATTALION, LONDON REGIMENT (ROYAL FUSILIERS).

Died on 7th October 1916, aged 28, during fighting at Lesboeufs.

Walter was born in Australia, one of eight children of John Archibald and Jane Campbell (née Gordon) of Melbourne, Australia.

He entered the Melbourne Preparatory School in 1899 and then the Senior School. Afterwards he and his brother managed the Dungalear Station, near Walgett, New South Wales.

After coming to England he trained with the Inns of Court OTC and went to France in March 1916. In a letter to his brother he wrote: *I am now in a dug-out trying to keep warm. One gets little sleep under these conditions, but we will go to the reserve trenches, where it is not so strenuous, for four days before having another turn. 'Fritz' gives us a bad time with his guns, and I have lost three men out of my platoon so far... Last night I was out on a patrol in 'No Man's Land,' and had to be in a shell hole full of water for over half-an-hour, as our guns began to 'strafe' the Huns, and some were falling short, and not far from where we were. That was not our only trouble, as on coming in at the arranged place our own people in the trenches threw a bomb at us, thinking we were Huns. This, to my mind, is the most dangerous thing about patrolling... The patrol might be out three hours, and on coming in it might be fired on by a 'nervy' man. A listening post out in front of the wire is so nerve racking that a man is very apt to fire at anything he sees.*

The award of the Military Cross was gazetted on 28th July 1916: *For conspicuous gallantry. On reconnaissance, and when leading a covering party to mark new lines, though wounded, he showed great courage and resource. It was not till he had made every effort to carry out his duties that he consented to go back and have his wounds dressed.*

He was shot in the temple as he jumped up to lead his men out of the trench to attack.

A fellow officer wrote that *He was as brave as a lion and as daring as anyone I have ever known.*

His brother, **Donald Gordon Campbell**, Second Lieutenant, 51st Battalion, Australian Infantry, A.I.F., died on 3rd September 1916, aged 31.

He is commemorated on the Villers-Bretonneux Memorial.

ERNEST REGINALD CLIFFORD

PRIVATE, 2862, 1ST/2ND BATTALION, LONDON REGIMENT (ROYAL FUSILIERS).

Died on 1st July 1916, aged 20, during an attack on Gommecourt.

Ernest was the youngest of at least nine children of Frederick (a printer's compositor) and Ann Eliza Clifford (née King).

Enlisting in London, he served in Malta from 31st December 1914 and then went to Egypt until moving to Gallipoli on 13th October 1915. Afterwards he spent time in hospital in Egypt before going to France on 24th April 1916.

He wrote many letters to his parents during his time on active service. On 17th March 1915, while in Malta, he wrote: *At present there is great excitement here over this Dardenelles business. We have had most of the battleships in here for repairs; I have been over one of them, the "Inflexible." She came in to have two new guns put in her bows. Another one that came in was the "Invincible" and the sailors told me that the transports landed at least a hundred thousand men to take over the forts that they have captured… We have nearly finished our firing and I have come out overall sixth out of about 200; and considering that we have got a lot of old soldiers, some of whom have been in action several times, I feel rather proud of myself.*

8th April 1915: *I have just received your parcel for which I thank you. Needless to say I have already made a big hole in it. All the biscuits are gone and the pudding is well on the way.*

8th May 1915: *You say as things are so unsettled you didn't expect to get any letters. I didn't know there was any chance of the mails being stopped. What gave you the idea we were going to Egypt? We had a rumour out here that we were going but so far we haven't heard anything official, but if we do I will let you know as soon as possible.*

From Gallipoli: *It's turning very cold out here and we have been issued out with some warm clothing but we haven't had any socks and as I haven't got one sound pair to my name my feet get cold. So I should be awfully obliged if you would send me out a couple of pairs of thick socks. We had a storm the other night and we were all flooded out so we had to walk about and dry ourselves as best we could. We were up all night as our dug-outs were half full of water… I daresay by the time you get this you will be thinking about Christmas; so shall we (perhaps), if we remember & have an extra bit of jam on our biscuit that morning if we're lucky.*

His last letter was dated 28th June 1916, it included: *I am writing this now as I have a few minutes to spare. The weather here is absolutely rotten, we are having on an average three showers a day; consequently, we are up to our eyes in mud. It has just started again. Taking the weather as a whole it's pretty rotten for the time of the year.*

ALEXANDER FRASER

Private, 2849, 1st/2nd Battalion, London Regiment (Royal Fusiliers).

Died on 1st July 1916, aged 23, during a bombing attack on German trenches at Gommecourt.

Alexander was the eldest of at least three children of Jemima Fraser of Forres, Morayshire.

Employed as a journalist on the *Forres Gazette*, he then became the personal secretary to Mr. Charles Roberts, MP for Lincoln.

He enlisted at Westminster on 2nd November 1914 and went to Egypt on 30th August 1915. He served at the Dardanelles and against the Senussi in North Africa before going to France in May 1916.

Whilst in training he wrote to a friend: *I have spent to-day wheeling coal in a barrow. This I find is a different occupation to having my tea on the Terrace of the House of Commons, but I am doing my bit, and hope shortly to be in the trenches.*

His employer wrote: *I know you will be very sorry to hear that poor Fraser was killed as long ago as July 1st. I have only just heard. He was leading a bombing party, and was killed by a bomb. One of his friends in his platoon wrote to me, and I am afraid there can be no doubt about it. It is a real grief to me, and I am afraid will be a tragic blow to his people.*

In an obituary, the *Forres Gazette* described him as having: *commanding qualities as a pressman. During his later years he was on the reporting staff of the paper and discharged his duties with great ability. He had the journalistic instinct in a very high degree and he had a keen desire to pursue a literary career. He had every prospect of his highest ambition being realised.*

A Lincoln friend wrote: *How did he, of all men, come to be leading a bombing party. For Alec Fraser was a giant of peace. A Scotchman of the Scotch. Not given to many words, a quiet deep-thinking, intellectual man. A democrat, whose vision was on the distant future when wars shall be no more. A hater of militarism in all its forms. During the time which I have known him we have argued long, and sometimes bitterly, on the military question. His contention was that the bigger the armies the bigger the danger of international relations coming to the arbitrament of force. Almost a peace-at-any-price man. And he met his death, after fighting in three continents, whilst leading a bombing party. The irony, the glorious irony of it!... And thus he fell. A modest, unpretending, simple hero.*

CHRISTOPHER COLEMAN

PRIVATE, 3465, 7TH BATTALION, LEINSTER REGIMENT.

Died on 3rd September 1916, aged 33, during an attack on Guillemont.

Christopher was one of nine children of Michael (a publican) and Mary Coleman (née O'Donoghue).

He married Adelaide Elizabeth English in 1908 and they had three children, born between 1909 and 1912. After his death Adelaide and the children started a new life in America.

This picture of Christopher is from a chalk drawing done by Adelaide. It was used in an advertisement placed in British newspapers seeking information as to his whereabouts. Adelaide was so desperate for news of him that she travelled to England and searched hospitals and recovery sites for the wounded.

A publican in Queenstown, Co. Cork, he enlisted in Cork and went to France on 18th December 1915.

A soldier in the Royal Engineers found and buried Christopher's body a few days later and wrote to his wife: *...well dear madam it's a very strange thing how I fell across him. My company was sent to Guillemont to clear a way for traffic after the place was taken...my duty was to go round & see all tools was collected & I can tell you I was always on the look out for any one that may have been wounded or killed & missed which I know often is the case as there is so much to do & of course the lads cannot do everything. However I came across this fellow in a shell hole (a very large one) & passed him as I passed others that lay about & something struck me to go back & see him, as he lay there as if resting from a long walk...then I pictured myself in his place. how if it was me & suppose he has just got missed altogether how will his friends ever know... I thought of his top pocket that all I could get to & with my knife I cut it down & I saw a piece of paper I got it out & read it & to my great relief I saw an address...& then I opened the other & the label of him was inside. this label I refer to is one they all have to wear when wounded & as he was wounded in the hand... I hope dear madam you will forgive me of taking liberties with your dear husbands body. but you can rest assured (I will give you my word of honour.) that he is buried & I buried him the best I could. not so well as some but better than thousands. I was at this time up at the ruined church...& found a lovely square stone from the ruins with 5 crosses engraved on it. then I claimed it & took it for his grave after writing his name & regiment in copying ink pencil as best I could. hoping & trusting that if I was called away myself some-one would be sure & come across him & probably would let you know.*

EVELYN HERBERT LIGHTFOOT SOUTHWELL

CAPTAIN, 13TH BATTALION, RIFLE BRIGADE.

Died on 15th September 1916, aged 30, during fighting near Delville Wood.

Evelyn was the only son of the Rev. Canon Herbert Burrows Southwell and Sarah Anne Southwell (née Willis) of Worcester.

Educated at Eton, he then went to Magdalen College, Oxford, taking a First in Moderations and a Second Class degree in Literae Humaniores.

He stroked his college boat (1905 and 1906), and rowed twice in the University Boat Race (1907 and 1908). He also took part in the Steward's Challenge Cup (1907) and was a member of the Leander Crew (1908). The same year he was also the spare man for the Olympic crew. In 1910, after leaving Oxford, he was a classics master at Shrewsbury. *Two men*, a memoir, with letters written by him and his contemporary, Malcolm White*, was published by the Oxford University Press in 1919.

He joined the battalion on 24th April 1915 and served abroad from 1st October. Initially he was in the trenches near Ypres and had to spend time in hospital in November and December. In January 1916 he was home on leave and returned to take command of D Company on 10th February, prior to the move from Belgium to France. He was gazetted captain in April.

On 12th July 1916 he wrote: *White* is killed, I suppose…we had heard that his Battalion was very badly cut up. He was my greatest friend, and loved Shrewsbury… I have faced the casualty list daily without tremor for two years now, and now, when I am hard hit myself, I cry out!*

On 6th September 1916 he wrote: *This first visit to the wood was the most unpleasant time we have had, in some ways, which is consoling – now it's over!! … Horrors? Well, yes I suppose so: but there seems no useful purpose in recalling them. Even from the most lamentable remains of brave men, blown to every sort of bits, and accusingly unburied beneath the stars, it was not hard to catch a rather obvious inspiration.*

An officer wrote: *The battalion advanced and did splendidly and they could go no further. Evelyn was in front of them with one sergeant and another officer close to him. They were in fact the farthest advanced of any body and they got into a shell hole for cover. Your son was shortly afterwards hit by a sniper's bullet and was killed immediately.*

*Malcolm Graham White, Lieutenant, 6th Battalion attached to 1st Battalion, Rifle Brigade, died on 1st July 1916, aged 29. He is also commemorated on Pier and Face 16C.

HENRY TRYON

CAPTAIN, 15TH BATTALION ATTACHED TO 8TH BATTALION,
RIFLE BRIGADE.

Died on 15th September 1916, aged 42, during the
fighting at Delville Wood.

Henry was one of seven children of Captain Richard and
Jane Anna L. Tryon (née Ewart) of Oakham, Rutland.

When the war broke out he was farming in British
Columbia but he immediately returned to England. He was
granted a commission as a lieutenant in the 15th Battalion,
Rifle Brigade, on 1st December 1914, and went to France with the 8th Battalion on 7th August
1915.

On the night of 23rd November he was on patrol with three men; one was hit and had to

he helped back by another of the party. A little later Henry was
shot through the neck but Corporal Alfred Drake stayed with him
and bound up the wound. Both men were found later by a rescue
party, Henry was unconscious but alive and bandaged, Alfred was
dead beside him, riddled with bullets. The award of the Victoria
Cross to Alfred was gazetted on 21st January 1916. The citation
concludes: ...*he had given his own life and saved his Officer.* **Alfred
George Drake VC,** Corporal S/107, 8th Battalion, Rifle Brigade,
was aged 21. He is buried in grave I.C.2 in La Brique Military
Cemetery No. 2.

Henry recovered from his wound and returned to light duty again in France on 26th July
1916. He was promoted to captain in September.

His Colonel wrote: *It was owing to the way Capt. Tryon led his men and the glorious example
set by him that they went on after he fell and accomplished what they did that day.*

His brother, **Richard Tryon**, Captain, 6th Battalion attached to
2nd Battalion, Rifle Brigade died on 10th January 1915, aged 46.
He is commemorated on the Le Touret Memorial.

HORACE WYNDHAM THOMAS

SECOND LIEUTENANT, 14TH BATTALION ATTACHED TO 16TH BATTALION, RIFLE BRIGADE.

Died on 3rd September 1916, aged 26, during an attack to the north of the river Ancre.

Horace was one of ten children of the Rev. Morgan Thomas and Mary Priscilla Thomas (née Jones) of Bridgend, Glamorgan.

He was educated at Bridgend Intermediate School, Monmouth Grammar School and King's College, Cambridge, where he obtained a Second Class degree in the History Tripos. He also gained his rugby Blue and had a short career as a Welsh Rugby International.

In 1913 he took up a commercial post in Calcutta, India. During the three years he spent in India he was elected captain of the Calcutta football team. In 1914 he joined the Calcutta Port Volunteer Corps as a private. In 1915 he returned to England and on 17th December applied for a temporary commission. On 4th January 1916 he was posted as a temporary second lieutenant to the 14th Battalion, Rifle Brigade. After training he was attached to the 16th Battalion, joining up with it in France on 12th June.

In his last letter he wrote: *At last has come the chance for which I came home. To-morrow we go over to pay what I trust will be a permanent visit to the Boche trenches… I've no doubt our visit will not be very welcome, but they will doubtless, give us a warm reception… Very fortunately, I have so far just a delightful feeling of longing to kill some of them – not a very Christian-like feeling, is it? But I can't help it at the moment. I only hope I shall be spared to tell you all about it. If not, then you must be comforted to know what a happy death it will be to me. Without wishing to be dramatic or boastful, I can say, truthfully, that I am not afraid of death at all. Let this always be the greatest comfort to you all. My life has been a happy one… All my best love and deepest thanks to you all from the bottom of my heart, and please find comfort, should I die, in the way I die.*

A private described how Horace *was with me in the 1st line of German trenches…when he was hit by a shell being blown to bits and killed outright… He had just called out, "Come on boys, and we've got them beat!" when he was hit. Then someone sang out "Retire" and we went back. I am afraid he will be posted as missing… I am quite sure he was hit. He was very popular and gave all the platoon cigarettes the day before we went into action.*

A plaque at Twickenham Stadium commemorates the twenty seven **Rugby Internationals** who lost their lives during the war. Horace and six others are commemorated on the Memorial. The stories of two of those, **Alfred Frederick Maynard** [1A] and **Richard Thomas** [7A], appeared earlier.

ADDENDA PANELS

The Memorial was created to hold over 73,000 names; given the scale of the task, it was to be expected that errors would be discovered. To allow for those names that had been omitted from the regimental listings, the extreme southern edge of Pier and Face 4C was set aside.

When this space was filled, further names were subsequently added at the base of 5D, 8D, 9B and 12B.

Later, new panels were added on the Terrace; these panels were updated in 2012.

WILLIAM PENN-GASKELL

Captain, 25th Battalion attached to 18th Battalion, Manchester Regiment.

Died on 12th October 1916, aged 44, during an attack on Bayonet Trench near Eaucourt l'Abbaye.

William was the eldest son, one of at least three children of Peter and Kathleen Mary Penn-Gaskell (née Stubbs) of Shanagarry, Co. Cork.

The family line was directly descended from William Penn, founder of Pennsylvania.

He was educated at Rugby and then at Westminster School. Afterwards he was employed by Messrs. Antony Gibbs and Son at Iquique and at Antofagasta, in Chile. Later he held a number of other posts across Chile.

On the outbreak of war he returned to England in order to join the Army. He was given a captaincy in the 18th Battalion, Manchester Regiment on 19th February 1915, was transferred to the 25th (Reserve) Battalion in November of the same year but was attached to his old battalion and went to France in August 1916.

He went over the parapet in support of the Royal Scots Fusiliers, who were held up for a time by intense enfilade and machine gun fire. Not seeing any of their officers, he decided to push on, and he stood up to rally the line and take the whole forward, when he was shot in the arm. While his servant was dressing the wound, a shell burst near and both were instantly killed.

His colonel wrote: *I admired his pluck and energy very much indeed in setting to work at his age to fit himself for the Front, and I always considered him a magnificent example to all of us and a pattern of everything an Officer and a gentleman should be. His fine example and gallant death, while he rallied his men, made the greatest impression upon all his comrades. His influence on his men was most inspiring.*

In March 1917 his body was found by a member of an Australian unit, the only means of identification being a compass inscribed with his name. His body was buried on the battlefield but the grave was subsequently lost.

CEDRIC CHARLES DICKENS

Major, 13th Battalion, London Regiment (Kensington Bn.).

Died on 9th September 1916, aged 27, leading his company into action at Leuze Wood.

Cedric was the youngest of at least five children of Sir Henry Fielding Dickens and Lady Marie Dickens (née Roche) of Chelsea, London. Sir Henry was one of the children of the writer Charles Dickens.

He was educated at Mr. Tabor's school at Cheam, Mr. Roper's school at Bournemouth, at Eton College, and at Trinity Hall, Cambridge. While at Cambridge he was coxswain of one of the University Trial Eights and got his Leander colours. He qualified as a solicitor in November 1913 and became managing clerk with a firm in Mincing Lane, London.

On 20th April 1909 he joined the 13th Battalion as second lieutenant, was promoted to lieutenant on 1st December 1910 and captain on 20th February 1914. Mobilised in August 1914, he went to France in November. He was wounded at Laventie on 22nd February 1915, but returned to the Front and was promoted to major on 18th December. He was mentioned in despatches for gallant and distinguished service in the field.

He survived the fighting at Gommecourt on 1st July 1916. At 13.00 he sent the following message: *Shelling fearful. Trench practically untenable, full of dead and wounded. Very few men indeed left. Must have instructions and assistance.* Another message, sent later after enduring

many hours of bombardment, said: *I have, as far as I can find, only 13 left besides myself. Trenches unrecognisable. Quite impossible to hold. Bombardment fearful for last two hours. I am the only officer left. Please send instructions.*

In the action at Leuze Wood he was shot through the heart and buried in a shell hole where he fell. A year later a cross was erected. After the war the family bought the land and erected a new cross. In 1948 attempts were made to exhume the body for reburial in a cemetery but no remains were found. His name was therefore added to the Memorial.

In 1995 the cross was moved and a new cross was erected in 2005, which bears the inscription: *In Loving memory of our darling Ceddy. Major Cedric Charles Dickens, 1/13th Kensington Btn. the London Reg. Born 8th March 1889. Killed in action Leuze Wood 9th Sept 1916.*

ORRELL TAYLOR DUERDEN

PRIVATE 17870, 11TH BATTALION, EAST LANCASHIRE REGIMENT.

Died on 1st July 1916, aged 21, during an attack at Serre.

Orrell was the only son, one of at least six children of James (a cotton weaver) and Eliza Ann Duerden (née Taylor) of Accrington, Lancashire.

He was employed as a weaver at Hambledon Mill, off Whalley Road, Accrington. Enlisting in Accrington in November 1914, he served in Egypt early in 1916 and arrived in France on 8th March.

A comrade wrote: *I have been making enquiries…and he is placed among the missing. This came as a great shock to me, after saying he was only wounded, but it seems there has been a mistake, as this wounded man turned out to be a certain R. Duerden. I am only sorry I cannot give you fuller details, but I will ask the corporal who was with him and is at present in hospital, if he can give you any further news. There were a few of our men taken prisoners and I hope he was amongst these, but I do not want to give you any false hopes, only to have them dashed to the ground again… I hope you will hear some definite news of him soon, as the suspense to you must be awful.*

A corporal wrote: *I am sorry I cannot give you any definite news, but I will tell you how we fared till we had to part company. There were three of us, signallers, with Z Company, and we went over the top with the rest of the lads. We had gone but about a hundred yards when a shell burst about a hundred yards away. The force of the explosion knocked me down. Orrell and the other chap said 'Are you hit?' I said 'No! I am O.K.' and we went forward again. We could see the lads dropping all around and we remarked that it was marvellous how we were being missed. We passed over three lines of trenches and got to the Germans' first line when I got hit in the hand by a bullet. Orrell and I got in the trench and he helped me to bandage my hand. He then said, 'Will you take this piece of shrapnel out of my head!' I was surprised, for it was the first he had said about it, and he must have got it from the shell that knocked me down. I took it out; it was only a small piece, and although it was near the temple he said it didn't hurt. Anyhow, he did not look any the worse for it. He envied me having received such a nice 'Blighty,' but you must not think that it was cowardly to do so, for it was simply awful. While we were in the trench a shell came and knocked the parapet in, burying two chaps and almost smothering us. Orrell and I, after the chaps had got out, said that it was rather unhealthy there, so we had to part, he to go forward to keep communication, and me to the dressing station… We shook hands and wished each other the best of luck. Beyond that… I cannot say what happened.*

Orrell's name also appears on an addenda panel, on Pier and Face 4C.

HARRY WYMAN

Rifleman, 372761 (5523), 1/8th Battalion, London Regiment (Post Office Rifles).

Died on 7th October 1916, aged 25, during an attack on Snag Trench near the Butte de Warlencourt.

Harry was born as Hans Henry, the son of Miranda Hephzibah 'Effie' Henry. Effie was a waitress. Sometime later the family name was amended to Weiman and subsequently to Wyman.

Prior to the war, the family lived in Kennington, London.

Employed as a Post Office assistant, Harry enlisted in Lambeth and went to France on 5th July 1916.

His mother appealed for information and his photograph was printed in the *Territorial Service Gazette* (T.S.G.). A comrade replied to the appeal and his letter was included in the issue dated 3rd February 1917: *I am an old chum of your son's, and spent a good time with him at Fovant, also while he was in France. Perhaps you wonder how I managed to get your address, which I couldn't obtain before or I would have written earlier. Well, it happened this way: I was on a fatigue yesterday (Jan 11) cleaning out our medical hut, and I was picking up the paper lying about when one piece caught my eye, which I noticed had photos. of soldiers on. So I looked at it, and, much to my surprise, one of the photos. was that of my old chum Wyman. ("T.S.G.," Jan. 6.) I read the few words which were underneath and much to my surprise, I saw that he was still "missing." I knew that you wouldn't give up, as more times than not these missing cases are reported afterwards, now wounded, or now prisoner. But it is as far back as Oct. 7, so that we know he can't be "wounded" but we can still believe and hope and trust that he may be a prisoner. It was on July 6 last that your son, myself and many of the other boys came out here. I had the good fortune of being with Harry for many months, we first being with the Q.V.R.'s... We kept together until the day before we made the attack; we got parted then owing to Harry being in the Company and I in the Lewis Gun Section, but all the same, we were not far from each other, and on the afternoon of Oct. 7 we both went over the top. I didn't see him go, but I knew he was there, and the part he was going across the Germans were shelling very heavily, and also sweeping the ground with machine gun fire. I heard no more until we came away from the trenches, which was two days afterwards. The roll was called, and Harry was not there to answer it, so he was put down as "missing." I made several inquiries among the boys, asking if they had seen anything of him, but not one of them could give me any news. Unfortunately, he was not the only one who couldn't be accounted for, and I believe that his company suffered the most casualties. That is all I can tell you about him. It isn't very much but perhaps some of the other boys have corresponded with you and can tell you more?*

CHAPTER FOUR

THIEPVAL PROJECT

Until the opening of the Visitor Centre in 2004 there was nothing at Thiepval to tell visitors, especially the increasing numbers of school children, what happened on the Somme in 1916. All they could see was a magnificent memorial inscribed with the names of men who disappeared on a battlefield, and the graves of 300 French and 300 British soldiers - nothing about the other 50,000 British soldiers who have graves, nothing about why they were there, or about Kitchener's Army and the Pals battalions.

The exhibition within the Centre hopes to correct this by providing visitors, as simply as possible and in three languages, with a greater understanding of the events of 1916 and the sacrifices made. The events of 1918 are also covered, when a fearful reverse was turned into the Hundred Days advance to the Armistice.

The concept is not to add another memorial to this already much visited and hallowed site, but to provide a centre where visitors can find historical information about Thiepval and what it represents, and also rest, reflect and find refreshment and associated facilities in a suitable setting.

Initially a joint venture, the Centre has, since 2006, been managed by the Historial de la Grande Guerre in Péronne on behalf of the Conseil Général de la Somme.

The Centre houses *The Database of the Missing*, a unique computer based collection of photographs and biographies of men commemorated on the Memorial. This supplements the information currently available in the Commonwealth War Graves Commission's registers. The collection was started in 2003 and has grown every year since.

Thiepval Memorial

Database of the Missing

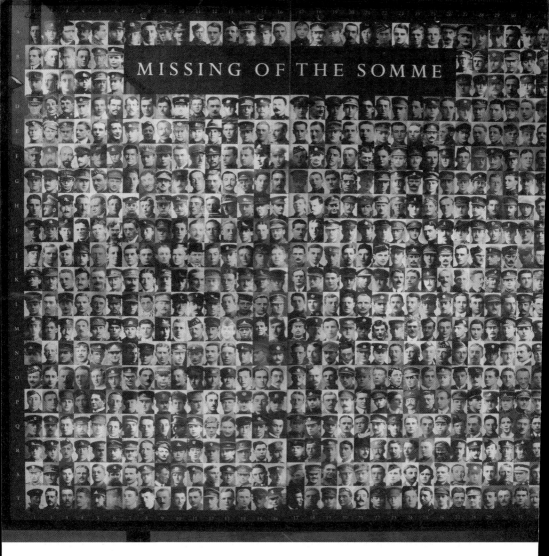

MISSING OF THE SOMME

One of the permanent display panels within the exhibition features 600 head and shoulders pictures taken from the database. These were selected in 2004 to provide a fair representation of the men commemorated on the Memorial.

If you have information you would like to share with the project, then please contact us.

Pam and Ken Linge
Drystones
Heugh House Lane
Haydon Bridge
Northumberland
England
NE47 6HJ

Email: pam_ken.linge@btinternet.com

CHAPTER FIVE

RESEARCHING THE 'MISSING'

This chapter does not provide a comprehensive guide to researching First World War service personnel. Instead it sets out the main sources of information we use in our research and it may therefore provide a useful checklist for others.

As Thiepval commemorates only men from British and South African regiments, no reference is made here to records of the other Commonwealth countries.

It is also worth noting that new sources of information continue to become available as contemporary records are digitised and provided online, through a mix of free and subscription services, or sold via CDRom. Many local libraries now offer free access to some subscription services.

The centenary of the outbreak of WW1 has served as an impetus and no doubt other records will be released over the coming years.

FAMILY HISTORY

Many families have retained information but often it has become fragmented as items have been passed down to different family members. It is therefore worth a call to other members of the family to see what facts they know or items they may hold. Of course in some families information and items have been lost; whilst in other families there is an interesting archive waiting to be discovered. One word of caution is that the accuracy of all family stories needs to be checked against other records wherever possible, as facts can get slightly distorted with the passing of the years.

COMMONWEALTH WAR GRAVES COMMISSION

The *Debt of Honour Register* [www.cwgc.org] lists each of the 1.1 million casualties with their place of burial or commemoration. Information on rank, service number, regiment and date of death are also included. In addition, the age at death and next of kin information may also be provided. In the case of the men commemorated on the Memorial, these latter two pieces of information are only present in around 47 per cent of the records.

Recently the records have, where appropriate, been linked to scanned copies of Burial Returns, Grave Registration Reports and Special Exhumation Reports, which provide additional details.

WW1 SERVICE PAPERS

Officer papers are held at the National Archives and are not currently available through online services. Papers relating to other ranks serving in the Guards regiments can be obtained (although restrictions do apply) from the appropriate regiment on payment of a fee. For men from other regiments the central archive was significantly damaged during the London Blitz in the Second World War. Around two thirds of the records were completely destroyed and the information that was saved was fire damaged to varying degrees. These became known as the 'Burnt Records' and are held at the National Archives; they have also been digitised and are available through subscription services.

MEDAL INDEX CARDS

These were compiled during the latter part of the war when the Army Medal Office began a system of making out an index card for each individual, recording their entitlement to campaign medals and gallantry medals. In some cases the card also has the date on which the individual first went overseas on active service and their date of death. For officers there may also be a note of the date of their commission as well as details of their next of kin with an address. A reference may also be made where a Silver War Badge (see below) was issued. Copies of the cards are available from the National Archives and subscription services.

SILVER WAR BADGE

These were issued from September 1916 to officers and men who were discharged or retired from the military forces as a result of sickness or injury caused by their war service. Lists of the awards are available from the National Archives and through subscription services.

SOLDIERS DIED IN THE GREAT WAR

This database contains basic details on over 703,000 officers and other ranks of the British Army. For the latter it may provide places of birth, residence and enlistment as well as a note of previous service in other regiments. Information is available on CDRom and through subscription services.

WILLS

Copies of soldiers' wills have been made available online via the Probate Service and can be downloaded for a fee. The Probate Service also holds copies of wills that may have been proved through the normal process. Copies of probate registers are available through the Probate Service and subscription services. Copies of the actual wills can only be obtained through the Probate Service.

UK ARMY REGISTERS OF SOLDIERS' EFFECTS

This database contains records detailing the money owed to soldiers of the British Army who died in service between 1901 and 1929. Records typically include the name of the soldier, the next of kin and their relationship, the date of death and sometimes the place. The next of kin information is particularly useful to confirm the identity of a specific casualty. Payments went first to widows, or if the soldier was unmarried, to a parent or sibling(s). Copies of the registers are held at the National Army Museum and are available through subscription services.

CIVIL RECORDS

As with any genealogical research, the census returns provide snapshots of families and individuals in ten-year steps from 1841 to 1911. Individuals can also be tracked through the registration of births, deaths and marriages. Census and registration information is usually available in local libraries or through one of the subscription services. Overseas Death Certificates for war casualties are available (for a fee) from the National Register Office; but these often do not contain much new information.

The immediate pre war Electoral Registers provide an address for those who matched the restricted eligibility criteria. The post war registers provide the same information for a larger number of people reflecting the widening of the criteria. The 1918/19 Absent Voters Lists indicate those eligible to vote at the compilation date who were still in military service, often indicating their rank, regiment and service number, as well as the address at which they would have been eligible to vote. These lists will also include men posted as missing and not yet officially declared dead. Some Electoral Registers are available in local libraries and a full set of the local registers should be available at the various County Record Offices.

NEWSPAPERS AND MAGAZINES

Local newspapers provide a contemporary source of information which is important in that the articles are written 'of the moment' and without the benefit of hindsight. Articles may appear (sometimes with photographs) when individuals enlisted, wrote letters home, were wounded or killed. A note of caution is that some newspapers were better at reporting war news than others. Some will have long obituaries with photographs and others might have just a few words. Any of the longer articles written will tend to include facts about an individual's education, employment and military training that cannot be found anywhere else. Articles obviously reflect the sense of the times (so can seem strange to a modern eye) and they are written based on the limited, sometimes contradictory, information which the family or the journalist had to hand. As a result they do contain errors as men are reported killed and later reported as alive (and vice-versa) but they do remain a valuable source. Indeed a local newspaper may contain the only surviving photograph of an individual.

The British Library's Newspaper archive can be accessed at St Pancras and, to a lesser extent, at their facility at Boston Spa. One downside is that access to original newspapers is rare, which means that for the majority of the time access is via microfilm and any copies taken are thus dependent on the quality of the copying machine. Some newspapers have been digitised and in these cases copies can be made which are of a higher quality. One advantage of digitised archives is that they are usually searchable for a particular name. Non digital copies need much more work to find any specific articles. As well as the British Library, local libraries and County Record Offices usually have newspapers on microfilm and may have access to some of the digital archives available through subscription services.

Although local newspapers are likely to have the most information, the national newspapers also reported on individuals, often picking up on a story previously carried in one of the local papers. Others, such as *The Times, The Scotsman* and *The Irish Times,* carried obituaries each day for Fallen Officers, with the occasional other rank.

There were a number of 'glossy' magazines (e.g. *The Illustrated London News, The Sphere* and *The Graphic*) that included 'society' articles as well as portraits of the fallen (usually only officers). There were also the regimental magazines and many specialist magazines covering sports, the arts etc.; and the likes of staff magazines produced for companies, all of which could include articles relating to servicemen.

ROLLS OF HONOUR

After the war many local communities, schools, universities and other organisations produced volumes often containing lists of 'their' men who served and information (with or without pictures) relating to those who fell. Early in the war *The Bond of Sacrifice* aimed to record all the deaths of officers but the sheer scale of the losses overwhelmed the compilers and only two volumes were produced, which have an incomplete record of deaths up to June 1915. After the war the *De Ruvigny Roll of Honour* was produced, covering the fallen for the whole period of the war. However its five volumes only include 26,000 obituaries, of which 7,000 have a photograph.

Original copies of these Rolls of Honour may be available from specialist military booksellers; some modern copies are available in either book or CDRom format. Some digital versions can also be accessed through subscription services.

MEMOIRS

In a few cases families produced privately published memoirs which often included letters/poems written by the individual as well as appreciations written by family members, friends and comrades.

EXISTING RESEARCH

It is also worth checking if someone else has already done some or all of the research. There are local communities, organisations or individuals who have done specific research of the fallen which they have placed online. It is worth looking for any references using one of the many internet search engines.

CHAPTER SIX

THIEPVAL

In pre war years Thiepval was a relatively tranquil village which had grown up around its chateau. It is believed that the first chateau was established in the 8th century by a local Lord Thiedu (or Thierri or Theodebald). By the 13th century the area was known as the Val de Thibault and it presumably had this name when Henry V established a camp nearby in 1415, just a few days before the Battle of Agincourt. The British, and their military, therefore have a long association with the area.

In 1725 a large chateau was built, with its parkland sweeping down into the valley of the River Ancre. With the chateau came the need for workers to maintain the building and its grounds, which resulted in the growth of the village.

Thiepval first felt the impact of European conflict during the Franco Prussian War in 1870, during which it suffered much damage. After peace returned, the chateau and village passed into the hands of the family of the Comte de Bréda. Over the years Thiepval, and nearby St

487 — THIEPVAL (Somme) - Le Château — The Castle.

G. Leloup, 11, Rue St-Martin, Amiens

Pierre Division, grew in size and prosperity, with around 400 inhabitants and two churches. The village included a presbytery, café, school and a sugar refinery; and the local farmers were known to produce cider as well as honey.

This way of life ended in August 1914 as the war drew closer. At that time the population had fallen to around 200 as local men were called up and other villagers decided to leave ahead of an expected German invasion.

Given that Thiepval occupies a dominant position relative to the surrounding areas, it attracted the German Army to the high ground around the chateau and village. The French Army occupied the lowlands around the river Ancre. Both sides consolidated their positions, the German Army spent its time significantly enhancing their defences with a range of bunkers and strong points that were to prove such major problems during the fighting in 1916.

Interestingly, the first victim of the fighting around Thiepval was **Boromée Vaquette**, a local farmer from Authuille, who was killed by French troops who mistook him for a German soldier.

The defence work around Thiepval meant that it was no place for civilians and all of the remaining inhabitants left their homes. It would be many years before they returned in any significant numbers.

The major change in 1915 was that the British Army gradually replaced the French in the trenches of the Thiepval sector as the BEF gradually took up responsibility for more of the line from their allies. During the preparation for the Somme attack the area was subjected to sustained artillery attack which progressively reduced the fine chateau and the surrounding buildings, to rubble.

These two pictures show the impact on the chateau, although there were obviously times when it was safe enough for the German troops to pose for a group picture!

G. Lelong, 21, Rue St-Martin, Amiens

The village also suffered, as shown in the contrast between this pre war postcard and a snapshot taken by a German soldier in 1915. Again there was time between the shells to stand around and take a souvenir picture in the village or outside the ruined school.

By the time the village was taken by British troops on 27th September 1916 there was only rubble where the various buildings had once stood. When King George V visited the area in July 1917 he was pictured on the site of the Thiepval Church; all that remained of the building was a piece of shapeless metal.

The war moved on, leaving Thiepval in ruins, like so many of the other villages along the Somme Front. For a brief time it again fell under German occupation in 1918; but then peace descended.

For the next ten years Thiepval was a 'ghost town' with perhaps only one resident who, in a postcard of the time, is described as the *heroine of the ruins*. The general rebuilding started in the early 1930s as farmers and their families moved to the area. It is understood that only five pre war families returned to the area, so the village really started afresh. The Church was completed in 1931 and its design is unusual in that the memorial for the six men from the village who were killed in the war is integrated into the fabric of the building rather than being a separate monument.

Less than a decade later the area was once again under German occupation; but this time the wholesale destruction was not repeated. The Germans also respected the Memorial and all the local war cemeteries.

After the liberation the village grew slowly, as shown in this picture taken sometime in the 1950s.

The village is now home to just over 200 people; but over 160,000 visitors pass through it each year as they come to visit the Memorial.

Among those who came to the area in the inter war years were the Potié family and they continue to be influential members of the community. The land on which the Visitor Centre stands was made available by **Madame Geneviève Potié MBE**, who was then Mayor of Thiepval.

With our thanks to Vincent Laude (Manager of the Thiepval Visitor Centre) for the historical information.

ACKNOWLEDGEMENTS

We would like to thank the following organisations for allowing the use of their pictures which appear on the following pages:

[31 & 212] - University of Reading, Special Collections (www.reading.ac.uk/special-collections); [38] - Repton School (www.repton.org.uk); [46] - John Taylor Bell Foundry Museum; [73] - Malvern Remembers; [76] - Soldiers of Gloucestershire Museum (www.sogm.co.uk); [81] - University of Glasgow Archive Services, University Chaplaincy collection, GB0248 CH4/4/2/2/180.

We would like to thank the following individuals for their contributions in respect of the following pages:

[12] - Norman Coleman & family; [25] - Margaret Cole & Daphne Smith; [27] - Paul Armstrong; [28] - Pam Bailey; [29] - Elizabeth Cook & Elaine & Rob Kirk; [37] - Paul Armstrong; [41] - Winifred Harker; [49] - Richard Roberts; [52] - Gordon Howells; [53] - Judith Beastall & Phil Mist; [54] - John Waters; [55] - Rob Thompson; [56] - Kathleen Kay; [57] - Phil Brooks; [60] - Joe Devereux, Arnold Kingston & Matthew Wilson; [63] - Joe Devereux; [70] - Dennis Sutton & Mark Wright; [72] - Paul Hughes; [76] - Robin Stayt; [80] - Elizabeth Dean; [84] - Jenny Bussey; [86] - Gillian Stone; [87] - Alison Caton; [92] - Pamela Dymock; [93] - Pat Kidd; [94] - James Day; [96] - David Swindlehurst; [97] - Clifford & Kathleen Bellwood; [101 & 102] - Gordon Hodgson; [102] - David Locker; [108] - Neil Dowson ; [111] - Michael Webster; [112] - Ernie Noakes; [115] - Chris Sheldon; [116] - Mrs J. S. Corton; [117] - John Mawer; [122] - Judith Golding; [124] - Ian & Mark Spelman; [127] - James Carvile; [133] - Gillian King; [134] - Valerie Evans; [136] - David Davies; [139] - Sandra Waterworth; [141] - Glyn Warwick; [146] - Val Sawyer; [147] - Michael Holtham & family; [149] - Wendy Nelson; [153] - Johanna Lindsay-MacDougall & family; [154] - Steve Wright; [162] - Judith Allen; [163] - Paul Williams; [168] - Eileen Baker; [177] - Malcolm Worrall; [179] - Lenore Campbell; [180] - Irene Shardlow; [181] - Malcolm Anderson; [182] - Angela Chapman & John Sheen; [188] - David Hedley-Goddard; [190] - Jean Hutchinson; [193] - Kathryn Fowler; [194] - John Richardson; [206] - Louise Coatta & Bridget Sudworth; [208] - Christine Adamson; [211] - Rebecca Marlow & Michael Thoms; [214] - Stephen Jenkins; [221] - Michael Halford Clark; [223] - Frank

Braidford; [228] - Christopher Dixon; [231] - Sheila Morris; [238 & 242] - Alan Curragh; [243] - Michael O'Devlin; [246] - Seth Rhodes; [251] - Jerome Lee; [255] - Simon Acors; [257] - Tom McCarthy.

Last, but by no means least, our personal thanks also go to:

• **Sir Frank Sanderson**, for his work in bringing about the Visitor Centre, his continued support and for agreeing to write the foreword;

• **Vincent Laude and Dawn Drouin**, for the professionalism of their work at the Visitor Centre and the knowledgeable assistance they provide to visitors throughout the year;

• **Paul Ainsley and Steve Frater**, for their friendship and encouragement and the diligence with which they undertook the proof-reading of the content; and

• **Brother Nigel Cave**, for his diligent review of the content and the resulting improvements to the text.

INDEX OF NAMES

Names in **bold** indicate the individual or organisation around which a biography in Chapter Three is based. Other names connected with each biography, or those mentioned in the other chapters, are shown in *italics*.

REGIMENTS AND THEIR PIER AND FACE

REGIMENTS MAY ALSO BE REPRESENTED ON THE VARIOUS ADDENDA PANELS

1st (Royal) Dragoons, *1A*
1st King Edward's Horse, *1A*
1st Life Guards, *1A*
2nd Dragoon Guards (Queen's Bays), *1A*
2nd Dragoons (Royal Scots Greys), *1A*
2nd King Edward's Horse, *1A*
2nd Life Guards, *1A*
3rd Dragoon Guards (Prince of Wales's Own), *1A*
4th (Queen's Own) Hussars, *1A*
5th (Royal Irish) Lancers, *1A*
5th Dragoon Guards (Princess Charlotte of Wales's), *1A*
6th Dragoon Guards (Carabiniers), *1A*
6th Dragoons (Inniskilling), *1A*
7th Dragoon Guards (Princess Royal's), *1A*
8th (King's Royal Irish) Hussars, *1A*
9th (Queen's Royal) Lancers, *1A*
10th (Prince of Wales's Own Royal) Hussars, *1A*
17th Lancers (Duke of Cambridge's Own), *1A*
20th Hussars, *1A*
21st (Empress of India's) Lancers, *1A*

Argyll and Sutherland Highlanders, *15A & 16C*
Army Chaplains' Department, *4C*
Army Cyclist Corps, *12C*
Army Ordnance Corps, *4C*
Army Service Corps, *4C & 5C*
Army Veterinary Corps, *4C*

Bailey's Sharpshooters, *Addenda Panel*
Bedfordshire Regiment, *2C*

Black Watch (Royal Highlanders), *10A*
Border Regiment, *6A & 7C*

Cambridgeshire Regiment, *16B*
Cameron Highlanders, *15B*
Cameronians (Scottish Rifles), *4D*
Cheshire Regiment, *3C & 4A*
Coldstream Guards, *7D & 8D*
Connaught Rangers, *15A*

Devonshire Regiment, *1C*
Dorsetshire Regiment, *7B*
Duke of Cornwall's Light Infantry, *6B*
Duke of Lancaster's Own Yeomanry, *1A*
Duke of Wellington's (West Riding Regiment), *6A & 6B*
Durham Light Infantry, *14A & 15C*

East Lancashire Regiment, *6C*
East Surrey Regiment, *6B & 6C*
East Yorkshire Regiment, *2C*
Essex Regiment, *10D*
Essex Yeomanry, *1A*

General List, *4C*
Gloucestershire Regiment, *5A & 5B*
Gordon Highlanders, *15B & 15C*
Grenadier Guards, *8D*

Hampshire Regiment, *7B & 7C*
Hampshire Yeomanry (Carabiniers), *1A*
Herefordshire Regiment, *12C*
Hertfordshire Regiment, *12C*
Highland Light Infantry, *15C*
Honourable Artillery Company, *8A*
Household Battalion, *1A*

Huntingdon Cyclist Battalion, *12C*

Irish Guards, *7D*

King's Own (Royal Lancaster Regiment), *5D & 12B*
King's Own Scottish Borderers, *4A & 4D*
King's Own Yorkshire Light Infantry, *11C & 12A*
King's Royal Rifle Corps, *13A & 13B*
King's Shropshire Light Infantry, *12A & 12D*

Labour Corps, *5C*
Lancashire Fusiliers, *3C & 3D*
Leicestershire Regiment, *2C & 3A*
Leicestershire Yeomanry, *1A*
Leinster Regiment, *16C*
Lincolnshire Regiment, *1C*
London Regiment, *9C, 9D, 12C, 13C & 16B*

Machine Gun Corps (Cavalry), *5C*
Machine Gun Corps (Heavy Branch), *5C & 12C*
Machine Gun Corps (Infantry), *5C & 12C*
Machine Gun Corps (Motors), *5C*
Manchester Regiment, *13A & 14C*
Middlesex Regiment, *12D & 13B*
Monmouthshire Regiment, *16B*

Norfolk Regiment, *1C & 1D*
Norfolk Yeomanry, *1A*
North Staffordshire Regiment, *14B & 14C*
Northamptonshire Regiment, *11A & 11D*
Northern Cyclist Battalion, *12C*
Northumberland Fusiliers, *10B, 11B & 12B*
Northumberland Hussars, *1A*

Ox & Bucks Light Infantry, *10A & 10D*

Queen's Own (Royal West Kent Regiment), *11C*
Queen's Own Oxfordshire Hussars, *1A*

Rifle Brigade, *16B & 16C*
Royal Army Medical Corps, *4C*
Royal Berkshire Regiment, *11D*
Royal Dublin Fusiliers, *16C*
Royal Engineers, *8A & 8D*
Royal Horse & Royal Field Artillery, *1A & 8A*
Royal Fusiliers, *8C, 9A & 16A*

Royal Garrison Artillery, *8A*
Royal Inniskilling Fusiliers, *4D & 5B*
Royal Irish Fusiliers, *15A*
Royal Irish Regiment, *3A*
Royal Irish Rifles, *15A & 15B*
Royal Marines, *1A*
Royal Munster Fusiliers, *16C*
Royal Naval Volunteer Reserve, *1A*
Royal Navy, *1A*
Royal North Devon Hussars, *1A*
Royal Scots, *6D & 7D*
Royal Scots Fusiliers, *3C*
Royal Sussex Regiment, *7C*
Royal Warwickshire Regiment, *9A, 9B & 10B*
Royal Welsh Fusiliers, *4A*
Royal Wiltshire Yeomanry, *1A*

Scots Guards, *7D*
Seaforth Highlanders, *15C*
Sherwood Foresters (Notts and Derby Regiment), *10C, 10D & 11A*
Shropshire Yeomanry, *1A*
Somerset Light Infantry, *2A*
South African Infantry, *4C*
South Irish Horse, *1A*
South Lancashire Regiment, *7A & 7B*
South Staffordshire Regiment, *7B*
South Wales Borderers, *4A*
Suffolk Regiment, *1C & 2A*
Sussex Yeomanry, *1A*

The Buffs (East Kent Regiment), *5D*
The King's (Liverpool Regiment), *1D, 8B & 8C*
The Loyal North Lancashire Regiment, *11A*
The Queen's (Royal West Surrey Regiment), *5D & 6D*

Welsh Guards, *7D*
Welsh Regiment, *7A & 10A*
West India Regiment, *4C*
West Kent Yeomanry (Queen's Own), *1A*
West Yorkshire Regiment (Prince of Wales's Own), *2A, 2C & 2D*
Wiltshire Regiment, *13A*
Worcestershire Regiment, *5A & 6C*

York and Lancaster Regiment, *14A & 14B*
Yorkshire Regiment, *3A & 3D*